This Is the Route of My Forefathers

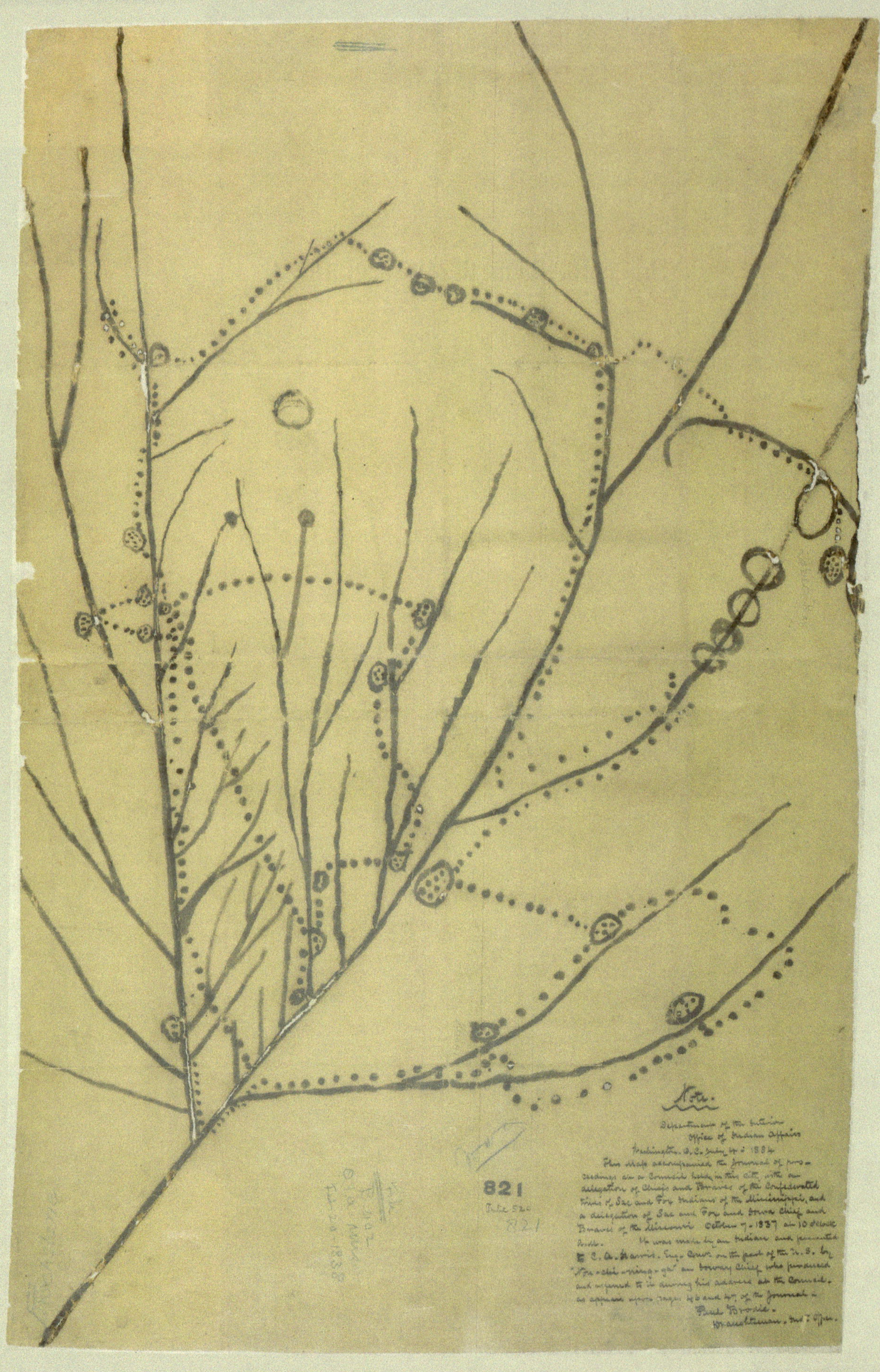
Note.
Department of the Interior
Office of Indian Affairs
Washington, D.C. July 14th 1884
This map accompanied the Journal of pro-
ceedings in a Council held in this City with a
delegation of Chiefs and Braves of the Confederated
Tribes of Sac and Fox Indians of the Mississippi, and
a delegation of Sac and Fox and Iowa Chief and
Braves of the Missouri October 7 - 1837 at 10 o'clock
A.M. It was made by an Indian and presented
to C. A. Harris, Esq. Comr. on the part of the U.S. by
"Non-che-ning-ga" an Ioway Chief who produced
and referred to it during his address at the Council,
as appears upon pages 46 and 47 of the Journal.
Paul Brodie.
Draughtsman, Ind. Offic.
821

This Is the Route of My Forefathers

The 1837 Ioway Map

William Green

CONTRIBUTIONS BY

Lance Foster and Saul Schwartz

UNIVERSITY OF IOWA PRESS, IOWA CITY

University of Iowa Press, Iowa City 52242

uipress.uiowa.edu
Printed in the United States of America

Design by Karen Copp
Typesetting by Rebecca Evans

Printed on acid-free paper

Names: Green, William, 1953– author. | Foster, Lance M., 1960–2025, contributor. | Schwartz, Saul (Ph.D.), contributor.
Title: This Is the Route of My Forefathers: The 1837 Ioway Map / William Green; contributions by Lance Foster and Saul Schwartz.
Description: Iowa City: University of Iowa Press, [2026] | Includes bibliographical references.
Identifiers: LCCN 2025022067 (print) | LCCN 2025022068 (ebook) | ISBN 9781685970451 (paperback) | ISBN 9781685970468 (ebook)
Subjects: LCSH: Iowa Indians—Middle West—Maps. | Iowa Indians—Middle West—History—19th century.
Classification: LCC E99.I6 G74 2026 (print) | LCC E99.I6 (ebook)
LC record available at https://lccn.loc.gov/2025022067
LC ebook record available at https://lccn.loc.gov/2025022068

Frontispiece: The 1837 Ioway map. Records of the Bureau of Indian Affairs, Record Group 75, Central Map File 821. National Archives and Records Administration, Cartographic Branch, College Park, Maryland.

For the Báxoje people,
past, present, and future

Contents

List of Figures

Acknowledgments

MY JOURNEY TO AND WITH the Ioway map involved a happy accident and many helpful people. I am a city boy, Chicago born and bred, the son and grandson of refugees from European fascism and genocide. I developed an interest in archaeology, especially North American archaeology, because I wanted to know who had preceded my family and me on this land and to learn what I could about our predecessors here despite the seeming absence of written records. My move to Iowa in 1987 and appointment as State Archaeologist brought me close to where my father grew up and gave me an opportunity, really a mandate, to explore the unwritten (so I thought) histories of his home state.

I embarked on the Ioway map project in the early 1990s in a secondhand bookstore in Chicago. I chanced upon *Mapping the North American Plains* and saw G. Malcolm Lewis's chapter with its full-page copy of the 1837 map along with Malcolm's geographic interpretations.[1] Here was the first Native-made map of Iowa I had ever seen. It was full of stylized rivers, village symbols, and connecting routes. My professional life changed then and there. I knew I had to bring my archaeological training to bear on that map. I learned that no Iowa archaeologist had paid any attention to the map, so I added a new research agenda to my portfolio. Over the next few years, I corresponded with Malcolm Lewis and received many helpful comments and suggestions about the map. I was most gratified to receive his handwritten letter stating that my 2001 article about the map was "excellent, particularly the archaeological insights."[2] Sadly, Malcolm passed away in 2022.[3] His studies of Native American maps inspired the present work, and my gratitude is immense.

Numerous other individuals, institutions, and organizations assisted in my three-decade engagement with the Ioway map. I thank members of the Iowa Tribe of Kansas and Nebraska and the Iowa Tribe of Oklahoma for their interest and encouragement. Foremost is my friend and colleague Lance Foster, who was a constant motivator regarding the map and all things Ioway since we first met thirty-some years ago. Patt Murphy, Pete Fee, Jimm GoodTracks, Dee Ann DeRoin, Rebecca Liberty, Marianne Long, Elaine Schroeter, Linda Big Soldier, Victor Roubidoux, and other tribal members helped in many ways, especially by connecting tribal history to current issues. I thank the Iowa Tribe of Kansas and Nebraska and the Kansas Humanities Council for the opportunity to discuss the 1837 map at the 1997 Báxoje Fall Encampment and Powwow and annual business meeting. I thank the Iowa Tribe of Oklahoma for the opportunity to discuss the map in 2007 with the tribe's Business Committee and at the annual Bah Kho Je Chena (Powwow).

For their assistance and encouragement, I thank current and former staff members, students, and faculty associated with the Office of the State Archaeologist and Department of Anthropology at the University of Iowa and with the Logan Museum of Anthropology and Department of Anthropology at Beloit College. I am especially grateful to Mary Whelan for her innovative GIS study of the 1837 map, Elizabeth Reetz, Lynn Alex, and Kris Hirst for their work on the 2007 Iowa Archaeology Month poster and website, Cindy Peterson for leading the Iowaville research project, Shirley Schermer and Larry Zimmerman for their leadership in Ioway and Oneota-related tribal consultations, Bill Whittaker for his research on settlement and trail locations and for reviewing a draft of part of this book, and John Doershuk for years of interest and support. Special thanks to my former student Saul Schwartz for his contributions to understanding Ioway history, language, and material culture and for agreeing to allow parts of his work to be incorporated into chapter 2.

I greatly appreciate Stephen Warren's helpful review and good suggestions on the manuscript. Several other archaeologists and historians—Colin Betts, Rob Bozell, Dale Henning, Patrick Jung, Alice Kehoe, John Ludwickson, the late Ron Mason, Tom Thiessen, Mark Warhus, and the late Ray Wood—also provided helpful information, advice, and questions. Many thanks as well to numerous archivists who helped me access documents housed at the American Philosophical Society Library and Presbyterian Historical Society in Philadelphia; the National Anthropological Archives (National Museum of Natural History, Smithsonian Institution), National Archives and Records Administration, and Library of Congress in Washington, DC; the Seeley G. Mudd Manuscript Library at Princeton University; and the Special Collections and Archives department at the University of Iowa Library. The interlibrary loan staffs at the Morse Library at Beloit College and the New Mexico State Library in Santa Fe were wonderfully helpful and generous.

Thanks also to Kelly and Tammy Rundle of Fourth Wall Films for inviting me to participate in their award-winning documentaries about the Ioway people. Presentations of those films afforded opportunities for productive and meaningful discussions about the Ioway map with tribal members and the interested public. Following the 2013 premiere of *Lost Nation: Parts 2 and 3* in Iowa City, one tribal member asked me, "So, when is your book about the map coming out?"—a question I hadn't anticipated and one that spurred me to think more expansively about the stories the map could tell.

Many thanks to the State Historical Society, Inc., of Iowa for generous financial support that aided production of this book, to the Iowa Archeological Society for assistance in securing that grant and for its own grant to facilitate distribution of this book to tribal members, and to the State Historical Society of Iowa for its

Research Grant for Authors that permitted research in Philadelphia and Washington in 2023.

And to everyone at the University of Iowa Press, as well as copyeditor Karen Fisher and indexer Kellyann Wolfe, thank you so much for ensuring this project got done and done well.

Most of all, I am grateful to my spouse, Linda Forman, for her understanding and support of my seemingly unending work on the 1837 map.

SPECIAL TRIBUTE

Lance Foster passed away unexpectedly on January 12, 2025, as this book was nearing the production stage. His loss was a shock and a tragic blow to the Ioway people and to the untold numbers of others he touched through his work in cultural and environmental preservation, language revitalization, and education. His training and expertise in anthropology, archaeology, art, landscape architecture, and Native American studies, along with his tribal and professional service, plus his publications and innumerable presentations and robust social media presence—to say nothing of his humble and gracious personality—made him a respected figure throughout Indian Country and well beyond. Just one indication of his esteem nationally was his receipt of the 2023 Secretary of the Interior's Historic Preservation Award for Tribal Historic Preservation Officers.

Lance's life, accomplishments, and contributions will be recognized and celebrated in many venues. For now, the tribute posted by the University of Iowa's Office of the State Archaeologist is a good starting point for learning about him.[4] In addition to his numerous publications, many of which appear in the bibliography, Lance's work on Ioway cultural heritage is well represented in the Ioway Cultural Institute website he created.[5]

I was honored to have known Lance for more than thirty years. I'll never forget one of our early conversations about the 1837 Ioway map. He said that study of the map could bring it to life, helping people trace Ioway movements just as maps of the Silk Road allow appreciation of ancient travel and connections. Early on, he thought the map was especially amenable to digital technology; years later, several University of Iowa colleagues applied GIS and interactive web methods to the map.

I so appreciate that Lance took time from his pressing duties to write this book's foreword and other introductory material, incorporated into chapter 1. Lance's generosity was legendary: Our final conversation centered on how to ensure this book served tribal preservation and education efforts. I'm glad he approved of the manuscript and am sad he isn't here to see the final product. Although we've lost Lance, he will always be with us in spirit and through his works. May his memory be a blessing.

Foreword

TRADITIONALLY, we introduce ourselves: who we are, where we come from, and what we are there for. That's what I want to do first. I am an enrolled member of the Iowa tribe, the Ioway people. I am one of many descendants of Ioway leaders, including No Heart. I have been the THPO (Tribal Historic Preservation Officer) for the tribe since 2013, and I served a term as vice chairman, 2019 through 2023.

My family was part of the Ioway diaspora, which scattered our tribal members across the country, after the slow erosion of our culture and sale of our reservation lands under allotment, with 90 percent of the reservation lost by the 1930s.

I began returning to our reservation with my grandparents in the 1980s in my twenties. I began to reconnect. That is also when I began to learn our language, starting with a little from my grandmother. She only remembered a little, having gone through boarding school, which took the language from her generation.

In the 1990s, I was a graduate student in anthropology at Iowa State University. I returned to visit on the reservation in Kansas often. My major professor at ISU was Dr. David Gradwohl. It was during that time that I met many of the archaeologists in Iowa, including Bill Green, who was then the state archaeologist for Iowa.

My cousin "Pete" Fee invited Bill to give a presentation at the Báxoje Fall Encampment powwow on the Iowa Reservation in Kansas in 1997 about the No Heart map that Bill had been researching. I attended and recorded the talk, although the wind was such that it is hard to hear Bill's presentation in the recording.

This is Bill's book about his discoveries about the map, which tells so much about our aboriginal homelands—and from our own chiefs' points of view.

We continue to uncover new information scattered all over the place that helps us better understand our past, about both the people and the land. I am glad that Bill has been able to put together his research at last of his journey and accumulated evidence from decades of hard work on the 1837 Ioway map. It has been seemingly an endless quest, and you still never know what new material might yet rear up its head to help enlarge or sometimes even shift the story.

Bill Green has provided the best account to date of this remarkable document, and we Ioway appreciate it deeply.

Lance Foster
September 19, 2024

Introduction

THIS BOOK IS ABOUT PEOPLE, history, and maps. Its focus is the Ioway people—the Native Americans for whom the state of Iowa is named. Ioway history has been told several times but too rarely from an Ioway viewpoint. Hence, maps—in particular, a map made by Ioways that depicts tribal history and defends tribal land claims. Drafted by Ioway leaders and presented to the U.S. War Department in 1837 to support the tribe's land claims, the map depicts places recalled from personal accounts, collective memory, and legendary history based on oral tradition.

Few other maps of that era combine geography and history as clearly and effectively as the Ioway map. When considered in its full context, few documents of any kind supply as much insight into Native American identity and historical memory. My goals are to tell the stories and histories associated with this map and its accompanying narrative and to spark further interest in Ioway and Native American history and cartography.

This book is also about betrayal. Broken treaties form a tragic and well-worn theme in Native American history. But the Ioway case reflects an even darker side of U.S.-Indian relations. Here was a small Indigenous nation that attempted to accommodate American territorial expansion and state authority: By 1837, it had remained at peace with the United States for over twenty years. Most tribal members abided by their leaders' treaty commitments, including cession of parts of their homeland. The Ioways treated the Americans like guests whose presence—permanent as it clearly would become—they could accept. But the Americans wanted more, and they wanted it as cheaply as possible. So, after another Native nation moved into Ioway lands—lands the Ioways never intended to abandon—the United States bought it from the newcomers, cutting the Ioways out of the deal. The Ioways viewed this as a betrayal of their loyalty to the Americans, and they resolved to remedy this breach of trust by demonstrating their long-held claim as the rightful owners of the disputed land. The 1837 map and the associated narratives proved the Ioways' point, but the United States was not willing to pay much for land it had already bought. The map's failure to help the Ioways obtain justice shows how the engine of Indian removal proceeded, heedless of historical connections.

The scope and methods of this book are interdisciplinary, and the intended audience is broad and diverse. I take an ethnohistorical approach, examining the 1837 map and its contexts through historical and anthropological (including archaeological) as well as geographic lenses. The ethnohistorical method, as Raymond DeMallie explained, "leads its practitioners to transcend disciplinary boundaries and ultimately to unify the past by coordinating the studies of anthropologists and historians." Because of this holistic approach, people interested in Native American history, in Iowa or Midwest history and archaeology, or in cartography and historical geography should find much of interest herein.[1]

Chapter 1, "The Ioways," provides background information about the Ioway people and their forebears of the Oneota tradition. Parts were written by Lance Foster, who was the Tribal Historic Preservation Officer of the Iowa Tribe of Kansas and Nebraska at the time of his premature death. As noted in the acknowledgments, Lance's perspective blended service to his tribal nation, expertise in archaeology and historic preservation, and educational, literary, and artistic accomplishments. Lance provided information about three of the tribe's nineteenth-century leaders who were instrumental in the events connected with the 1837 map. Lance's untimely passing means that these contributions are among his last published comments on Ioway history.

In chapter 2, "Washington, DC," we learn about the treaties and treaty councils that were essential cogs in the machinery of Indian land dispossession and removal. Saul Schwartz and I examine the Ioways' participation in the 1837 council, including their presentation of the map that they hoped would bolster their case, as they sought recognition of their rightful claim to their homelands and just compensation for its loss. Rejecting the government's meager offer, the Ioway delegates nevertheless continued their East Coast visit, which we describe based on firsthand accounts.

Chapter 3, "Mapping Time, Space, and Place," takes a close look at the map. What exactly does it depict? Can we identify general or specific places shown on the map? Can we assign dates or time ranges to the villages or the routes between them? Do independent lines of evidence assist in determining locations or dates? Integration of oral traditions, written records, and archaeological information addresses these questions and exemplifies the value of the interdisciplinary ethnohistorical approach.

Chapter 4 discusses another historic Ioway map, "Wawnonqueskoona's Map," drafted in 1847 or 1848 and published in 1853. Although the original version of this map is missing, the published version complements the 1837 map by filling a significant spatial and temporal gap.

Chapter 5, "Historicity," returns to the 1837 map, exploring the accuracy of the depicted rivers, lakes, villages, and routes. It addresses the kinds and sources of information the Ioways in 1837 would have used to make the map, focusing on oral tradition. The map and its associated narrative illustrate how oral tradition operates on three levels: personal accounts, group accounts or collective memory, and accounts of origin or legendary history. Because the map depicts Ioway movements across a vast area of the Midwest, chapter 5 also pays attention to movement: why the Ioways apparently were so mobile and how their mobility related to their identity and their "placemaking" on the land.

Chapter 6, "The Life of the Map," takes a life-history or biographical approach to explore the 1837 map's creation, early uses, long dormancy, and resuscitation late in the twentieth century. The map is inanimate, strictly speaking, but like other important objects and documents, it lives in the sense that it has generated a wide array of research, educational, artistic, and other efforts. But it also rested unused for many years. What I call the map's "significant silence"—its long absence from Ioway historical consciousness, land claims litigation, and scholarship—was particularly regrettable.

"Epilogue: Past and Future" summarizes what the map reveals about the past and asks what it can do next. I argue that the Ioway people themselves are the key decision-makers in determining how and for what purposes the map should be used in the future.

Regarding terminology, this book employs interchangeably the terms "Native Americans," "Indians," and "Indigenous." The term "tribe" is frequently used, but readers should understand that Native American tribes were considered nations from the earliest colonial encounters. Federally recognized tribes such as the Iowa Tribe of Kansas and Nebraska and the Iowa Tribe of Oklahoma are nations with sovereign status and government-to-government relationships with state and federal entities.

For ease of comprehension by non-Native readers, the names of most Ioway individuals are transliterated from the Ioway language at first use but are subsequently given as translated or understood in English. Most names of non-Ioway Native individuals are given in their own languages. Names of most tribal nations are given as they were used and spelled in original documents, for example, "Sac and Fox," although "Ioway" denotes the Iowa tribes and their members, as explained in chapter 1.

The online sources listed in the notes and bibliography were all accessible at the indicated URLs as of May 30, 2025.

Figure 1. Locations of present reservations of (1) the Iowa Tribe of Kansas and Nebraska and (2) the Iowa Tribe of Oklahoma. Map prepared by William Green.

CHAPTER ONE

The Ioways

William Green and Lance Foster

The Ioway People and Language

This book is concerned with Ioway history, especially the 1837 Ioway map, but we start by introducing the Ioways today. We do this to help dispel any belief that the Ioways—or any Native American people—are entirely of the past. They and hundreds of other tribal nations exist today. As many Indian people unfortunately have to remind members of the dominant society, "We Are Not Extinct."

The Ioways today constitute two sovereign, federally recognized tribal nations: the Iowa Tribe of Kansas and Nebraska and the Iowa Tribe of Oklahoma (figure 1). The Iowa Tribe of Kansas and Nebraska enrolls nearly 5,000 citizens and administers a reservation headquartered at White Cloud, Kansas, near the Missouri River between Kansas City and Omaha. The Iowa Tribe of Oklahoma, located on the Cimarron River at Perkins, between Tulsa and Oklahoma City, has over 800 citizens. Both nations operate governmental, business, social service, and cultural institutions and programs.[1]

The state of Iowa and the preceding Iowa Territory took their name from the Ioway people. The state's name was often pronounced "Ioway" even into the twentieth century—witness the "Iowa Corn Song" of 1921 ("We're from I-o-way, I-o-way. That's where the tall corn grows.") and "All I Owe Ioway" from the 1945 film *State Fair*. This pronunciation continued the "etymologically correct" pronunciation of the tribal name as it had been recorded as early as the seventeenth century.[2]

Today, while the state and even the official tribal names are spelled "Iowa" and pronounced "Eye-o-wuh," "Ioway" is the traditional pronunciation and spelling of the people and the language. The English "Ioway" is based on the French "Aiaouez" and its variously spelled homonyms, all of which include the terminal "ay" sound. "Aiaouez" is the French spelling of a Dakota (Sioux) term that might denote "sleepy ones." This was the first name the French knew for the Ioways, so it stuck. However, in their own language, the Ioways are the Báxoje (variously spelled

Bah-kho-je, Paoute, Páxoche, Pa-ho-che, etc.), which means "gray snow" or "ashy heads" people. In this book, we refer to the historical and present-day Báxoje and their ancestors as Ioway in recognition of their widespread identification with that term over nearly 400 years, and to differentiate the tribal nations and people from the state name.[3]

The Siouan language family contains several groups, one of which consists of the Ioway, Otoe, Missouria, and Ho-Chunk. (Another Siouan language group—the Dhegihan—includes the Kansa, Omaha, Osage, Ponca, and Quapaw; all but the last would become close neighbors of the Ioway.) The Ioway, Otoe, and Missouria speak Chiwere, after the Otoes' name for themselves, Jiwere ("the People of This Place"). The Otoe and Missouria people, now conjoined as the Otoe-Missouria Tribe, are the Ioways' closest cultural and linguistic relatives. Within the Chiwere language, there are only slight dialectical differences between Ioway and Otoe-Missouria. The Chiwere and Ho-Chunk languages are also quite similar, indicating that those two languages, and probably the associated cultural entities, separated from each other between 500 and 1,200 years ago. In view of this ancestral relationship, Ioways refer to the Ho-Chunks as their "fathers" or "grandfathers."[4]

The Ioway/Chiwere language was well documented in the nineteenth century. In 1835, a Baptist missionary to the Otoes, Moses Merrill, published Ioway translations of hymns and religious lessons. The Presbyterian missionaries William Hamilton and Samuel Irvin, who lived among the Ioways from 1837 into the 1850s, published a dictionary and description of the language in 1843. The linguist/ethnologist/missionary J. Owen Dorsey published a treatise on the Dhegihan group in 1890. As we will see, Hamilton, Irvin, and Dorsey also recorded cultural and historical, as well as linguistic, information about the Ioways.

As with many Native nations, U.S. government assimilation efforts caused the Ioway/Chiwere language to fall out of everyday use and become considered an endangered or dormant heritage language. Yet language is important in forming and maintaining group identities, so language preservation and revitalization are elements of many tribes' cultural heritage programs. Recently, Ioway and Otoe-Missouria tribal members and linguists have been working on documenting and revitalizing the language. This work is not without controversy, though. Some tribal members are adamant about recovering and preserving the language, while others view it with respect but as a past rather than present aspect of tribal culture.[5]

That the Iowa tribes' lands today are in Kansas, Nebraska, and Oklahoma rather than Iowa is a legacy of removal, dispossession, and factionalism. The Ioways endured colonization and the attempts at cultural erasure that the U.S. government inflicted on most tribes, especially tribes displaced from traditional homelands. Despite land loss, disease, poverty, and policies of assimilation, Ioways and other tribes endured and maintained their identity, a remarkable feat of not just persistence but "survivance," as Gerald Vizenor has dubbed the active work against efforts of subordination. Another way to understand Ioway and other tribes' resilient identities is through the lens of "peoplehood," an interweaving of four key factors: language, sacred history, religion, and land. Ioway peoplehood has been tenuous, with all four elements at risk of attenuation or loss, especially over the past 200 years, but we will see that the 1837 map served as one of the means the tribe employed to try to retain a measure of peoplehood.[6]

For insights into the saga of the Ioways over the past 200 years, Lance Foster's *Indians of Iowa*, his many other writings, and his Ioway Cultural Institute website, listed in the bibliography, are the best starting points. Mildred Mott Wedel's chapter in the Smithsonian *Handbook of North American Indians* distills her decades of research about the Ioways. For additional historical details, the principal source is Martha Royce Blaine's *The Ioway Indians*, complemented by Greg Olson's *The Ioway in Missouri* and *Ioway Life: Reservation and Reform 1837–1860*. The three-part documentary film series *Lost Nation: The Ioway* is well worth viewing, in large part because tribal members' voices are prominent. The websites and other online resources of both Iowa tribes are also excellent places to learn about tribal history and current conditions.[7]

To provide context for later chapters, the following summary is a general framework for tribal historical geography.

Oneota

Archaeological evidence, documentary records, and oral traditions indicate that the Ioways and their Chiwere and Ho-Chunk relatives, and probably some Dhegihans as well, descend from a widespread grouping of cultures archaeologists term the Oneota tradition. Ioway oral tradition refers to an ancient collective—perhaps the Oneota—as *hunge*, while Dhegihans might have pronounced it *hoⁿ'ga*. Oneota and closely related people lived throughout the Upper Mississippi valley, Lower Missouri valley, and Lake Michigan basin between about 1100 and 1730 CE. The ancestral Chiwere and Ho-Chunk people might have been the first Siouan group to transform in the archaeological record from the Woodland tradition to Oneota, beginning around 1100 CE. Many of the ancestral Dhegihans apparently took on Oneota lifeways in the 1400s–1500s, after their arrival in the central Plains from the Ohio Valley and the American Bottom (the St. Louis region). In general, the Oneota tradition is characterized by large, permanent village sites, investment in agriculture as well as large-game hunting, and manufacture of shell-tempered ceramic jars. The geographic spread of this tradition was at its maximum from about 1300–1500, when it dominated much of the upper Midwest. At that time, to the north and northwest of the Oneota tradition was the Psinomani complex, ancestral to the Sioux proper, the Oceti Sakowin (Dakota, Lakota, etc.). To the west and south was the Central Plains tradition, whose inheritors included the Caddoan-speaking Arikara, Pawnee, and Wichita.[8]

The term "Oneota" derives from its brief and unfortunate usage as a name for the Upper Iowa River, a river named for the Ioway people. The river temporarily acquired the "Oneota" moniker several decades after the 1845 publication of a book titled *Oneóta* by the early ethnologist Henry R. Schoolcraft, whom we will encounter later in this book. The Oneida Indians, who refer to themselves as Oneota (Oniotaaug, O-ne-a-ta-auk, or Oneota:haka; People of the Standing Stone), are Iroquoian people who never lived in Iowa. Moreover, nothing in Schoolcraft's *Oneóta* touches on Iowa. However, Iowa's pioneer geologist W. J. McGee believed—almost certainly incorrectly—that "Oneota" was a local Ho-Chunk term for the Upper Iowa River. Once the river's name reverted to "Upper Iowa," Iowa's pioneer archaeologist Charles Reuben Keyes appropriated the term "Oneota" for the archaeological culture because, he stated (again, mistakenly), this was "the Indian name for the Upper Iowa River, where the culture is most fully represented. . . . This good, original name having been rejected for the river, it may serve here to designate the people that once lived there."[9]

A few years after Keyes adopted this Iroquoian term for sites he believed were of Siouan affiliation, Iowa archaeologist and ethnohistorian Mildred Mott not only concurred with the Siouan attribution for the Oneota tradition but further suggested that the Oneota sites along the Upper Iowa River were seventeenth-century Ioway. Archaeologists later classified these Oneota sites of the early contact period as Orr focus and Orr phase, in honor of another important early Iowa archaeologist, Ellison Orr, while noting that the Orr phase may encompass other tribes in addition to the Ioway.[10]

If Ioways resided in the Upper Iowa River valley of northeast Iowa in the seventeenth century, how long had they lived there? Where did they live before then, and where did they live afterward? Chiwere and Ho-Chunk traditions recorded in the nineteenth and early twentieth centuries locate tribal origins in the Green Bay region of eastern Wisconsin. Ioways also indicated Lake Pepin along the Mississippi River between Wisconsin and Minnesota as an origin locale. Additionally, each Chiwere and Ho-Chunk clan had its own unique origin story. While these oral traditions might contain some elements of historicity, it may well be that there was no single origin location for these tribes or clans. Instead, communities likely coalesced, merged, and split off repeatedly throughout the precontact era. In this light, the formation of the Oneota tradition in several places around 1100 CE and its subsequent spread probably represent pan-regional cultural transformations and migrations.[11]

The earliest Oneota sites are located in the Red Wing locality (on both sides of the Mississippi River at the head of Lake Pepin) and in various parts of eastern Wisconsin. Oneota communities became established in central and northeast Iowa by the thirteenth century. By the fourteenth century, most parts of the Prairie Peninsula and adjacent areas were Oneota territories, from central Kansas to Lake Michigan, and from central Minnesota to central Missouri, except for several Mississippian (Cahokia-related) settlement clusters, holdovers from their twelfth- and thirteenth-century florescence. Over a period of about 250 years, Oneota people, who may well have been ancestral Ioway/Chiwere, built large villages—some with enormous longhouses—in the La Crosse region of western Wisconsin, as well as huge ridged-field agricultural complexes there. They hunted, or interacted with hunters, in the prairies of Iowa and Minnesota, bringing bison products back to their villages. By the time the earliest hints of European contact appear (glass beads and European metal objects are the easiest to spot archaeologically), the La Crosse villagers had apparently decamped to the Upper Iowa River valley and the Root River valley of southeast Minnesota. Other possible Ioway/Chiwere ancestors already might have been living in those areas and in the lakes region of northwest Iowa.[12]

The Postcontact Era

Seasonal shifts and village movements were standard practices in both the precontact and postcontact eras as the Ioways and their neighbors adjusted to constantly changing economic and political challenges and opportunities. Villages moved periodically between the Mississippi and Missouri River drainages, while hunting and raiding parties ranged widely, often covering hundreds of miles. Because of this residential and logistical mobility, generations of Ioways and their ancestors were familiar with and had close associations with the land that became Iowa and portions of all adjacent states. It is no wonder that two major rivers, Iowa Territory, and eventually the state of Iowa bore their name.[13]

At any given time prior to the 1830s, the Ioways probably maintained two or more main villages as well as numerous short-term seasonal camps and homesteads. Their economy was a mix of agriculture (corn, beans, squash, tobacco, sunflowers, and probably other crops), hunting of large and small game, fishing, and wild plant harvesting. Their villages were often situated in wooded valleys, while hunting ranged throughout the surrounding prairies. Local resource availability was always an important factor in village locations, but siting of villages also took note of trading opportunities and the whereabouts of neighboring tribes. Intertribal raiding occurred, but as a relatively small tribe, the Ioways' survival

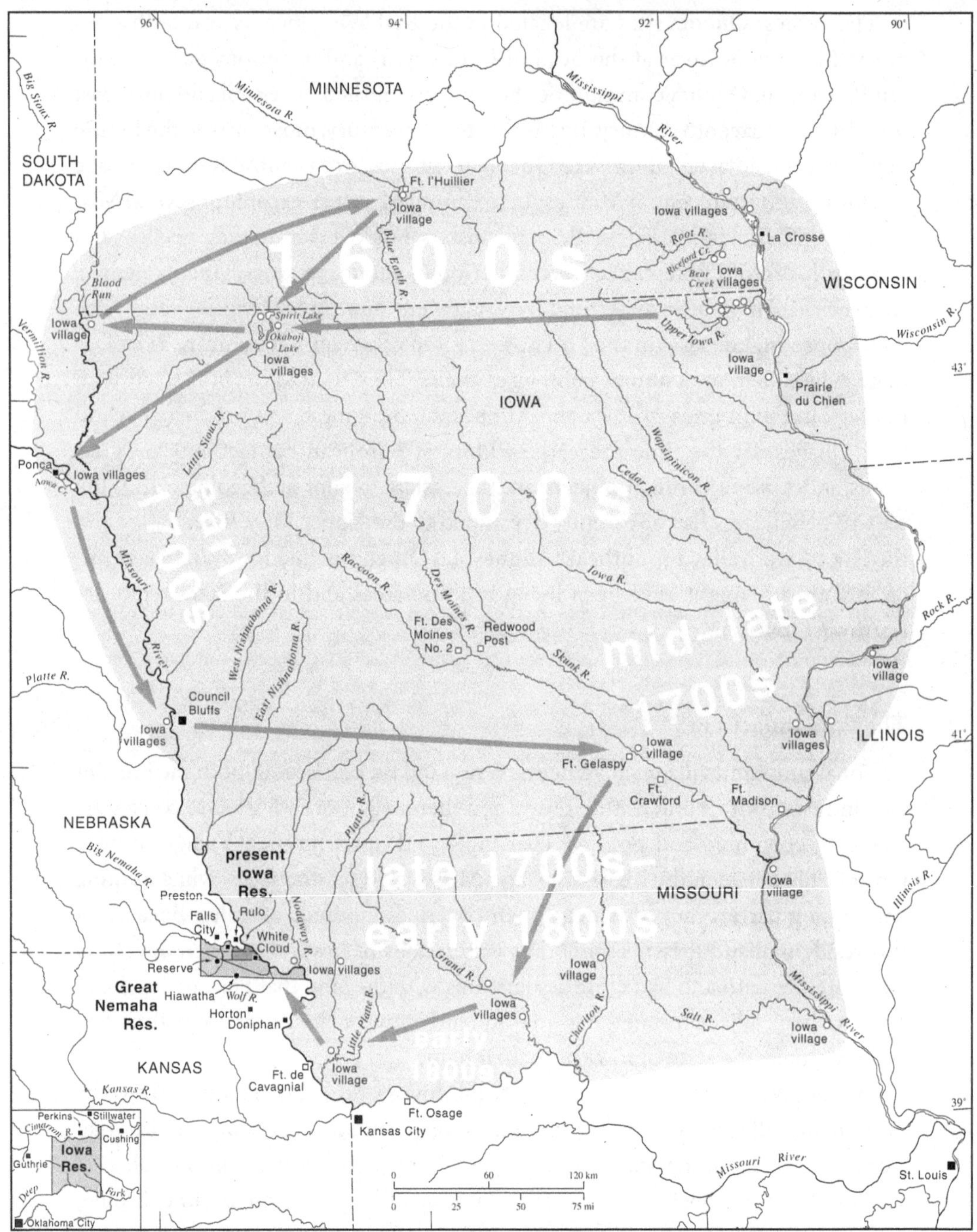

Figure 2. Ioway locations from the seventeenth through nineteenth centuries. From Wedel 2001. Original caption (minus references): "Villages, territory, and movements of the Iowa. Dates label areas of major population concentrations; additional villages were outside of these areas at various times. . . . The inset illustrates the area of the executive order reservation in Indian Territory for the Iowa between 1883 and 1891." Courtesy of Smithsonian Institution National Museum of Natural History.

depended more on alliances, geographic insulation, and residential mobility than on large-scale warfare.[14]

Ripples across the continent in the form of epidemics and population movements grew from the 1500s onward. Beginning in the 1600s, Algonquian-speaking groups in the Northeast were embroiled in wars with the Haudenosaunee (Iroquois). As a result, these Algonquian groups withdrew from the Northeast and expanded west. Such groups included the Ojibwa, Sauk, Meskwaki, Potawatomi, Kickapoo, Illini, and Miami, newcomers to Chiwere and Ho-Chunk lands. The disruption in the 1500s–1600s was a world changer for the Indigenous Midwest. The Ioways and their Siouan-speaking neighbors now had to contend and interact with numerous new groups, both Native and European. By the time Spanish and French explorers started documenting the area in journals and maps, it was a very different place than it had been in precontact times.[15]

For Ioway history from the seventeenth century onward, oral tradition and European written records become the principal sources of information, though archaeology still plays an important role. Figure 2, from Mildred Mott Wedel's 2001 summary of Ioway history and culture, depicts 200 years of Ioway settlements, migrations, and territory. It does not incorporate insights from analysis of the 1837 map but is an otherwise comprehensive depiction of Ioway places and spaces through time.[16]

Early French records indicate that Ioways resided in northeast and northwest Iowa and in the area around southwest Minnesota's red pipestone quarry in the seventeenth century. There might have been two separate groups—Aiaouez and Báxoje—that coalesced in northwest Iowa to form the Ioway (see this chapter, n. 3). Temporarily joining the Omahas, Ioways continued moving west and south under pressure from the Dakota, settling by the early eighteenth century along the Big Sioux and Missouri Rivers. The Ioways occupied villages in what is now eastern Nebraska until the 1760s, when they returned east and settled on the lower Des Moines River. The principal Ioway village between around 1770 and 1820, located between Eldon and Selma, Iowa, became known as Iowaville and has been the subject of extensive archaeological and historical research. Ioway villages also might have been established around that time on the east side of the Mississippi River in western Illinois. By 1820, Ioways were leaving the Des Moines River: Many returned to the Omaha region along the Missouri River, while others lived at various locations in northern Missouri into the 1830s.[17]

The relentless press of American settlement was codified in the 1830 Indian Removal Act. The federal policy of dispossessing Indians of all land east of the Mississippi River had a profound effect on the Ioways. No Ioways lived east of the Mississippi by that time, but forced relocation of the Sauk and Meskwaki (Sac and Fox) tribes into lands west of the Mississippi, as well as expanding American settlement, impinged on traditional Ioway territory during the 1830s. Treaties signed by the Ioways had ceded much of their land east of the Missouri River, but the tribe was fracturing: One segment continued residing in ceded lands in northern Missouri, while most Ioways abided by treaty provisions and relocated west of the Missouri River.[18]

By 1838, the Ioways had been forced to cede all the land they formerly occupied in what is now Iowa and Missouri. Many tribal members desired to move back to the Des Moines River, but most resided in a tiny tract—soon to become even smaller—in northeast Kansas near what eventually became the current reservation of the Iowa Tribe of Kansas and Nebraska. From 1836 to 1854, the Ioway lived in settlements scattered in what is now the northeast corner of Kansas between Iowa Point and the Highland area. Hamilton and Irvin's Presbyterian mission—built by Ioway annuities—was meant to civilize the tribe. The St. Joe Road of the Oregon-California Trail went right through the reservation. The associated epidemics of smallpox and cholera decimated the tribe.

With much of the original reservation taken via the treaty of 1854, the Ioways were moved north near the Big Nemaha River to establish a new town called Nohart, Nebraska, named for No Heart, the last surviving of the three principal chiefs of the late 1830s. The 1850s also was the violent Bleeding Kansas era, a prelude to the Civil War in which proslavery and abolitionist factions battled over land that had just been wrested from Native people.[19] During the Civil War, most Ioway men joined the U.S. Army, earning American citizenship through service to the Union.

After the Civil War, continued pressures from white settlers for the last of the reservation lands in Kansas split the tribe. The portion wanting to live more traditional lives left for lands in Indian Territory, forming the core of what became the Iowa Tribe of Oklahoma. The portion that was more attached to their lands in Kansas and Nebraska realized in order to live there, they would have to take on more of the white man's ways, including intermarriage. That was the only way they could keep the last of their lands. This is why there are two Iowa tribes.[20]

Three Ioway Leaders

Here we introduce the three Ioway leaders principally associated with the 1837 treaty council negotiations that are central to this book. It is important to understand that these leaders were human beings, just like the rest of us. They had personalities, intellect, and spirits, and they also left descendants who continue their legacies in different ways. Lance had been discovering more and more about them, slowly, over many years; here is some of what he learned.

Figure 3. Portrait of White Cloud II, "Young Ma-Has-Kah, Chief of the Ioways." After Charles Bird King, 1837; Albert Newsam, lithographer. From McKenney and Hall 1838b. Smithsonian American Art Museum 1985.66.153,227.

Francis "Frank" White Cloud (aka White Cloud II/Mahaska II, 1810–1852)

White Cloud II (Mahaska, Maxúshga; figure 3) was the son of the previous first chief White Cloud and, as the ranking Bear Clan member, also had the rank of first chief. There is a story that little White Cloud's mother died when they were both thrown from her horse, and his father found them. The child looked up and said, "My mother is sleeping."

His father dropped him off in 1824 at Saint Regis Academy in Florissant, Missouri, near St. Louis, to attend that Jesuit boarding school with two other Ioway youths. Unhappy, they tried to run away but were caught and taken back. He was baptized and given the name Francis after St. Francis, later shortened to Frank. Father Pierre-Jean De Smet was one of the priests who taught him there. Francis (White Cloud II) took on the position of head chief in 1834 after his father, White Cloud I, was murdered by other Ioways on the Nodaway River in Missouri or southwest Iowa. He avenged his father but was an inexperienced leader, so he relied on his uncle No Heart (younger brother of White Cloud I) as his key advisor.

Although we would call No Heart his uncle, in the Ioway kinship system, the brother of your father is also called "Father," as they are members of the same clan.

In 1836, White Cloud II signed the Platte Purchase treaty, ceding the last of the Ioways' Missouri lands, and led the tribe to the new reservation across the Missouri River. He realized change was inevitable, and he tried his best to accommodate in order to help his people transition to a life of restrictions and poverty.

One of the big events of his life was traveling with Walking Rain and several other Ioways to Europe, exhibiting their dances and skills in England, Scotland, Ireland, and France in 1844–1845. There they met the artist George Catlin, who had painted some of them while he was at Fort Leavenworth (Kansas) around 1830. They had gone to Europe to make some money to bring home to their people, as life was very hard and they didn't have enough to eat. Their time in Europe taught the Ioways much about the contradictions in white culture: How they were instructed to behave contrasted starkly with what they observed about life in Europe. They were also continually pressured by missionaries of different religious denominations to convert to Christianity.[21]

The disconnect between what was preached and what the Ioways observed of the terrible poverty and drinking in the streets of Europe seems to have shifted Francis White Cloud's thinking. Reports from the resident missionaries and Indian agents show that he began a growing opposition to their authority; in return, they began to erode his authority. The final blow was when Francis killed some Pawnees who were on a peaceful mission to obtain supplies from the government. This was the last straw for the government. The other chiefs, including No Heart and Walking Rain, were forced to remove him as chief. Of course, many in the tribe still regarded him as a chief.

There are different accounts of the last few of his years of his life. One is that in despair, he turned to drink and eventually died around 1852. Another story is that he was killed by a young Pawnee boy who shot him in the eye with an arrow.

Francis White Cloud had children with several wives. His wife Mary Robidoux was a daughter of Joseph Robidoux, the founder of St. Joseph, Missouri. Their children included Robert, Sarah, Eliza, Jefferson, James, Martha, and Mary. Jefferson would become a chief among the Ioways of Oklahoma, and James would become a chief among the Kansas-Nebraska group. Francis White Cloud's descendants are in the hundreds today, including families like the White Clouds, Rhodds, and Tessons.

No Heart (ca. 1797–1862)

Born at the Ioway village at Iowaville, Iowa, No Heart (figure 4) was the second chief of the Ioway at the time of the 1837 treaty council. A Bear Clan member, his name is spelled and translated variously: Nochiminge, Notchemine, Nacheninga,

Figure 4.
Portrait of No Heart, "No Heart (Nan-che-ning-ga)." By Charles Bird King, 1837. Oil on wood. Courtesy of Smithsonian American Art Museum 1985.66.258,362.

No Heart of Fear, and so on. It is generally spelled today Nahsje Ninge, "heart" + "nothing."

Some confuse him with another Ioway chief, Hard Heart (Wangewaha), but they were different people. Hard Heart lived in the Council Bluffs area in Iowa and Nebraska, and he was killed there by the Sioux in 1823. No Heart lived in Iowa and Missouri, and then from 1837 to 1862 on the Iowa Reservation on the border of Kansas and Nebraska.

No Heart's older brother was White Cloud I, the head chief who was one of the signers of the 1824 treaty that ceded most of northern Missouri. After the murder of White Cloud I, the next person to be head chief was his son White Cloud II. White Cloud II (Francis) was very young at the time, so No Heart became a sort of regent for him or assistant until he was old enough to be the primary chief. No Heart served as a second chief most of his life but was the tribe's de facto leader for many years—"the principal business-man of the nation" according to the missionaries Hamilton and Irvin—and he succeeded White Cloud II in 1849–50.[22]

Like all other Ioway men, No Heart's identity and reputation were tied to his war record. The accounts of his life given by chroniclers such as McKenney and Hall are of war expeditions, enemies defeated, and horses stolen. Once he was on the reservation, however, he took a peaceful road.[23]

Figure 5. Later portraits of No Heart. Left: "No Heart, Second Chief of the Iowa." By Thomas Easterly, ca. 1845–1847. Daguerreotype. Right: unknown photographer, prior to 1862 (original at National Anthropological Archives, Smithsonian Institution). From the William Henry Jackson Photographs Collection, Box 5, Special Collections and Archives, University of Iowa Libraries.

By the time of the 1837 move to the reservation, No Heart worked as a bridge between the Ioways and the government agent and missionaries, trying to help his people adapt to the new reality. He was supportive of the Presbyterian mission school. Although we have paintings and prints of him as a younger man, he is the only one of the three leaders that we have photographs of, including several daguerreotypes from one sitting in the 1840s, and one photograph taken not long before his death, when he was head chief (figure 5).

No Heart had several children, notably Joseph No Heart and Eliza No Heart, as well as an older son (perhaps adopted) called Naggarash (or British), who became head chief in 1862 after No Heart died. Joseph served in the Civil War along with most other Ioway men. Several families are descendants of No Heart, such as the Campbells, the Baradas, the Murrays, and related lines.

Walking Rain (ca. 1797–ca. 1852)

We know least about Walking Rain, a member of the Thunder Clan (figure 6). He served as the war chief, and often therefore the official orator. For much of his

Figure 6.
Portrait of Walking Rain, "Ne-O-Mon-Ne, an Ioway Chief." After Charles Bird King, 1837; I. T. Bowen's Lithographic Establishment. From McKenney and Hall 1838b. Smithsonian American Art Museum 1985.66.153,225.

life, he would have been counted as the third chief. His uncle was Hard Heart, who went to live near the Otoes during the War of 1812, when the neutral Ioways left under Hard Heart and the pro-British Ioways stayed near the Mississippi, including Iowaville.

The accounts of his life also are all about his war exploits, until he lived on the reservation after 1837. He accompanied White Cloud II on the trip to Europe in 1844–45, during which he served as the tribal spokesman.[24]

We don't know a lot about his descendants. He had a son, Watawebukana (translated as Commanding General), who accompanied him to Europe. He had a son who attended the Mission school but who was beaten and then ran away, never to be heard from again. We don't know if this son was Watawebukana.

Walking Rain—his Ioway name was written variously as Neomonni, Nyiyumanyi, and so on (Nyiyu "rain" + Manyi "to walk")—was also known as Kirutsche after he returned from Europe. Kirutsche may be a spelling of the Thunder Clan name XraHsji (Krah-Shsjay) "Real Eagle."

He became friends with the visiting Swiss artist Rudolph Kurz in the late 1840s. One of his daughters, named Witthae, was married off to Kurz in 1850 as Walking

Rain/Kirutsche wanted to go into a quarrying business with Kurz on the reservation. But that plan was thwarted as the young, unhappy Witthae ran away to relatives among the Otoes up north and got married there.[25] Broken-hearted, Kurz continued north and did more of his art among tribes further upriver.

Walking Rain died soon afterward. In 1852, the government agent noted the recent deaths of both Francis White Cloud and Walking Rain: "Both were men of decided talents, and the latter was particularly noted for shrewdness."[26]

CHAPTER TWO

Washington, DC

William Green and Saul Schwartz

Indian Removal and Indian Councils

In 1837, even in the throes of the worst financial crisis since the nation's founding, the largest single portion of the U.S. federal budget was devoted to Indian removal.[1] Why? Because Native people were viewed as impediments to the nation fulfilling its Manifest Destiny: "to overspread the continent allotted by Providence for the free development of our yearly multiplying millions." The Manifest Destiny doctrine promoted not only "spreading European American ideals, beliefs, technology, and institutions" but also supplanting Native peoples to permit establishment of a national empire.[2]

To fulfill this destiny and hasten its arrival, President Andrew Jackson and his Congressional allies established the policy and practice of Indian removal in 1830. Tribes were to vacate their lands east of the Mississippi River, and even western tribes were on notice to move. While Jackson was the originator and staunchest proponent of the formal Indian removal policy, he was by no means either the first or last advocate of the concept. The removal momentum continued and strengthened under his successor, Martin Van Buren, who was inaugurated on March 4, 1837. Treaties were the official removal documents, and treaty councils—formal, public, government-to-government discussions and negotiations—were often the venues for treaty drafting and signing. Under both Jackson and Van Buren, the power dynamics of treaty-making left few choices for most tribal nations: either accede to U.S. demands or return home with no resolution of their worsening situations.[3]

To the government, cost was no obstacle. Between 20 and 50 percent of federal spending in 1837 promoted or expedited Indian removal. Removal was literally the government's most important task. In the modern parlance of strategic planning, if Manifest Destiny was the American nation's vision, and promoting white settlement the government's mission, then Indian removal was the goal, treaties were the strategies, and treaty councils the tactics.[4]

The Ioways had a long history of treaties and treaty councils with the United States. None of these represented the kinds of treaties nations sign when they surrender after a military defeat. Instead, they were treaties of peace and friendship (as in 1815, signed at Portage des Sioux, near St. Louis) or, more often, cessions of specified parcels or interests in land. In return for land, the tribe would receive cash payments and other considerations. Such cessions were made in 1824 in Washington, in 1830 at Prairie du Chien (then Michigan Territory, now Wisconsin), in 1836 at Fort Leavenworth (near Kansas City), in 1837 at St. Louis, and in 1838 at the Great Nemaha Agency near the present reservation of the Iowa Tribe of Kansas and Nebraska. The 1824 treaty ceded the northern half of Missouri except the northwest corner (retained as the Platte Purchase); the 1830 treaty ceded lands in western Iowa and Missouri (though the Ioways were not supplied with an interpreter and did not know they had signed away those lands); the 1836 treaty relinquished the Platte Purchase (and in return the Ioways were assigned a reservation in Kansas); the 1837 treaty, signed during the tribal leaders' return trip from a failed council in Washington, ceded western Iowa; and the 1838 treaty ceded all remaining lands in central and eastern Iowa, as well as claims to Missouri. The Ioways also signed later treaties that ceded most of the Kansas reservation lands. Allotment then further reduced tribal holdings.

At treaty councils, tribes argued for fair treatment and protection and set out their grievances against the government or other tribes. The government portrayed itself as benevolent but powerful. Most councils resulted in the signing of treaties that led to tribes relinquishing land, compensated at rates far below fair market value. In the Old Northwest, dispossession and relocation generally proceeded peacefully. But if this reading of the treaty process seems relatively benign, Lance Foster encapsulates the standard sequence of government intentions, actions, and results as follows:[5]

1. Establish a legal relationship with tribes and exclude them from similar relationships with other countries like Britain and France.
2. Establish boundaries between tribes (there were rarely firm boundaries between tribes) and try to stop intertribal warfare, much of which was caused by westward migration of tribes being pushed out of their lands by white settlements and wars further east.
3. Once the tribal boundaries were fixed and relative peace was made, white squatters would begin to move in and occupy the best Indian farming areas and hunt out the wild game.

4. Once the best areas were taken by whites and game depleted, conflicts between tribes and squatters were inevitable.
5. Display or exert U.S. military power and deal with Indian/white conflicts by removing the Indians to more distant lands. The Indians sometimes went willingly along at this point because the best areas and the game had already been taken. When they resisted, the government would use the conflict to compel a settlement and remove the tribe to a more distant area, with promises that that would be the final removal.
6. Begin the next phase with Step 3, and repeat again and again. . . .

This sequence—part of the large-scale "political economy of plunder" that characterized early American expansion—played out with the Ioways in the 1820s and 1830s.[6] In addition to indignation about unfair treatment in the 1830 council, the Ioways were angry that the Sauk, newly arrived in what had been traditional Ioway territory, were now claiming and selling that land.[7] Frustration built to the point that by 1836, Ioway leaders petitioned President Jackson and the Congress to obtain redress for their grievances.

The 1836 Petition

The petitioners were faced with the challenge of presenting Ioway history in a way that U.S. officials could understand but also in a way those officials would find convincing enough to side with the Ioway in their dispute with the Sauk. The petitioners proved skillful representatives in this cross-cultural encounter, selectively and strategically translating historical knowledge rooted in Ioway consciousness for presentation to U.S. agents who operated according to very different cultural frameworks.[8]

The petition, dated December 14, 1836, is presented in full as appendix 1. It charged the Sauk with selling Ioway land to the United States. The Ioways objected that "large tracks of valuable Land have been ceded to the United States by the Sacs [Sauks], to the amount of many Thousands of Dollars," despite the Ioways only having granted them permission to hunt there. Not only did this land cession constitute an "oppression that has been in a most unsparing manner heaped upon them by their Red Brothers" but, they regretted to say, it was also "in a good degree fostered and cherished by their White Brothers." Trusting that the United States would consider the Ioway claims and that "ample Justice [would] be done," the Ioways also warned that if their demands for recognition of their land claim and recompense for its loss were not met, "they [would] have again to appeal to arms, and try to repossess themselves of their ancient possessions."

What lands did the Ioways claim and accuse the Sauk of usurping and selling? Essentially, the territory encompassed by the present state of Iowa as well as northern Missouri: "between the Mo. and Mississippi Rivers, from the mouth of Missouri, as high north as the head branches of the Calamut [Big Sioux], upper Ioway and Desmoines Rivers." What was the proof? "Go search at the mouth of the Upper Ioway River, (which has been the name of their Nation time out of mind) there see their dirt Lodges, or Houses, the mounds and remains of which are all plain to be seen, even at this day, and even more, the Country which they have just claim to, is spotted at various places with their ancient Towns and Villages, the existence of which no Nation can deny." The Ioways argued that they exclusively owned and occupied the disputed territory for a great length of time—"No Indians of any other tribe [would] dare build his fire or make a mocasin track" on it—and continued to own it even after they ceased occupying it.

They recognized their argument for ownership was a historical one requiring appropriate evidence to be convincing, and they drew on multiple lines of evidence to support their case. For example, they turned to the names of geographical features for support. They also used what we might call archaeological evidence, citing the remains of their old villages as material, public, and verifiable manifestations of historical Ioway presence on the landscape, marking the area to which "they have just claim."

The Ioway contention is a sophisticated piece of historical argumentation supported by carefully chosen evidence. But the Ioways no longer lived in the subject territory, so the claim needed to be more than historical. The petition's comments about Iowaville respond directly to this issue: "And even now their village on the Desmoines is held and occupied by the Sacs—which place the Ioways only left about 25 years ago, on search of Game on other parts of their land, but never intended to abandon their claim to the same or the bones of their fathers, which are yet to be seen there, and the Country has never been taken from them by Conquest."

Yet the situation in 1836, with the Ioways living far from the land they were claiming and the Sauk occupying precisely that land, calls into question the claim of hundreds of years of continuous Ioway occupation and ownership of Iowa. Recognizing their current absence from that land, the petition emphasizes that the Ioway only very recently left the contested area and mentions Iowaville on the Des Moines River precisely because it was the most recent well-known place they had inhabited in the disputed territory. Furthermore, the Ioways use the Sauk occupation of Iowaville as an opportunity to portray the Sauk as recent, illegitimate intruders on Ioway land. Not only do the Ioways refute the idea that they were conquered by the Sauk—saying they left the area "on search of Game" and that "the Country has never been taken from them by Conquest"—but they also construct the striking image of the Sauk living among the still visible bones or graves of Ioway ancestors. They cite physical and emotive evidence—"the bones of their fathers, which are yet to be seen there"—both to support their claim to the area and to construct a rhetorically persuasive image that furthers their own case while weakening that of their rivals.

Six Ioway men signed the petition. The first four signers are known respectively in English as the Orator, Plum, Walking Rain (figure 6), and Plenty of Meat. The fifth signer (Rube doux) is probably White Cloud II (figure 3). The identity of the sixth signer (O Kig Water, On kig wato) is unclear, but the county clerk who certified the petition identified him as one of the two signatory chiefs, so there is a good chance this name was an alternate, unrecorded appellation for No Heart (figure 4). At the time, White Cloud II, No Heart, and the Orator were the first-, second-, and third-ranking Ioway headmen, and Walking Rain was reportedly fifth in rank.[9]

Apparently believing the government could expeditiously settle their grievances and allocate the requested funds, White Cloud II and a young Ioway warrior known as the Sioux Killer (Shauhaunapotinia), along with Andrew Hughes and Major Joseph V. Hamilton, carried the petition to Washington. Accompanying them was Nesouaquoit (Ne-sawa-hkwatwa, Bear in the Forks of a Tree), leader of the Sac and Fox of the Missouri. Nesouaquoit had a complaint similar to the Ioways': the Sac and Fox of the Mississippi were benefiting from treaty payments owed instead to the Sac and Fox of the Missouri. When the small party stopped in St. Louis, they met with Superintendent of Indian Affairs William Clark, who addressed a letter to Hamilton that endorsed the Ioway petition. Clark wrote on January 5, 1837, that when he arrived in the area in 1803, he "found the Ioways in possession of an immense tract of country between the Mississippi and the Missouri rivers . . . which they have never abandoned, living on it from that time to the present . . . and as to their claim to the country in question, to the extent indicated by the treaty of 1825, it is, in my opinion, not to be doubted or questioned." Clark was well respected among Indian Affairs officials as well as tribes, although his allegiance was to the cause of white settlement expansion.[10]

After the five travelers arrived in Washington, Hamilton delivered the Ioway petition and Clark's letter to Indian Commissioner Carey A. Harris. White Cloud II, Sioux Killer, and Nesouaquoit remained in Washington for about ten days. There they received medals and sat for portraits painted by Charles Bird King. Nesouaquoit received assurance—whether verbal or written is unclear—that the Sac and Fox treaty provisions would be fulfilled. White Cloud II similarly "was promised"—again, by whom and in what form is unknown—"that his business should be attended to, and his grievances redressed." Apparently placated by those unofficial declarations, the tribal leaders returned home in mid-February.[11]

The 1837 Council

White Cloud II's diplomatic mission did not resolve the Ioways' complaints. Nor were the Ioway and the Sac and Fox of the Missouri the only tribes that wanted to settle important territorial and diplomatic issues. Because the U.S. War Department's Office of Indian Affairs was concerned that intertribal conflicts and unresolved land claims were hindering white settlement west of the Mississippi River, Commissioner Harris scheduled a council in Washington for the fall of 1837. Invitees included leaders of the Ioway, Missouria, Omaha, Otoe, Pawnee, Sac and Fox of the Mississippi, Sac and Fox of the Missouri, Santee Sioux, Winnebago (Ho-Chunk), and Yankton Sioux tribes. The Ioway, Sac and Fox, and Sioux delegates arrived in September, and the Ho-Chunk in October. The other tribes did not arrive until November, after the council had adjourned.[12]

The Ioway delegation consisted of four of the tribe's highest-ranking leaders: White Cloud II, No Heart, Walking Rain, and the Orator, plus the young warrior Plenty of Meat. All of them had the authority to sign agreements on behalf of the Ioway nation. The Orator, Walking Rain, Plenty of Meat, probably White Cloud II, and perhaps No Heart had signed the 1836 petition. All five of them had signed or would sign various of the Ioways' 1830s treaties: 1830 (Walking Rain and Plenty of Meat), 1836 (White Cloud II, No Heart, Walking Rain, and the Orator), 1837 (No Heart, Walking Rain, the Orator, and Plenty of Meat), and 1838 (White Cloud II, No Heart, and Plenty of Meat).

The trek from the Ioway settlement in northeastern Kansas to Washington—White Cloud II's second journey to the nation's capital within a year—took nearly a month. The delegation began its journey in August or early September by heading down the Missouri River to St. Louis. There, the Ioways were joined by "nine principal chiefs of the Sioux" and four or five headmen of the Sac and Fox of the Missouri. Accompanied by Joshua Pilcher, Indian agent for the upper Missouri, the entourage left St. Louis on September 7. They steamed down the Mississippi River, then up the Ohio, arriving in Cincinnati on September 12 and in Wheeling a few days later. Next, they traveled overland across the Appalachian Mountains, almost certainly on the National (Cumberland) stage road, as the Sauk leader Black Hawk (under military guard) had done four years earlier. The travelers arrived in Philadelphia on September 23, then finished the last leg of the journey by rail. They met President Van Buren in Washington on September 28.[13]

The council was held in the largest meeting hall available for government use in Washington, Rev. James Laurie's Presbyterian church, across F Street from the White House. The arrival of more than 100 tribal representatives, most of them clad in traditional regalia, captivated the local citizenry and the press. Newspaper coverage was extensive, both of the council itself and the delegations' various unofficial outings such as the theater and the racetrack. Traditional dance demonstrations also entranced the press and the public.[14]

The month-long treaty council was a theatrical event in its own right. On a platform at the front of the church, the Indian delegates, grouped by tribe, sat in a semicircle facing Secretary of War Joel Poinsett and other U.S. officials. To keep the audience to a manageable size, invitation cards were issued, though to whom is not clear. Seating on the main floor was "reserved for ladies, for gentlemen accompanying them, for members of Congress, and for other persons to whom invitations may be extended."[15]

Each day's session of the month-long council opened with the smoking and passing of the Calumet of Peace to each participant. (The calumet is the pan-tribal sacred pipe whose use solemnizes important events. Treaty signings also concluded with the passing of the calumet.) The council commenced on September 21 with the first-arriving delegation, the Santee Sioux. No other tribe was yet present, and the Santees signed a treaty on September 29. The proverbial fireworks began when the General Council commenced on October 5, attended by the delegations of the Santee and Yankton Sioux, the Sac and Fox of the Missouri, the Sac and Fox of the Mississippi, and the Ioway. Initial attention focused on a long-standing dispute between the Sioux and the Sac and Fox of the Mississippi that was threatening to spiral into a full-scale intertribal war as U.S. settlement pressure and resource depletion exacerbated the conflict. With those two delegations seated on opposite sides of the dais and with the calumet being passed from the commissioner to the Sacs and Foxes of the Mississippi, reaching the Sioux only after passing through the other two delegations, it is not surprising that things did not go well. The Sioux and Sac and Fox of the Mississippi leaders hurled accusations and insults at one another, the Sac leader Keokuk speaking initially and most forcefully for the Sac and Fox (figure 7). After refereeing a full afternoon of acrimonious disputation, Commissioner Harris exhorted both tribes "on returning home to throw away the war-club and bury the Tomahawk" and trusted that "I shall hear that the two great tribes now represented before me have smoked the pipe together and promised to remain at peace with each other"—a literal pipe dream. Neither side would relent, and the conflict continued until the Sac and Fox ceded their Iowa Territory lands in 1842.[16]

Both the intransigence of the Sac and Fox of the Mississippi and Harris's inability or unwillingness to impose a settlement boded ill for the Ioways. With ten days between their arrival in Washington and the opening of their council session on Saturday, October 7, they had plenty of time to hone their presentation. If they had not brought their map with them, they had opportunities to draft it in Washington. Their petition of the preceding year was a treatise in Ioway historical and cultural geography, and their 1837 presentation was going to echo that approach, this time

Figure 7. "Council Held in Washington in 1837 between the Ministers of the United States and the Chiefs of the Sauks-Foxes and the Sioux of the Mississippi." By Ferdinand Pettrich, ca. 1845–1856. Painted plaster frieze based on drawings Pettrich made in 1837. Keokuk stands at the head of his delegation with his arm outstretched, the U.S. government representatives are in the center, and the Sioux delegation is on the right. Pettrich's earlier drawing of this scene depicts Secretary of State John Forsyth (standing to the right of the table) smoking a long-stemmed calumet. In the frieze, no U.S. official is smoking, but the seated Sioux leader holds an object of similar size in the same position, though the bowl is of the pipe-tomahawk style rather than a spiked shape as in the drawing. Approximate size: 170 × 35 inches (430 × 88 cm). Anima Mundi (Vatican Ethnological Museum). Photo copyright © Governorate of the Vatican City State—Directorate of the Vatican Museums.

supported by a map, so the cartographic gambit likely was part of their council strategy from the outset. It would not be the first council in which Ioway delegates made a map to illustrate their claims: White Cloud I did the same at the 1825 treaty council. Because Indian delegations rarely made maps for treaty councils, the fact that the Ioways drafted and presented maps at two councils is a notable aspect of their diplomatic strategy. But even if they had not originally planned to use a map in 1837, witnessing the contentious October 5 session may have impelled them to develop such evidence to support their position, in which case they would have drafted their map on October 6.[17]

On the morning of the seventh, the Sioux having signed their treaty, the council platform was occupied solely by government officials and the Ioway and Sac and Fox delegations. "The church was crowded to excess, both below and in the galleries." Platform dignitaries included Vice President Richard Mentor Johnson and Secretary of the Treasury Levi Woodbury. Following the passing of the calumet, Commissioner Harris began the council by noting that the Ioway and the Sac and

Fox of the Missouri both had claims based on provisions of the treaty of 1825 and that he wished to hear from both tribes in hopes of addressing and settling their grievances.[18]

No Heart spoke first. Observers reported that he "put himself in an oratorical attitude, and in a very firm and dignified manner laid before the representative of his great father an account of the grievances of his tribe—consisting chiefly of oppressions inflicted by the Sacs and Foxes."[19] Walking Rain followed. Both of them focused on the Ioways' historic and continuing connections to the land between the Mississippi and Missouri Rivers, and both referred to the map that No Heart presented to Commissioner Harris at the beginning of his presentation. Several authors have published reviews and small segments of the Ioway testimony, but appendix 2 provides the entirety of No Heart's and Walking Rain's statements. This is the first time the complete presentations have been published.

"My Father this is the rout[e] of my forefathers," No Heart said as he presented the map to Harris. "It is the land that we have always claimed from old times. We have the history. We have always owned this land. It is ours. It bears our name." With these words, No Heart announced his strategy for the council. He argued that the Ioways were the rightful owners of the land in question because they were its original owners. He put the current Ioway claim in the context of a continuous historical claim ("It is the land that we have always claimed from old times"). He also argued that the Ioways not only continuously claimed but indeed continuously owned and occupied the land in the past ("We have the history. We have always owned this land.").[20]

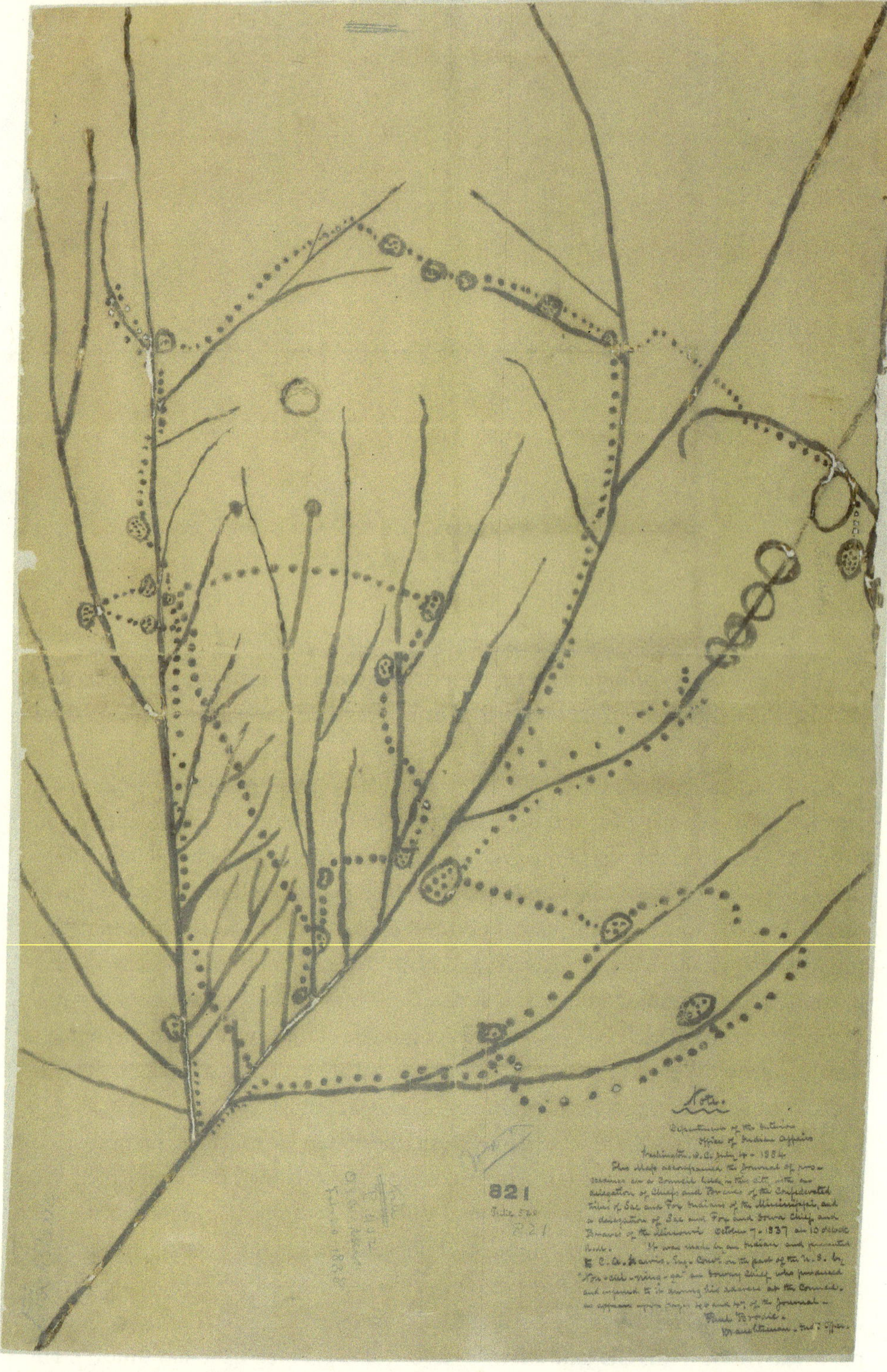

Figure 8. The 1837 Ioway map. Records of the Bureau of Indian Affairs, Record Group 75, Central Map File 821. National Archives and Records Administration, Cartographic Branch, College Park, Maryland.

As the Ioways had in 1836, No Heart recognized that his argument required historical evidence to be convincing. One piece of evidence he mentioned is the fact that the land is named after his people ("It is ours. It bears our name."). The map showing Ioway migrations across the region in the past ("This is the rout[e] of my forefathers") was also evidence for his assertion of continuity between past and present Ioway claims to and ownership of the land. Walking Rain also spoke, offering "another proof of our claim to this country. The Ioways named all the rivers."

No Heart and Walking Rain named and showed on the map several places where they or their forefathers had lived or visited: Green Bay, Lake Pepin, the Missouri River, the Des Moines River, the Illinois River, the Calumet River, and the Grand River. They identified several tribes the Ioways had lived with or visited, or with whom they were friendly: the Omahas, Otoes, Kickapoos, Sauk (of the Missouri), and Sioux (of the Mississippi). No Heart identified two specific places on the Des Moines River (the "dry field" and the "big groove," possibly "grove") that were theirs when "the Spanish & French came into the Country."

Chapter 3 examines the map in terms of Ioway testimony and traditions as well as other historical and archaeological information. Here, it is important to note that for No Heart and Walking Rain, their map and testimony not only proved that the Ioways had occupied Iowa for a great length of time but also that they retained a legitimate claim to the land even though they had recently relocated: "the Sacs and Foxes (of Mississippi) were invited through friendship to come and hunt to eat with us and divide the game but never understood they were to have our lands." The Ioways traditionally permitted others to hunt on their land if requested.[21] As No Heart noted, referring to the 1825 treaty, the Ioways "gave the game but not the lands." Regarding the 1830 treaty, No Heart and Walking Rain pointed out that the Ioways were not aware of the provision that allowed eastern tribes to settle on Ioway land, having been provided no interpreter at that council. In essence, No Heart said of the Sac and Fox of the Mississippi, "They steal from us and then sell to you." Regarding "my land," he asked, "I should like to know by what right they claim it."

We can't know what kind of answer No Heart expected, but Keokuk responded in a way that, according to one reporter, "explained away and controverted many of the Ioway's charges." Furthermore, "Ke-o-kuck had the advantage in powers of oratory, and produced upon the large audience assembled, a decided impression in his favor." This was not an isolated observation: Contemporary accounts frequently remarked on Keokuk's oratorical and diplomatic skills.[22]

Keokuk conceded previous Ioway occupation of the territory in question but upheld the Sac and Fox right to it, saying, "The country laying between the Missouri & the Mississippi river we fought for. We drove these people off. . . . This country I have gained by fighting. Therefore, I claim it." This understanding of territorial primacy applied as well to land lost by his own nation: "Our people once inhabited the country about the Great Lakes. We were driven off. You don't hear me claiming the country I was driven off from. . . . This is my country. I have fought for it." In a specific rebuttal to the Ioway map, Keokuk said, "They fled before us. We followed on their track. We have always pushed them before us. That is the reason they have marked so many villages on their map. . . . If I had not beg[g]ed them to come back they would have been off I don't know how far beyond the Mississippi." Keokuk's viewpoint on matters of land acquisition and ownership was well known. Fourteen years earlier, he had asked then-Secretary of War John C. Calhoun, "How did you Americans become possessed of this land which we now stand on, on whom did your claim first originate, was it not at the point of the spear, & did not the mouths of your big guns proclaim that you were masters of the soil"? He continued, "By that same right we claim the Country which we conquered." Presaging his argument against the Ioway claim, he had asked Calhoun "by what right the Osages sold to you a Country which we had conquered, and were then in possession of." And applying the same reasoning he would use in 1837, he said the Sac and Fox did not claim their former Wisconsin homeland "because our fathers were conquered and it fell into the hands of other people"—asserting, as he would in 1837, that they were forced to move west of the Mississippi River and were not simply bullying the nations that already lived there.[23]

Wapello, the Meskwaki headman, followed Keokuk and responded to the Ioway presentation, alleging, "It is very recently that I heard of those people claiming the lands spoken of. I was very much surprised. It cannot be their own doings, they must have been advised so to do by the white people. It is very strange that we did not hear of their claim before this. My forefathers never heard such talk before. If so we never knew of it. I was surprised to see you bring forward this paper (alluding to the map presented by the Ioway Chief). Some persons have pushed your head towards mine."[24]

After adjourning for a day of reflection and deliberation, Commissioner Harris reconvened the council at 11 a.m. on Monday, October 9. "All seats in the church, both on the floor and in the galleries, were occupied, and many gentlemen remained standing in the aisles during the entire proceedings." Vice President Johnson was again in attendance, as was Secretary of the Navy Mahlon Dickerson. Responding to Harris's request for any additional comments, No Heart simply said, "My Father, I am well pleased to see you. I came with my Father, your agent. I was much pleased to receive your invitation. What my people have told you respecting our having once occupied that country is true." Commissioner Harris presented a draft treaty to the Ioways, but they rejected it because it did not offer what they considered just compensation for the land the Sac and Fox were selling and because it stipulated that payments to the tribe (consisting of 5 percent interest on a principal sum) be appropriated for farmers, teachers, and blacksmiths, which the Ioways deemed unnecessary and to which they strenuously objected.

Thus ended the Ioways' participation in the 1837 council, except to attend the ceremonial closing session on October 21 at which delegates whose tribes had signed treaties received medals. The United States had betrayed the Ioways again: After having cheated them in the 1830 treaty council by not providing an interpreter, the United States rejected their 1837 claim, implicitly accepting conquest as conferring right of possession and offering a pittance for the Ioway homeland—see steps 5 and 6 of the treaty process as outlined by Lance Foster earlier in this chapter.[25]

The heart of the Ioway case supporting their claim was the cartographic chronicle of their history in the present state of Iowa and portions of all neighboring states. Other tribes sharing the land were considered guests. Keokuk did not dispute Ioway settlement history but claimed Sac and Fox pressure had forced the Ioways to move between the villages on the map. These alternate narratives of Ioway history both cite the map. But only one side prevailed, as Keokuk reminded the War Department officials that the Sac and Fox perspective on the perquisites of conquest matched that of the United States.

The rhetoric exchanged between the Ioways and the Sac and Fox of the Mississippi had been barbed but, to the ears of those in attendance, relatively civil: "In manner, and in the great matter of sticking to the point, these [Ioway] speakers, and Keokuck, who replied to them, furnished good models for imitation." "The discussion was conducted with great decorum and courtesy on both sides; and I could not help thinking that our legislators might profit by the example set them in the councils of these savages." Having thus entertained and perhaps edified the residents of Washington, but failing in their diplomatic mission, the Ioways and their Sac and Fox allies, as well as their Sac and Fox antagonists, headed off to Baltimore by train on the evening of October 22 to begin a postcouncil East Coast tour.[26]

The Ioway map remained in Washington.

Touring the East

The week-long East Coast tour generated another series of public spectacles in Philadelphia, New York, and Boston. Thousands of urbanites witnessed the exotic visitors at a circus in Philadelphia; at Scudder's American Museum and the newly opened George Catlin Gallery and Lecture Room at Stuyvesant Institute in New York; at Boston Common, Faneuil Hall, and the Massachusetts State House in Boston; and in various theaters in those cities. Not surprisingly in view of their ongoing enmity, and especially after the combative council sessions, the delegations were seen to "keep entirely separate, have their separate interpreters . . . and hold no intercourse with each other." Keokuk once again won over the audiences. In Boston he was dubbed "one of nature's best orators," speaking with great verve and "manly suavity" even while those attending the public talks had difficulty comprehending his interpreter's remarks. Keokuk presented to Massachusetts Governor Edward Everett "a bow, quiver and arrows, in a token of amity"; other Sac and Fox delegates also presented gifts. In contrast, when the "Chief of the Ioways" (probably No Heart) followed Keokuk, "his manner and gesture were more vehement than Keokuck's though he looked less of the savage. There seemed to be an arch sarcasm in the close of his speech to which the interpreter did not give the point of the original." By the time of this October 28 gathering, No Heart's sarcasm might have stemmed from having heard quite enough from the Sac and Fox of the Mississippi over the previous three weeks. He also seemed exasperated or exhausted by the public's expectations: "Alluding to the presents which Keokuck and his chiefs had brought, the Ioway said that they brought no presents. They had been advised by their white brethren to act like white men, and they were trying to do so. They had accordingly laid aside their Indian apparel, and appeared in the dress of the white man, and as white men give no presents, they had brought none, to be like the white men." The Ioways left Boston on October 30, the Sac and Fox a few days later.[27]

As the smallest delegation, the Ioways received less public attention, at least outside of the council sessions, than the Sioux and the Sac and Fox. They did not leave the Eastern Seaboard without making an impression, though. Henry R. Schoolcraft—of "Oneota River" fame, as we saw in chapter 1—was, among his polymathic pursuits, a poet and collector of poetry. He reported the following from one of the cities on the Ioways' eastern tour:

> A young lady who went to see the Warriors of the Forest at the City Hotel took with her, as did other ladies, various presents for them. A young Indian whose name upon inquiry was "No Heart" particularly attracted her notice: She gave him a bracelet which apparently pleased him exceedingly and when she returned home wrote the following verses, which a Friend begs leave to offer for publication.

TO A YOUNG IOWA CHIEF CALLED "NO HEART"

Can the sweetness that dwells in thy voice and thy smile
Like the offspring of culture but charm to beguile?
Can thy glance of the Eagle, thy step of the Deer
Be the types of a spirit which crouches in fear?

I will read Thee young Chieftain thy hand clasp'd in mine
For the bravest and best of the Warrior line.
Thou thirsted not "No Heart" for glory alone
Gentle pity is there with her whispering tone.
And thy soul sees
The hunting grounds where the red man no more sleep
With thee then my Chief to the forest I'll fly
And still trust to the language that speaks in thine eye
For affection to truth and for valour to aid
Through its tangles—the "pale face" and Ioway Maid.[28]

Even more than they had in Washington, the delegates used the East Coast tour to connect with large audiences, dignitaries as well as the general public, most of whom had never interacted with Indians. Yet whatever its Native participants might have felt, and whatever the audiences might have experienced or learned, the tour was primarily a War Department scheme to promote Indian removal. After incorrectly reporting that all of the visiting tribes' claims had been "happily adjudicated" in Washington, a Boston journalist praised the government for having "wisely and humanely provided for [the Indians] visiting the principal cities," urging that they "be treated with the respect we would award to a delegation of distinguished men from any nation with whom we wished to be on terms of reciprocal amity . . . that they may feel that we are their friends and not their foes." But the ultimate rationale was subjugation:

> that they may see the strength of our people . . . and how vain it is for their feeble tribes, though every man of them might be brave, to contend with this mighty nation. The impression made on the minds of these men who are evidently sagacious and observing, (particularly if they are treated with respect by the multitude) must be favorable to a determination on their part to trust the magnanimity and justice of the United States for redress in any future wrongs, rather than resort to war, which must end in their extermination.[29]

This "disobey us at your peril" attitude echoed government policy, as Superintendent Harris wrote that fall:

> It is believed that the visits of the several tribes to [Washington, DC], and to others upon the seaboard, has had, and will have a most salutary effect. So far as a correct judgment can now be formed, they will return to their kindred with just ideas of the strength and resources of the country, and of the friendly dispositions of our people towards them, and impressed with the conviction of the propriety of remaining at peace with us and with each other.[30]

Home

The Ioway delegates began their return home with no resolution of their grievances. When they reached St. Louis in late November, they agreed to sign a treaty extinguishing their rights to a tract in western Iowa Territory. But they still refused to sign away their interest in central and eastern Iowa, even with Commissioner Harris offering to sweeten the deal with an extra thousand dollars. With the Ioways continuing to claim and even seek restoration of their Des Moines River lands, they were described as "obstinate" in their rejection of the deal. A sympathetic reporter in Missouri wrote that that region "is held in high estimation by the Ioways, 'tis the land of their fathers, and they are endeared to it by many ties and considerations. . . . They have lost confidence in the whites . . . and they will not part with [the Des Moines River country] . . . without . . . a fair and liberal consideration." The Ioways held out for nearly a year until October 1838 when, under threat of starvation, they signed a treaty relinquishing their claim to the rest of their former homeland in Iowa.[31]

CHAPTER THREE

Mapping Time, Space, and Place

WHILE THEIR MAP DID NOT HELP the Ioways achieve satisfaction in 1837, its presentation was an important element of their diplomacy. Yet despite all that has been written about the Ioway people and about Native American cartography in general, little has been published about this map's significance as a historical record and cultural product. In this chapter, I employ oral history and oral tradition, documentary records, and archaeological evidence to understand what the map depicts. We will see that the map chronicles 200 years of Ioway history and helps situate the Ioways within the complex and dynamic historical and sociopolitical environments of the early contact and removal eras.

The map the Ioway delegation presented on October 7, 1837, measures 69 by 104 centimeters (27 by 41 inches). It was boldly drawn in ink on two sheets of paper joined by an adhesive prior to drafting (figure 9). The map depicts an area that encompasses about 700,000 square kilometers (around 270,000 square miles) of the Upper Mississippi valley and lower Missouri River valley, comprising what is now the entire state of Iowa, plus large portions of all adjoining states: from Lake Michigan on the east to the North Platte River on the west, and from southern Wisconsin and Minnesota on the north past the mouth of the Missouri River on the south (figures 10–12). The map shows fifty-four rivers, nine lakes, and twenty-three settlements as well as routes connecting the settlements. There are two faint notations in pencil as well as an inked description added in 1884. While No Heart's and Walking Rain's presentations, as summarized in the Journal of Proceedings, constitute the principal contemporary sources for identifying many of the physical and cultural features represented on the map, additional historical and archaeological evidence is crucial for specifying several places, dates, and events.

The descriptions presented here discuss the places depicted on the 1837 map, estimate when the Ioways occupied or visited those places, and situate these sites in relevant historical and cultural contexts. I assigned each settlement a unique letter designation in alphabetical order from earliest to latest according to its apparent temporal position. Each river and lake received a number, beginning in the east

Figure 9. The 1837 Ioway map. Numbers added to indicate physical features (rivers and lakes) identified in Table 1; letters added to indicate settlements discussed in text.

MAP REFERENCE NUMBER AND FEATURE	
1	Mississippi River
2	Illinois River (lower)
3	Illinois River (central)
4	Sangamon River
5	Rock River
6	The "Four Lakes" (Madison, Wisconsin)
6a	Lake Kegonsa
6b	Lake Waubesa
6c	Lake Monona
6d	Lake Mendota
7	Green Bay
8	Lake Winnebago
9	Fox River (of Wisconsin)
10	Wisconsin River
11	Cuivre River
12	Salt River
13	North Fabius or Wyaconda or Fox River (of Missouri)
14	Des Moines River
15	Raccoon River
16	Middle Raccoon River
17	North Raccoon River
18	Storm Lake
19	Des Moines River or West Fork Des Moines River
20	Boone River or East Fork Des Moines River
21	Skunk River
22	Cedar River
23	Iowa River
24	South Fork Iowa River
25	Turkey River
26	Upper Iowa River
27	Root River
28	Chariton River
29	Grand River
30	Weldon River
31	Thompson River
32	Twelvemile Creek (uncertain)
33	Platte River (of Missouri)
34	Hundred and Two River
35	Nodaway River
36	East Nodaway River
37	West Nodaway River
38	Nishnabotna River
39	East Nishnabotna River
40	West Nishnabotna River
41	Boyer River
42	Blackhawk Lake
43	Little Sioux River
44	Floyd River
45	Big Sioux River
46	Rock River (of Iowa)
47	Beaver Creek or Skunk Creek
48	Missouri River
49	Bow Creek or White River
50	Platte River
51	North Platte River
52	South Platte River
53	Kansas River
54	Republican River
55	Osage River
56	Gasconade River
57	Iowa "Great Lakes" (Spirit Lake, Okoboji Lakes, etc.), or Storm Lake, or stylized representation of these or other northwest Iowa lakes

Table 1. Identification of hydrographic features depicted on the 1837 Ioway map.

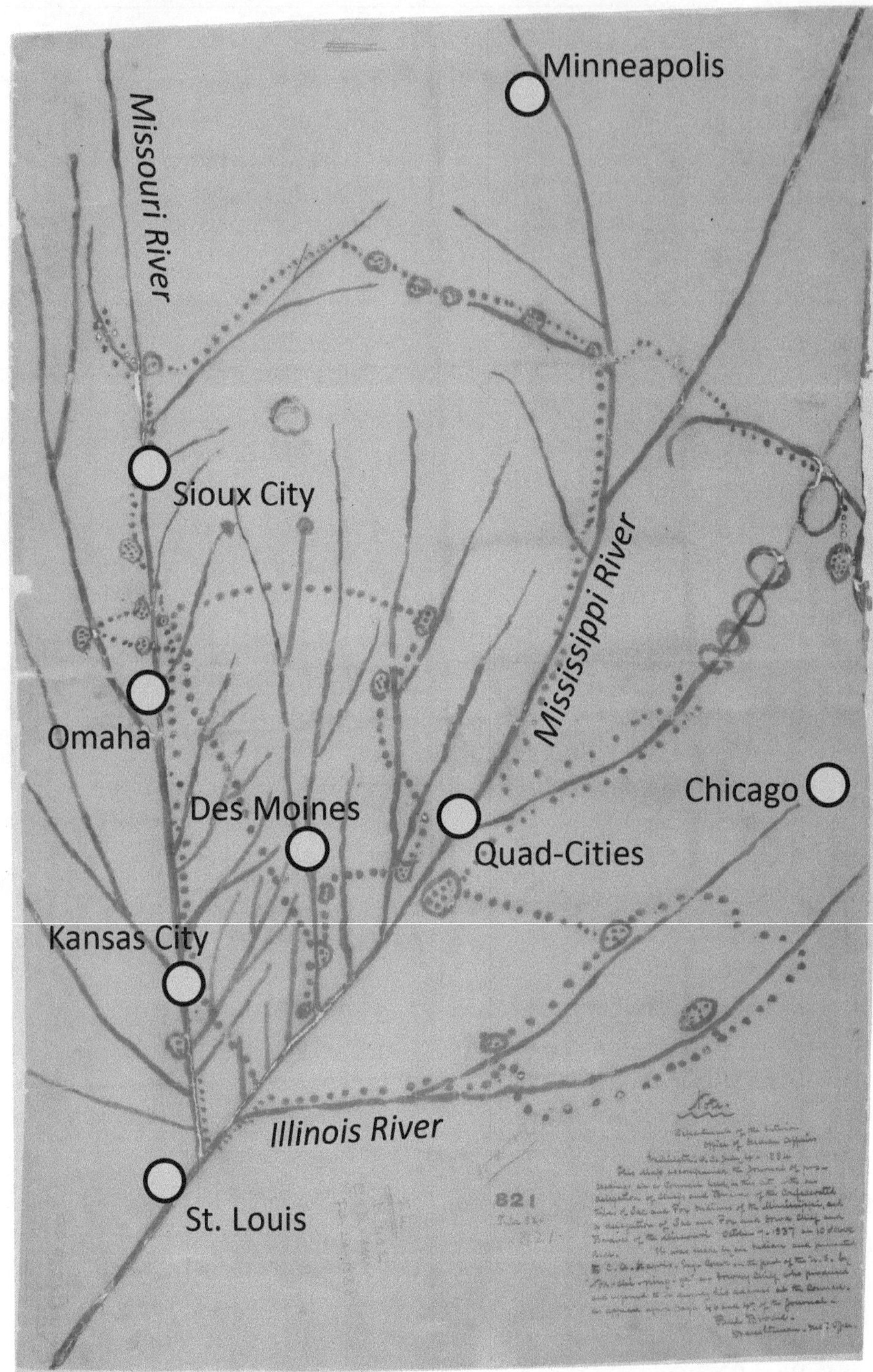

Figure 10. The 1837 Ioway map with river names and modern city locations added.

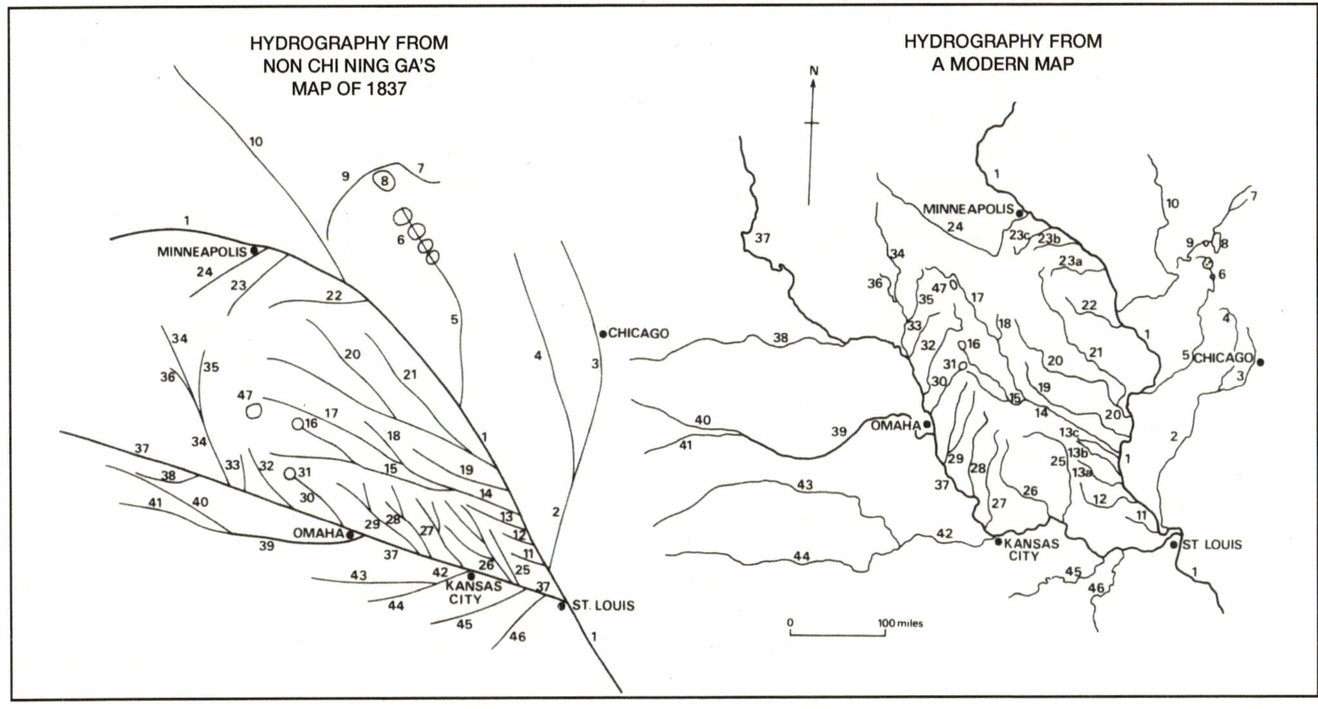

Figure 11. Interpretation of the hydrography on the Ioway map as identified by G. Malcolm Lewis (1979).

1 Mississippi R.
2 Illinois R.
3 Des Plaines R.
4 Fox R. (Illinois-Wisconsin)
5 Rock R. (Illinois-Wisconsin)
6 Series of Small Lakes and Swamps on the Upper Rock R.
7 Greenbay?
8 L. Winnebago
9 Fox R. (Wisconsin)
10 Wisconsin R.
11 Cuivre R.
12 Salt R.
13 A) South Fabius or B) Wyaconda or C) Fox (Iowa) R.
14 Des Moines R.
15 Raccoon A. (with W and E Forks)
16 Storm L.
17 West Fork Des Moines R.
18 East Fork Des Moines R.
19 Skunk R.
20 Iowa R.
21 Cedar R.
22 Turkey R.
23 A) Root or B) Zumbro or C) Cannon R.
24 Minnesota R.
25 Chariton R.
26 Grand R.
27 Platte A. (Missouri)
28 Nodaway R.
29 Nishnabotna R.
30 Boyer R.
31 Blackhawk L.
32 Little Sioux R.
33 Floyd R.
34 Big Sioux R.
35 Rock R. (Minnesota-Iowa)
36 Skunk Creek?
37 Missouri R.
38 Niobrara R.
39 Platte R.
40 North Platte R.
41 South Platte R.
42 Kansas R.
43 Republican R.
44 Smoky Hill R.
45 Osage R.
46 Gasconade R.
47 Heron Lake

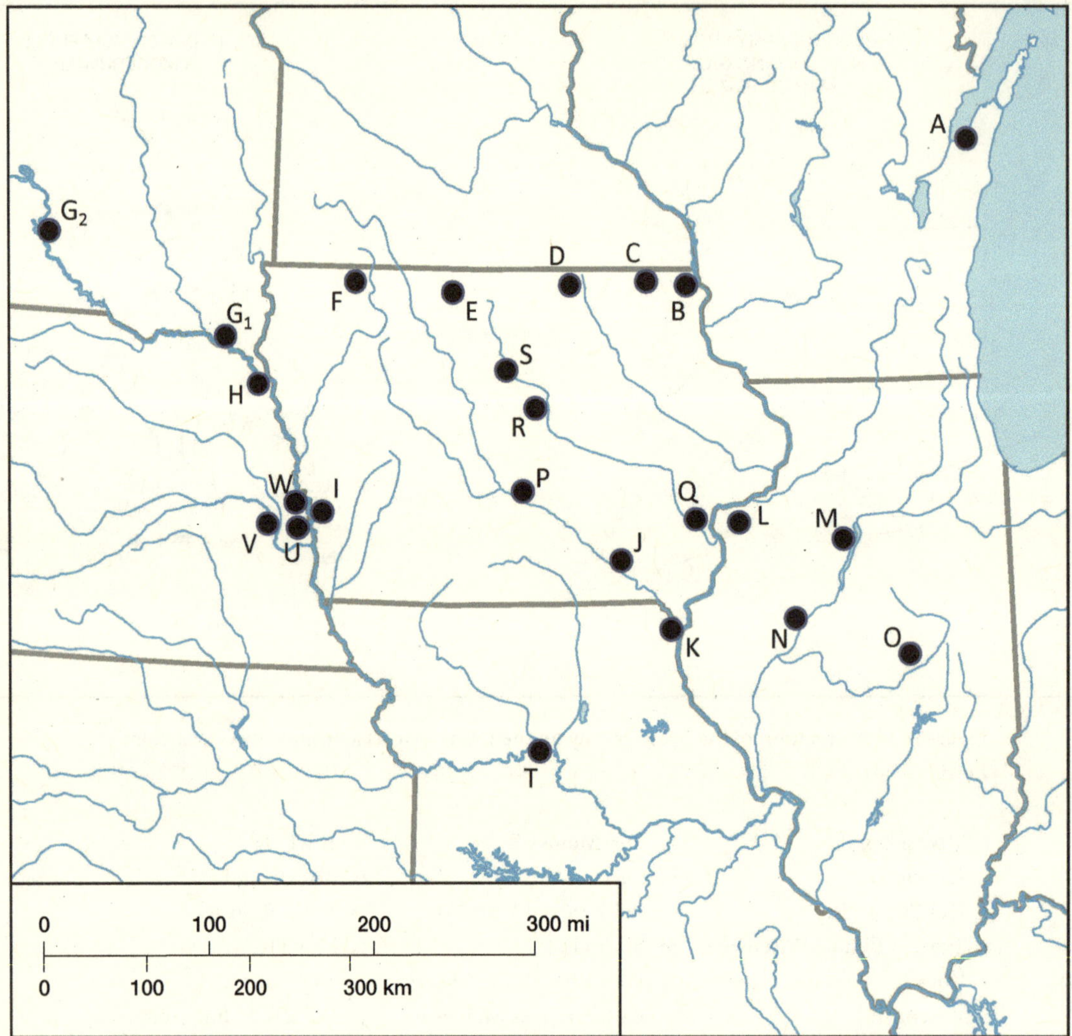

Figure 12. Inferred and estimated locations of settlements depicted on the 1837 map. Base map from the *National Atlas of the United States of America*, U.S. Geological Survey 2024.

with the Mississippi and Illinois Rivers and moving generally to the west. These designations and labels differ slightly from those used in earlier publications, particularly those by G. Malcolm Lewis, because they are based on more recent historical and archaeological analyses.

This narrative contains many qualifications such as "likely," "probable," and "may be." Few of the sites' locations and dates are absolutely certain, but most attributions are at least plausible or supported by a preponderance of evidence. Several previous studies have discussed the map's importance as an example of Native American cartography and as an element of Ioway diplomacy and political negotiation strategies. In contrast, this chapter constitutes a comprehensive effort to identify the settlements and other features depicted on the map and to estimate the dates when the Ioways inhabited or visited those places. In effect, it elucidates and updates the 1836 Ioway petition and 1837 testimony with information derived from oral traditions, documentary histories, and archaeology.[1]

Site A

The transcript of No Heart's chronicle states, "This village (pointing to a few dots on his map) was the residence of our forefathers. If I should try I could not tell you the number of villages our people made. They built one on the banks of Lake Pepin. The Sacs call it Green Bay, we call it Lake Pepin."[2]

Every map purporting to trace a population movement that ends someplace must also show it to begin someplace. The map's chronicle of Ioway history begins at Site A.[3] This site is located below the mouth of the Fox River on the right (east) bank of Green Bay in eastern Wisconsin (figure 13). The transcript of No Heart's presentation evinces confusion in the record between Green Bay and Lake Pepin. Lake Pepin is in the Mississippi River valley about 330 kilometers (205 miles) west of Green Bay. The Lake Pepin region is home to some of the earliest known Oneota sites, and No Heart may well have mentioned it as an ancestral location that predated European contact and the Ioway presence at Green Bay. The Orator also referred to crossing Lake Pepin as the earliest episode he knew about in Ioway traditional history.[4] It is also possible that living on or crossing Lake Pepin referred to a time after departure from the ancestral origin at Green Bay. Regardless, both Lake Pepin and Green Bay factor into Ioway traditional origins. But contrary to the council transcript, the Ioways never referred to Green Bay as Lake Pepin, nor did the Sauks ever refer to Lake Pepin as Green Bay. "Green Bay" is penciled lightly on the map next to Site A, superimposing a penciled and erased "Lake Pepin" (figure 14). These labels were almost certainly added to the map at the time it was presented, and the handwriting matches that of Chauncey Bush, Commissioner Harris's secretary. Bush evidently was trying to take notes on the translated Ioway testimony while simultaneously annotating the map. It is no wonder that he was confused regarding No Heart's reference to Lake Pepin. Despite the mixup, erasure of the Lake Pepin label and its replacement by "Green Bay" correctly identifies the eastern Wisconsin location of the earliest mapped village. The position of the Lake Pepin/Green Bay label also indicates that during the council, the map was viewed in landscape rather than portrait orientation. For convenience on the printed page, most studies of the map, including the present one, employ portrait orientation.

Did the Ioways originate or live at Green Bay? If so, when? According to the Jesuit Father Louis André, reporting from the St. Francis Xavier Mission at Green Bay,

Figure 13.
Site A and vicinity
on the 1837 map.

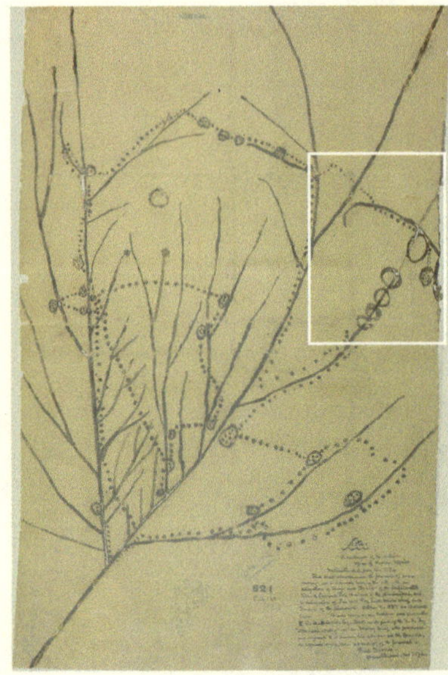

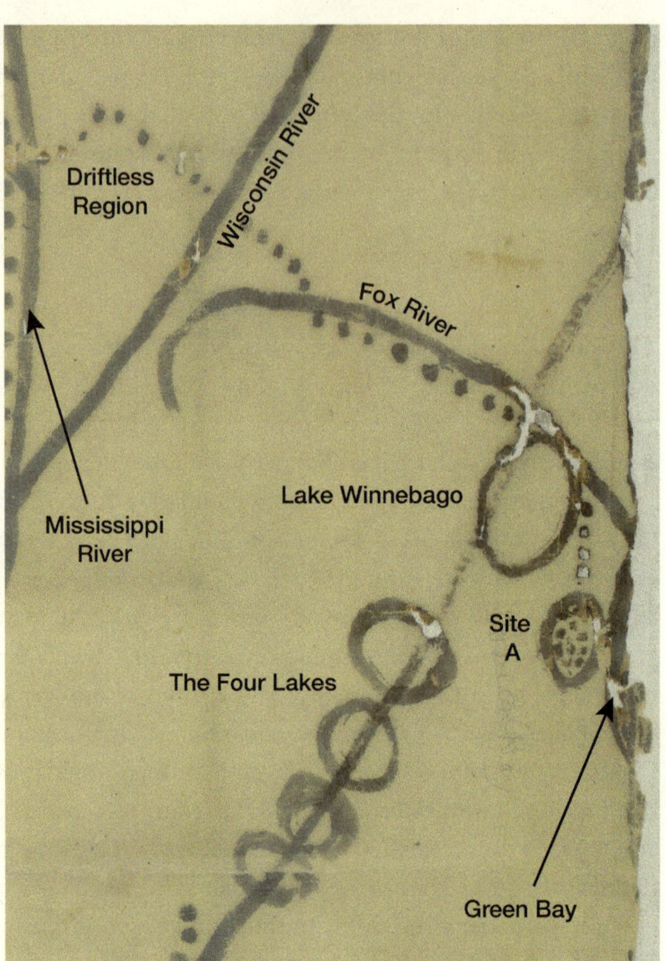

Figure 14.
Close-up of the
1837 map showing
"Lake Pepin"
overwritten by
"Green Bay."

at least seven Ioway families resided there in 1676. Small quantities of Allamakee Trailed pottery, a type probably made by Ioways in the seventeenth century, have been found in the Red Banks area near Green Bay. Yet the main Ioway villages in the late 1600s were west of the Mississippi River, in the Upper Iowa River or Root River valleys (Sites B–D) or even farther west. It is likely that the mapped 1837 chronicle of Ioway migrations originates at Green Bay not because (or not only because) some Ioways lived there in the late seventeenth century but because Green Bay figures in oral tradition as the Ioway people's original home, Moka'shutzê. Ethnologist Alanson Skinner, working among the Ioways in the early twentieth century, reported that this term denotes "Red Earth, the traditional eastern home of the Iowa . . . the mythical point of origin of the Iowa, thought by them to have been in Wisconsin on the shore of Lake Michigan." In 1935, the ethnologist William Whitman also recorded an Ioway tradition of an eastern origin and Mokashudje as a place from which westward movement occurred. Ioway elder Emma Kent stated in 1952 that she learned from her father and grandfather that "the beginning is what they call Red Hill . . . where the Iowas history began . . . where we begin all our history." Even though she did not know its exact location, she knew "there were great lakes on the northern part of Red Hill." Ioway oral traditions continue to identify MakaShuje (Mokashudje; Red Banks/Red Earth/Red Dirt) as the place where the ten original clans converged to form the Ioway nation. The same place (Móogašúč, Red Banks) is also traditionally the origin locus of the Ho-Chunk.[5]

When and where this legendary gathering of the clans and formation of a proto-Ioway–Chiwere–Ho-Chunk collective might have occurred can only be conjectured. Their common ancestral language probably split between 500 and 1,200 years ago (see chapter 1, n. 4). Despite decades of careful searching, the Red Banks locality on Green Bay has yet to yield evidence of a large Oneota archaeological site that would evince a major village or coalescent center, though several small sites have been identified. Moreover, "Red Banks" might refer to any number of locations. Also, as noted, many early Oneota sites have been recorded in the Lake Pepin region, and early Oneota sites also appear in several other parts of the Midwest. A single Oneota (or *hunge*) origin is probably an archaeological chimera, as Oneota beginnings seemingly involved pan-regional cultural transformations within a dynamic demographic, environmental, and ideological milieu. Nevertheless, the fact that Site A—as depicted on the 1837 map—contains more dots (people? dwellings? clans?) than any other settlement indicates the importance of Green Bay in Ioway origins.[6]

On the 1837 map, the route out of Green Bay or Red Banks takes one past Lake Winnebago and up the Fox River into what is now south-central Wisconsin. Instead of using the Fox-Wisconsin portage to reach the Mississippi River via the Wisconsin River, the route crosses the Wisconsin River and enters the Driftless

Region of southwestern Wisconsin (figure 13). No villages are mapped in that region even though archaeological sites evince extensive Oneota (apparently ancestral Ioway) occupation in the La Crosse locality from the fourteenth century into the early seventeenth century. The route crosses the Mississippi River near the mouth of what is likely the Upper Iowa River at the northeast corner of what is now the state of Iowa (figure 15). There, the route encounters the terminus of another route, one that originated at Site L before it ascended and descended the Rock River and then ascended the Mississippi River. I discuss that route under Sites L–O, but it is relevant to the identification of the Upper Iowa River. The 1836 Ioway petition stated, "Search at the mouth of the Upper Ioway River, (which has been the name of their Nation time out of mind) there see their dirt lodges, or Houses, the Mounds and remains of which are all plain to be seen, even at this day"—a description indicating not only that tribal members had recently visited the mouth of the Upper Iowa River but also that they considered that place to be among their ancestral residences. This is why the river paralleling the route into Iowa is more likely to be the Upper Iowa River than another east-draining river such as the Root River or Minnesota River.[7]

Sites B and C

These sites are the first mapped villages on the route after departing the origin point at Site A. They are located along the lower and middle portions of the Upper Iowa River in the Paleozoic Plateau landform region of what is now northeast Iowa (figure 15). They likely represent Ioway occupation of the region at least as early as the 1650s, though Oneota occupation in the region began centuries earlier. Oral tradition as well as documentary and archaeological evidence indicate Ioway residence in the Upper Iowa River valley in the middle to late seventeenth century. The earliest Upper Iowa River sites with European trade items date to what archaeologists term the "protohistoric" period, that is, the time of initial contact in which interaction with Europeans occurred indirectly, almost exclusively through Native intermediaries. Mildred Mott Wedel and subsequent researchers identified the Orr phase of the Oneota tradition as consisting of several villages and burial sites that date to this period in the Upper Iowa River valley and along the nearby Riceford Creek, a tributary of the Root River in southeast Minnesota. Archaeologists believe the Oneota inhabitants of the La Crosse locality left their villages on the east side of the Mississippi River (the Valley View phase) to take up residence along the tributaries west of the Mississippi just when the earliest European goods and other foreign influences arrived in the region. These other stimuli might have included heightened interest in bison hides and other Plains/Prairie prod-

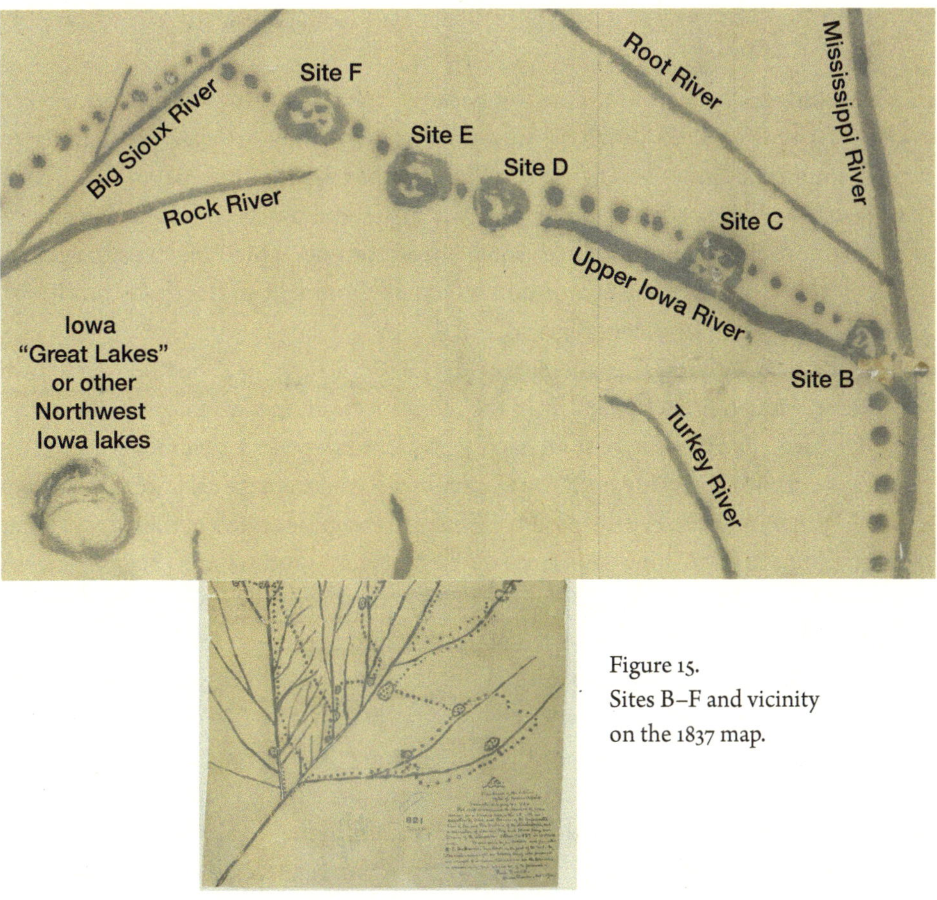

Figure 15.
Sites B–F and vicinity on the 1837 map.

ucts, territorial pressures from displaced eastern tribes, and novel microbe-borne diseases.[8]

Sites B and C probably represent seventeenth-century villages that Ioways in the 1830s knew about through cultural memory or recent site visits. There are too many Orr phase Oneota sites in the Upper Iowa River valley to permit specific identification of the mapped locations with particular archaeological sites. It is also important to reiterate that the 1837 map's purpose was to document historical Ioway residence relevant to the lands subject to ongoing treaty negotiations, not necessarily to chronicle the tribe's entire settlement history. Therefore, it is understandable why the map did not depict villages outside that area, such as the Riceford Creek sites, historically attested villages in eastern Minnesota, and sites in western Wisconsin that archaeologists identify as precontact Ioway, though there is no mention of these locations in recorded tribal historical memory.[9]

Sites D, E, and F

These sites are located in the region between the Upper Iowa River and the Big Sioux River watershed, in what is now north-central and northwest Iowa and possibly southern Minnesota (figure 15). They are the only sites not mapped on a river or lake. Site E in particular is not near any mapped drainage. The sites' positions appear to indicate a headwater or small-stream setting, which matches the generally poorly drained and wetland-dominated environment of north-central Iowa's Des Moines Lobe landform region.[10]

Documentary and archaeological evidence for the Ioways in north-central Iowa is sparse, though French maps from the 1680s locate an Ioway village on the upper Cedar River. Perhaps the best archaeological candidate for a seventeenth-century Ioway occupation outside both the Upper Iowa River drainage and northwest Iowa is the Wanampito site (13BM16). This village or camp is located in the upper Cedar River drainage in the Iowan Surface landform region, southwest of the Upper Iowa River cluster of Oneota sites. The 1837 map depicts only the lower portion of the Cedar River. The Wanampito site's material culture is similar to that of the Ioway as well neighboring groups, so it is possibly but not definitively an Ioway site.[11]

Site F, the westernmost of this group, and possibly Site E, might represent the Ioway village(s) documented in the late seventeenth century around the "Iowa Great Lakes" region. French accounts and maps place the Paouté near those lakes and the nearby headwaters of the Little Sioux River in the 1670s and 1680s, with the Aiaouez appearing in that region around 1685. A village mapped around the turn of the eighteenth century and attributed to the "Aiaouez or Paoutez" is situated just south of West Okoboji Lake on the Little Sioux River, which French sources label the Riviere des Aiaouez (figure 16). Colin Betts argues that the Paouté and Aiaouez were two related groups that resided in separate regions until they merged in the Iowa Lakes locality in the 1680s, the Aiaouez having recently relocated from their mid-seventeenth-century homeland in northeast Iowa. The route from northeast Iowa to the Lakes region and beyond, indicated on the 1837 map by the standard dotted line, appears on early French maps as the Chemin des Voyageurs, the travelers' way or road, a network that probably comprised several east-west Native trails.[12]

Several archaeological sites in northwest Iowa probably reflect Ioway (both Paouté and Aiaouez) and possibly Otoe occupation in the middle to late decades of the seventeenth century. These sites—Milford (13DK1), Gillett Grove (13CY2), and Harriman/Burr Oak (13CY1), constituting what archaeologists term the Okoboji phase—are located south of the Lakes district along the Little Sioux River. At these sites, seventeenth-century European trade goods are associated with Native-made Oneota material. Because of the proximity of Site F to the upper part of the Big

Figure 16. Detail of De L'Isle's 1718 map. Arrows indicate, from right to left: the Chemin des Voyageurs across northern Iowa; an Aiaouez/Paoutez village near the "Iowa Great Lakes region" in the Little Sioux River valley ("R. des Aiaouez"); an Aiaouez village on the left (east) bank of the R. du Rocher (Big Sioux River), probably Blood Run, with an Omaha village on the opposite bank; and an Aiaouez village on the left bank of the Missouri River below the mouth of the James River. Guillaume De L'Isle, *Carte de la Louisiane et du Cours du Mississipi*. Library of Congress, Geography and Map Division.

Sioux River, it is also possible that Site F represents an occupation west of the Lakes region in the Big Sioux River drainage. The Ioways had a long and deep association with the well-known catlinite quarry at Pipestone National Monument, located along Pipestone Creek, a Big Sioux River tributary, in what is now southwest Minnesota. Site F might refer to this connection even though the quarry is located north of the subject territory of the 1837 council (but see Site G).[13]

The large lake depicted north of Storm Lake and near the head of several rivers (the Des Moines, Raccoon, Floyd, and Little Sioux; see figure 15) might be a stylized representation of the Iowa Lakes district, which is adjacent to the upper portion of the Little Sioux River drainage. It might also represent the numerous other lakes and perennial wetlands that dotted the Des Moines Lobe.[14] The fact that this lake is so far from the Little Sioux River and the late-seventeenth-century villages is puzzling but might indicate the Ioway delegation's interest in showing village locations in relation to rivers and other well-known transportation routes.

Site G

The route from Site F to Site G crosses the Big Sioux River and proceeds south along its right (west) bank (figures 15, 17). The route veers west below the mouth of the Rock River, perhaps near the modern village of Akron, Iowa, and reaches the Missouri River near the mouth of what is probably Bow Creek. Site G is situated opposite the mouth of Bow Creek in what is now southeastern South Dakota.

At the 1837 council, Walking Rain referred specifically to Sites F and G and the route between them: "When we left this place (pointing to a Village on his map) we crossed the Calumet river, built a Village on some river running into the Missouri." In the early 1800s, and certainly long before, the Big Sioux River was known as the Calumet or Redstone River in recognition of its proximity to the source of red catlinite used for calumet pipes. One of the largest recorded Oneota sites, and one that contains a notable quantity of catlinite objects, is the Blood Run/Rock Island site (13LO2/39LN2), situated along both sides of the Big Sioux River just south of the city of Sioux Falls, South Dakota. The straight, relatively short route from Site F to the Big Sioux River implies that Site F was more likely to have been located in the Lakes district or upper Little Sioux valley than near the pipestone quarry. This is because the point at which the route crosses the Big Sioux likely represents Blood Run, which would require a southwestern journey from the quarry, whereas reaching Blood Run from the Lakes district simply involves a continuation of the direct westerly overland route that became the Chemin des Voyageurs as the 1837 map appears to depict.[15]

Blood Run was probably established around the early sixteenth century, possibly by ancestral Omaha and Ponca people. It grew into a regional interaction and ceremonial center and multiethnic community by the seventeenth century. While Ioways may have dwelt at Blood Run by 1650, documentary records indicate a Paouté presence by the 1680s and Aiaouez probably in the first decade of the eighteenth century (see both on figure 16). Ioway occupation apparently was not long-term, as the site's inhabitants departed by 1714. Pressure from the Dakota (Sioux) probably was a key factor in the decision to move, not only from Blood Run but from the Pipestone vicinity as well. Blood Run, now a National Historic Landmark, is recognized as a significant ancestral place by the Omaha, Ponca, Ioway, and Otoe-Missouria tribes and has associations with many additional tribes.[16]

The Ioways continued their westward movement. No Heart stated, "I went and settled at Omaha village on the Missouri river," and Walking Rain indicated Site G was located "on some river running into the Missouri," although their map shows the village opposite the mouth of that tributary rather than on it. Why doesn't the transcript identify "some river" by name? We cannot tell if that was Walking Rain's term because he did not know the river's name (possible, although the map shows

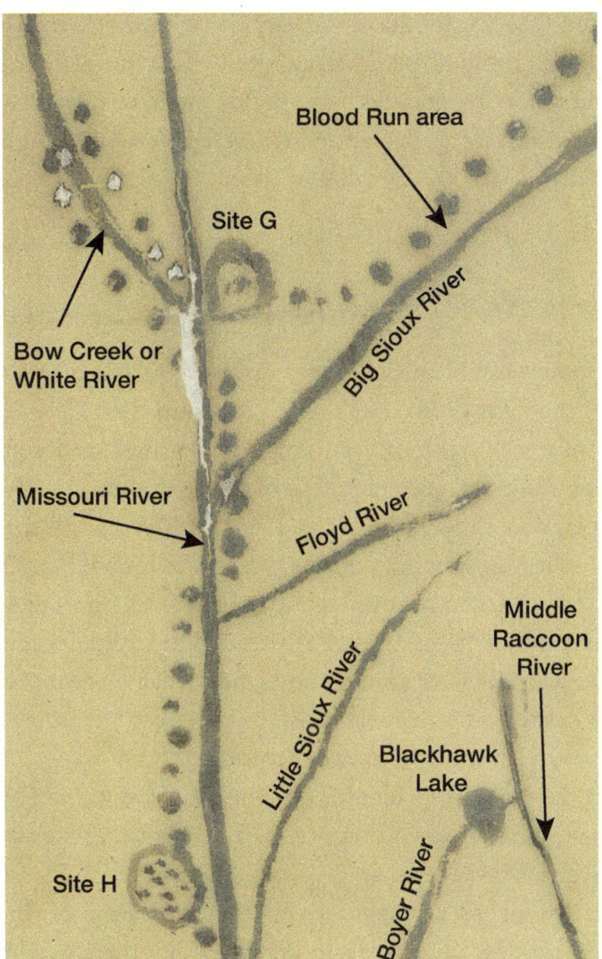

Figure 17.
Sites G and H and vicinity on the 1837 map.

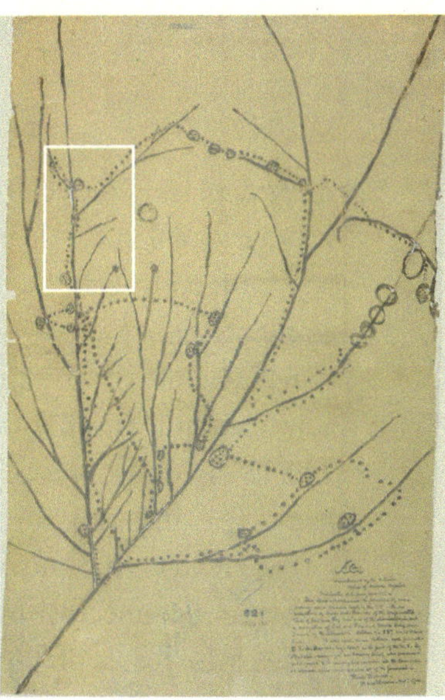

routes ascending and descending the river), if the translator omitted or bungled the river's name, or if Secretary Bush wasn't able to record the name for some other reason. Regardless, there is ample evidence that when the Ioways and Omahas left the Big Sioux River (Blood Run), they moved together but as distinct groups up the Missouri River. The Omahas, with the Ioways likely with them as No Heart mentioned, first established a village near the mouth of the White River, near what is now Oacoma, South Dakota, that became known as "the place where the snowbirds came" or "the place where snowbirds were shot." Around 1720, the Omahas left that village and built one near the mouth of Bow Creek (near what is now St. Helena, Nebraska) that became known as Bad Village. The Ioways had apparently established their own village by that time, siting it on the left (north) bank of the Missouri River near the mouth of the James or Vermillion River approximately opposite the mouth of Bow Creek, between the modern cities of Yankton and Vermillion, South Dakota (the westernmost Aiaouez village on figure 16). The Oneota component at the Vermillion Bluff Village site (39CL1) might connect with that occupation, and other Oneota sites in the region might be related as well. Site G appears to represent this location (labeled G1 on figure 12), although it could also be the earlier village with the Omahas at the White River (G2 on figure 12).[17]

Site H

After departing Site G, the Ioways established a village on Aowa Creek, a small tributary named for them on the right (west) bank of the Missouri River. Site H probably represents the Aowa Creek village (figure 17). This location is about 8 miles west of Sioux City, Iowa near the present village of Ponca, Nebraska. The Omaha name for Aowa ("Ayoway") Creek (also termed "Iouwa River") and the adjacent land, *Ma'xude waa i te* or *Máqude-wa'aí,* means "where the Iowa farmed." The Ioway village was reportedly situated near the mouth of the creek on its east bank. The time of occupation probably would have been around the third decade of the eighteenth century. Despite intensive search efforts, no archaeological site that might connect with the Ioways' Aowa Creek village has yet been identified. The erosive forces of the Missouri River might have destroyed it.[18]

The Aowa Creek village is the most likely identification of Site H, but Site H's position on the 1837 map is below the Floyd and Big Sioux Rivers. Aowa Creek actually enters the Missouri River above rather than below the mouths of the Floyd and Big Sioux. There is a major eighteenth-century site, the Big Village of the Omaha (Tonwantonga, 25DK5), below the Floyd and Big Sioux, but there would have been no reason for No Heart and Walking Rain to map an Omaha village rather than an Ioway village along that stretch of the Missouri River. It is therefore likely that they mapped the early eighteenth-century Aowa Creek site too far downriver.

Site I

In the early to mid-1700s, the Ioways established a new village near what is now Council Bluffs, Iowa, or Omaha, Nebraska. There might have been two villages, one on the west side of the Missouri River and one on the east side, occupied sequentially or simultaneously. The 1837 map depicts a single village and locates it on the east side of the river in what is now the Council Bluffs area (figure 18). However, Native oral histories indicate the presence of an Ioway village situated on the west side of the Missouri "near the place where Florence now stands," which is on the north side of the city of Omaha. A French trader's recollection from 1816 also indicates an old Ioway village "on the right [west] bank of the Missouri about eighteen miles above the river Platte on the lands of the Mahas [Omahas]." Eighteen river miles (in the current channel configuration) would place the village almost exactly where Interstate 80 now crosses the Missouri between Omaha and Council Bluffs. Eighteen direct miles would place the village near Florence or, if it was on the east side of the river, just north of Council Bluffs. The discrepancy between the map and the documentary records cannot be easily reconciled, other than to note that the village on the west side of the river was only briefly occupied and probably of less importance to the Ioways in 1837 who, as noted earlier, were primarily interested in asserting their claim to lands east of the Missouri River.[19]

Further documentation of the Ioways in this vicinity in the eighteenth century supports a village location east of the Missouri. In 1804, William Clark recorded an "Old Village of the *Aiaawaz*" on the east side of the river. H. M. Brackenridge made a similar mention in 1811. The precise whereabouts of this site have been debated. Some researchers identify a location in the city of Council Bluffs, while others suggest locations just north or south of the city. It might never be possible to know exactly where the fabled "old Ioway village" of Lewis and Clark was located in relation to Council Bluffs, but the correspondence of the village to Site I is fairly clear. The Ioways lived in the locality well into the 1750s, departing only about forty years prior to Lewis and Clark's visit. Clark's identification of the vacant site's inhabitants as Ioways likely had support from knowledgeable locals: On the day he noted the Ioway village in his journal, expedition members met with a Missouria man who

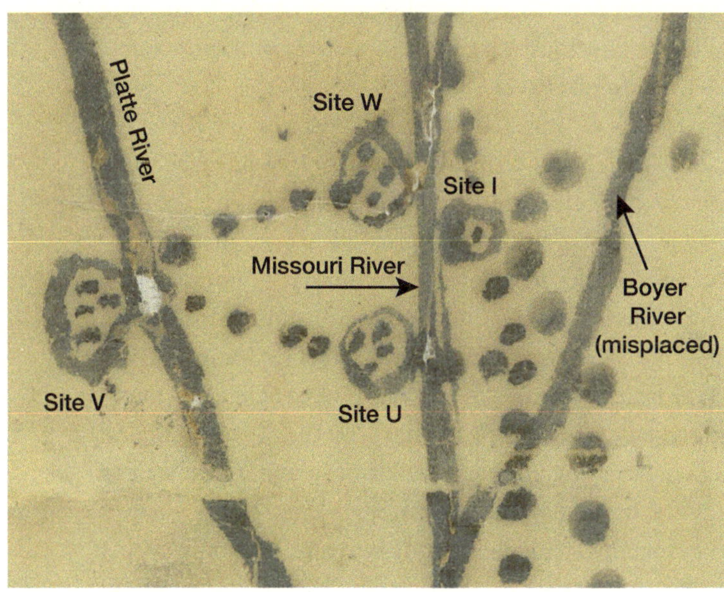

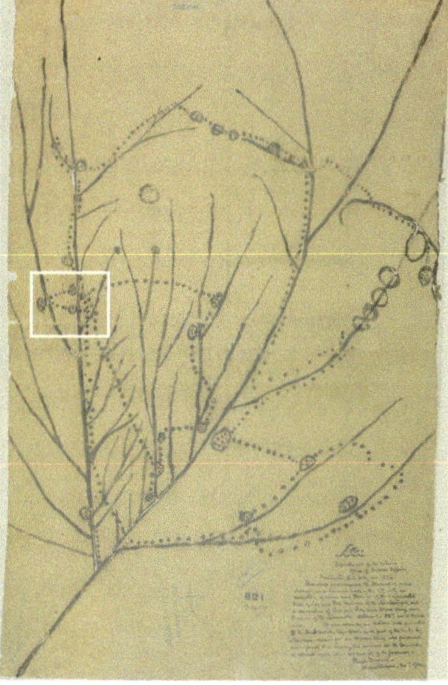

Figure 18. Sites I and U–W and vicinity on the 1837 map.

lived at a nearby Otoe village, and Clark identified another place as a former village of the Otoes.[20]

Another complication related to the placement of Site I on the 1837 map stems from the site's mislocation on the map above rather than below the mouth of the Boyer River. Before it was channelized, the Boyer River entered the Missouri about 6 miles north of Council Bluffs, not south of it as the 1837 map would indicate. But we can be confident Site I represents a Council Bluffs–area site rather than a location north of the Boyer River for two reasons: (1) the Council Bluffs/ Omaha locale was the sole documented mid-1700s Ioway occupation, intermediate between the early 1700s Aowa Creek (Site H) and late 1700s Des Moines River (Site J) villages, and (2) Site I is directly across the Missouri River from Otoe villages (Sites V, W) near Omaha and the lower Platte River. The Council Bluffs and Otoe sites are located below, not above, the Boyer River. Therefore, when the Ioway mapmakers added villages and routes to the map, the Little Sioux River was probably mistaken for the Boyer, resulting in placement of the Council Bluffs and Omaha-area sites too far north.[21]

Site J

In an effort to improve their economic position vis-à-vis Spanish and British interests and to reduce conflicts with tribes along the Missouri River, the Ioways moved their main village back to the east in the 1760s (figure 19). By that time, trading opportunities had become greater for them along the Mississippi River and its tributaries in southeast Iowa than they were along the Missouri. The route from the Council Bluffs area (Site I) to the new location (Site J) is a direct overland course across southern Iowa to the Des Moines River.[22]

The principal village the Ioways established along the Des Moines River became known as Iowaville. This village was probably the birthplace or early home of the Ioway delegates to the 1837 council. Certainly, residing there was part of their lived experience, unlike most if not all of the Ioways' previously occupied villages. No Heart testified, "My home is in the middle of that country"—"home" likely referring to his personal origin there and "the middle of that country" meaning a centrally located place within the tribe's land claim, that is, the Des Moines River, rather than his current (1837) home west of the Missouri River. The 1836 Ioway petition mentioned that the village on the Des Moines—by that time "held and occupied by the Sacs"—was a place the Ioways had left only about twenty-five years earlier, that is, around 1812. In 1814, William Clark labeled the site as "Ioways Old Village," indicating either that the Ioways had lived there for a long time or that they no longer lived there. Other documentary evidence indicates departure from the Des Moines around 1813 by one Ioway faction (the tribe was split between pro-

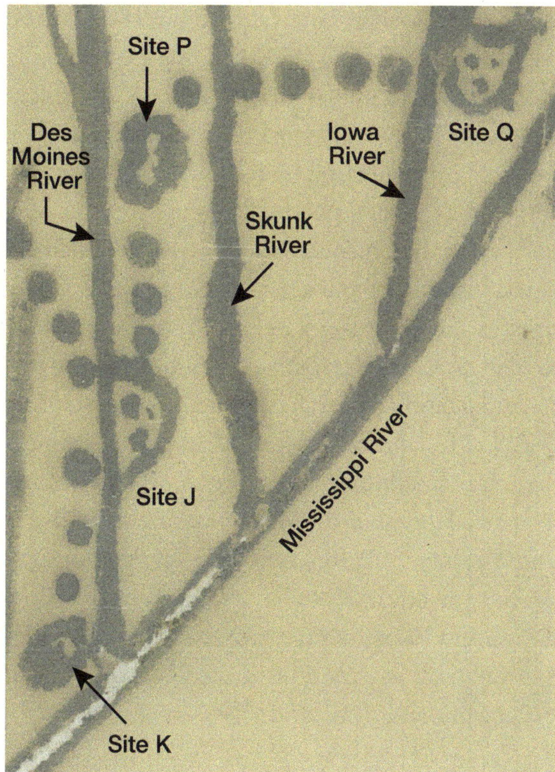

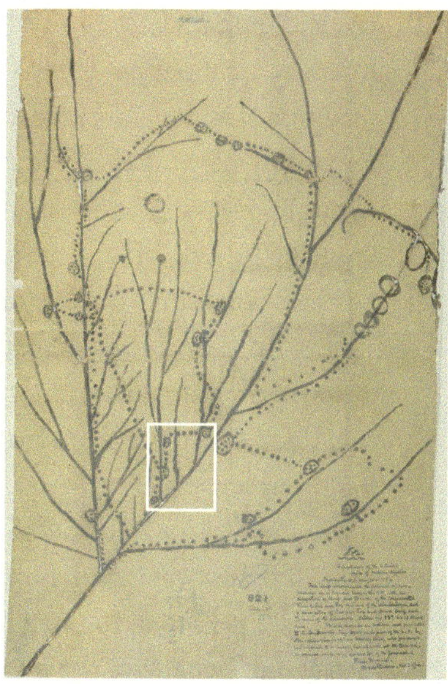

Figure 19.
Sites J, K, P, and Q and vicinity on the 1837 map.

British and pro-American sentiments), but some Ioways may have returned by 1819 or may have continued to reside there into the 1820s.[23]

The Ioways' main Des Moines River village site gained the name Iowaville shortly after the Ioways departed the region. Acknowledging the Ioways' former residence at that place, the toponym is the name by which nearby Sauk and Euro-American communities became known. What did the Ioways call their Des Moines River villages? No Heart specified in 1837, "There is a place called the dry field on the des moine river, another place called the big groove. It was ours at the time the Spanish & French came into the country [i.e., 1760s]. I have been there." We cannot be certain whether "dry field" or "big groove [grove?]" denoted Iowaville, but "dry field" characterizes the Iowaville archaeological site's (13VB124) high terrace position and its well-drained soils that formed under prairie vegetation. The Chiwere term for "dry field," and perhaps the site's original toponym, is *má^{n}xe-xége*. Also, because the Ioway name for the Des Moines River system was Raccoon River (Mingke Nyi), "the Ioway village on the Des Moines might have been called *Mingke China* (Raccoon (River) Village)."[24]

The Iowaville site is located on the left (north) bank of the Des Moines River between the present communities of Eldon and Selma. Documentary and archaeological evidence of Ioway life at this site is abundant. During the main period of Ioway occupation (1770–1820s), Iowaville featured at least two (sequentially occupied?) village areas, each protected by a circular ring consisting of a ditch, embankment, and possible palisade wall. Villagers farmed nearby, hunted widely throughout southern Iowa and northern Missouri, and traded and negotiated with Spanish, British, and American officials at several nearby forts and in more distant locations such as St. Louis and Prairie du Chien. Ioway women often married traders from St. Louis–based French families, which expanded kinship networks and concomitant social understandings and obligations. Yet the Ioways' move back east did not insulate them from conflict. Intertribal relations continued to be in flux and often tense as Euro-American colonization placed new pressures on resources and as territories became squeezed due to land dispossession and forced relocations of tribes westward. Diseases such as smallpox afflicted the community. Some Ioways left to live in the Grand River area (their hunting and wintering grounds) in the second decade of the nineteenth century. Still, for about three generations the Ioways parlayed their Des Moines River position effectively, playing Spanish, British, and American interests off each other to maintain relatively stable and prosperous livelihoods that retained Ioway traditions and integrated Euro-American goods and relationships into Ioway culture on Ioway terms.[25]

Site K

Site K is the only site other than the origin (Site A) and terminus (Site W) with just one route leading to or away from it (figure 19). This dead end implies that the site was not positioned on a migration or travel route but was connected to one other site by out-and-back movement. Therefore, Site K, located near the confluence of the Des Moines with the Mississippi River in what is now northeast Missouri, apparently represents a site that was connected to Site J and thus coeval at least in part with the Iowaville occupation (ca. 1770–1820). A seventeenth-century Peoria (Iliniwek) village is located at the mouth of the Des Moines River in northeast Missouri, but no village from the Iowaville era has been identified there. Rather than signifying a village, Site K could represent a location used on a temporary or short-term but perhaps recurring basis. Interestingly, an Ioway map produced in 1847 or 1848 (the Wawnonqueskoona map, published in 1853; see chapter 4) noted a nearby site of a "council with several tribes held by Gen. Clark" on the west side of the Mississippi just above the mouth of the Des Moines River (rather than just below it, as on the 1837 map). The most likely location for such a council near the mouth of the Des Moines would be Fort Madison, a U.S. Army installation active between 1808 and 1813, or nearby Sauk villages.[26]

The site originally intended for the military and trading center that became Fort Madison was close to a Sauk village above the Des Moines Rapids on the Mississippi River near present-day Montrose, Iowa. American authorities considered this to be a strategic location for Indian commerce and control because it was within easy reach of not only the Sauks but also the Ioways and Meskwakis. At a meeting in St. Louis in 1808, leaders of all three tribes ceded a small plot of land to the government for construction of the fort. But upon inspection, government authorities found that location and another nearby site prone to inundation and decided instead on a place farther to the north, which the United States then acquired from the Sauk and Meskwaki. Upon completion of the fort and associated factory (trading house), Ioways visited regularly for trade and, in at least one instance in 1809, for a council with the fort's captain, Horatio Stark. The Ioway leader Hard Heart was Stark's main antagonist during that contentious meeting. William Clark, by then the Louisiana Territory's St. Louis–based agent for Indian affairs, was neither present for that council nor, apparently, for any meeting at Fort Madison, despite the notation on Wawnonqueskoona's map. Several other U.S. officials did hold Indian councils in the Fort Madison area, though, including territorial governor Meriwether Lewis in 1808 at Quashquame's (Sauk) village, located near Montrose. Because of Lewis and Clark's close affiliation, Wawnonqueskoona, who drafted the map about forty years after Lewis's council, or Seth Eastman, who redrafted the map, may have simply mistaken Lewis for Clark.[27]

Site L

Although the 1837 map and its presentation focused on locations within the purview of the October council, the Ioway delegates did call attention to several sites beyond the land being contested at the time. Four sites in Illinois are among them: Sites L, M, N, and O (figure 20). All can be plausibly connected with locations Ioways visited or possibly occupied between the 1760s and the first ten to fifteen years of the nineteenth century.

Site L is the only mapped site on the east bank of the Mississippi River. As noted in regard to Iowaville (Site J), Ioways moved their settlements back to eastern Iowa around the 1760s after nearly 100 years along the Missouri River and its tributaries. The 1837 map shows a direct, overland route from the Council Bluffs area (Site I) to Iowaville, but Iowaville might not have been the first site occupied during the eastward resettlement. Travelers' accounts and maps indicate that Ioway villages were established along the Mississippi River in the 1760s. The 1837 map appears to show a circuitous route from Site I down the Missouri then up the Illinois River and overland from Site M to Site L on the Mississippi. However, that route's south-

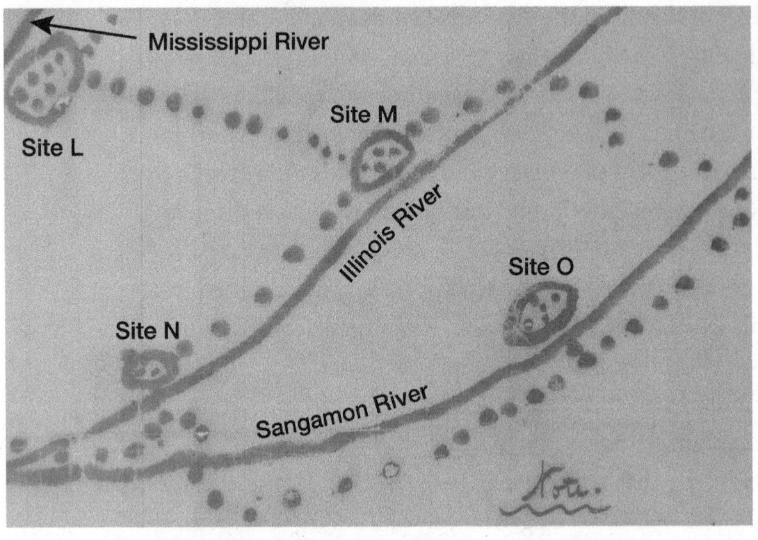

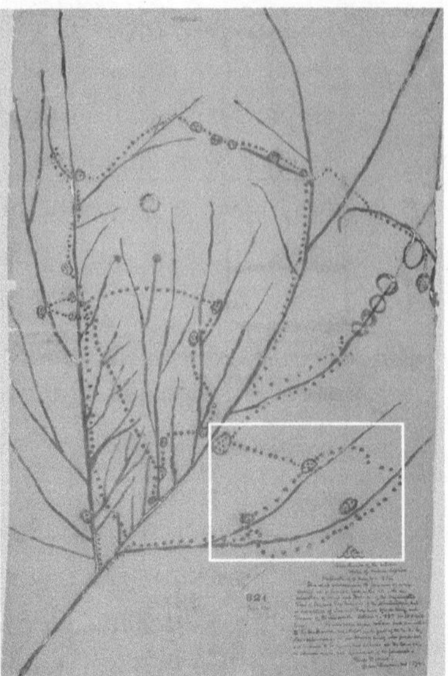

Figure 20. Sites L–O and vicinity on the 1837 map.

ern terminus near St. Louis does not actually intersect with the route that descends the Missouri—the two routes probably were added to the map at different times. Similarly, the northern terminus of Site L's route network (Site B at the mouth of the Upper Iowa River) abuts but does not connect with the previously discussed east-west route that became the Chemin des Voyageurs. And the route between Sites L and M appears to emanate from Site L but is not part of the network connecting Sites M–O. What this means is that the Illinois sites stand apart from the main migration narrative, as does the lone site in northern Missouri (Site T).

Ioways reportedly had a presence in Illinois as early as 1762, and McKenney and Hall noted that "there was a small tribe of Ioways in the Illinois country" around 1779. Two Ioway villages in western Illinois first appeared on a 1778 map that was based on surveys conducted around 1769–1771 (figure 21). The cartographer, Thomas Hutchins, designated each village Iowa Town. The southern Iowa Town, identified as having a population of 300 men, was located opposite and 3–5 miles below the mouth of the Des Moines River. The other Iowa Town, with "400 Men," was about 40 miles to the north, about 15 miles below the mouth of the Iowa River. Both sites may have been situated near the east bank of the Mississippi. While the two villages had been settled by the early 1770s, their terminal dates are not known despite the appearance of the Iowa Towns on maps for several more decades. All post-1778 references to "Iowa Towns" ultimately lead back to Hutchins's map as the sole source. Hutchins's survey shows that these sites were at least partly coeval with, and perhaps slightly earlier than, the Iowaville site occupation.[28]

Upper and Lower Iowa Towns, as the two places came to be known on post-Hutchins maps, could have been precursors to Iowaville, serving as the Ioways' initial eastern settlements upon their having departed the Council Bluffs area. The Mississippi River sites were quite conveniently situated in relation to the St. Louis–based trade (especially Lower Iowa Town, below the Des Moines Rapids) and perhaps more so to British trade (from Upper Iowa Town through Prairie du Chien to Green Bay and Michilimackinac) because of their location on the east side of the river in nominally British territory. However, after a few years, as early as the early 1770s, the proximity of Sauk villages to the Ioways' Mississippi River sites may have become too close for comfort. Ioway-Sauk relations were sometimes amicable but often strained, as the 1837 council proceedings make clear. Iowaville, being inland along the Des Moines River, was more distant and better insulated from Sauk villages yet still easily accessible to Mississippi River trade.[29]

The specific locations of Lower and Upper Iowa Towns have not been ascertained. A search for the Lower Town site in the 1980s identified possible but unverified locations about 4 miles south of Warsaw, Illinois, just where the site would

Figure 21.
Detail from Hutchins's 1778 map showing "Iowa Towns." From Thomas Hutchins, "A New Map of the Western Parts of Virginia, Pennsylvania, Maryland, and North Carolina. . . ." Library of Congress, Geography and Map Division, https://www.loc.gov/resource/g37070.ar078901/.

be expected on the basis of Hutchins's map. For the Upper Town site, no physical evidence or specific site locations have yet been obtained or determined.[30]

It is important to note that Site L might not represent Upper Iowa Town or any Ioway settlement at all. Hutchins's survey placed the Upper Town below the mouth of the Iowa River, but Site L is located north of the mouth of the Iowa, approximately midway between the mouths of the Iowa and Rock Rivers. This discrepancy casts doubt on identifying Site L as Upper Iowa Town. Instead, Site L might well represent a non-Ioway site, most likely the large Sauk village of Saukenuk, known archaeologically as the Crawford Farm site (11Ri81). Saukenuk was located on the east side of Milan, Illinois, along the left (south) bank of the Rock River, about 4 miles upriver from the Rock's confluence with the Mississippi. This extensive community, often referred to as a town, was occupied throughout much of the eighteenth century into the early 1830s. It was the largest Sauk settlement and has been the subject of extensive historical and archaeological study. Saukenuk attracted visitors from many tribes, including the Ioway for an intertribal council in 1812 and probably other times. The mapped location of Site L north of the mouth of the Iowa River and close to the south bank of the Rock River, the routes connecting it to Site M and to other locations upriver along the Rock and Mississippi, and the fact that it is the largest settlement depicted on the 1837 map all argue in favor of Site L representing Saukenuk rather than one of the Iowa Towns of Hutchins's survey.[31]

Sites M, N, and O

Site L connects to three other sites in Illinois as well as to the long route between the mouth of the Missouri River and the mouth of the Upper Iowa River. The three sites—M, N, and O—are not Ioway villages but are places Ioways visited occasionally or periodically during the late eighteenth and early nineteenth centuries (figure 20). The route also indicates additional places the Ioways visited in that period in Missouri, Wisconsin, and Iowa.

Site M, which connects to Site L by a direct overland route, is located on the right (west) side of the Illinois River in the central Illinois River valley. Site M represents one or more places in the Peoria locality, a hub of Native and European activity in central Illinois from the late seventeenth through early nineteenth centuries. The Native and French communities at Peoria were large and long-lived. Ioways were not noted as residents of the Peoria area, but in the 1760s, Ioways from the Mississippi River and some Peorias (Iliniwek) who were residing with them were accused of "annoying" and "insulting" the French at Peoria. Alternatively, Site M could represent the Potawatomi villages of the 1790s through early 1830s that were located upriver from Peoria. Members of other Algonquian tribes such as the Kickapoo and Miami periodically resided in those villages as well. The

Potawatomi village named for its leader Gomo, located about 20 miles north of Peoria near the head of Peoria Lake, was occupied from around 1792 until its residents left in 1813; the U.S. military burned it shortly thereafter. A Kickapoo village was located nearby around 1812. An overland "beaten road" across the prairie linked that location to the lower Rock River near Saukenuk at least as early as 1812. The journey reportedly took only one day on horseback and two days on foot—or less if traversed by the "Indigenous prairie runners" of the region. The "beaten road" corresponds to the route on the 1837 map that connects Sites L and M.[32]

Downriver from Site M, Site N is also situated on the right bank of the Illinois River. It is upstream from the mouth of the Sangamon River, placing it in the vicinity of the Spoon River, where several lakes occupy the Illinois River floodplain. Several Algonquian tribes lived in that region in the early nineteenth century. Potawatomis resided at the mouth of the Spoon River around 1830 at a site known as Captain Hill (or Capt. Hill's village) and had been present along the Spoon River for two decades previously.[33]

Site O is located on the north side of the Sangamon River, a major eastern tributary of the Illinois River. During several decades straddling the turn of the nineteenth century, Kickapoo villages were present on small streams in the northern part of the Sangamon basin. The most thoroughly documented of these villages is the Rhodes site (11Lo8), located under what is now the Interstate 55 interchange on the west side of Lincoln, Illinois. Also well documented is the mid-eighteenth–early nineteenth-century "Grand Village" of the Kickapoo and its associated fort (11Ml5 and 11Ml21) near LeRoy, Illinois. Like Gomo's Potawatomi village on Peoria Lake, they too were burned by the U.S. military during the War of 1812 because of their residents' putative nativist or pro-British sentiments.[34]

In the 1837 council, No Heart referred to Sites M, N, and O and the route connecting them by saying, "We went around the Illinois to the Kickapoo." Secretary Bush lightly penciled the label "Illinois" to indicate the river's name next to Site N, again indicating that the map was presented in a landscape orientation (figure 22). While Ioways might have journeyed to those places many times, the early 1810s is a particularly well-documented time of Ioway visits to Illinois, as well as to Wisconsin and St. Louis. Ioways met with other tribes, notably the Kickapoo, during the unrest associated with the nativist movement of Tecumseh and his brother Tenskwatawa (the Shawnee Prophet) and the onset of the War of 1812. Also in the second decade of the nineteenth century, some Ioways met often in St. Louis with U.S. territorial officials, traveled annually to Prairie du Chien, mined lead near Dubuque, resided temporarily with their Ho-Chunk "grandfathers" at Four Lakes (Madison, Wisconsin), and, as noted, met with many tribes at Saukenuk. Yearly journeys to Prairie du Chien would have facilitated visits to the nearby mouth of the Upper Iowa River, where, according to the 1836 Ioway petition, their

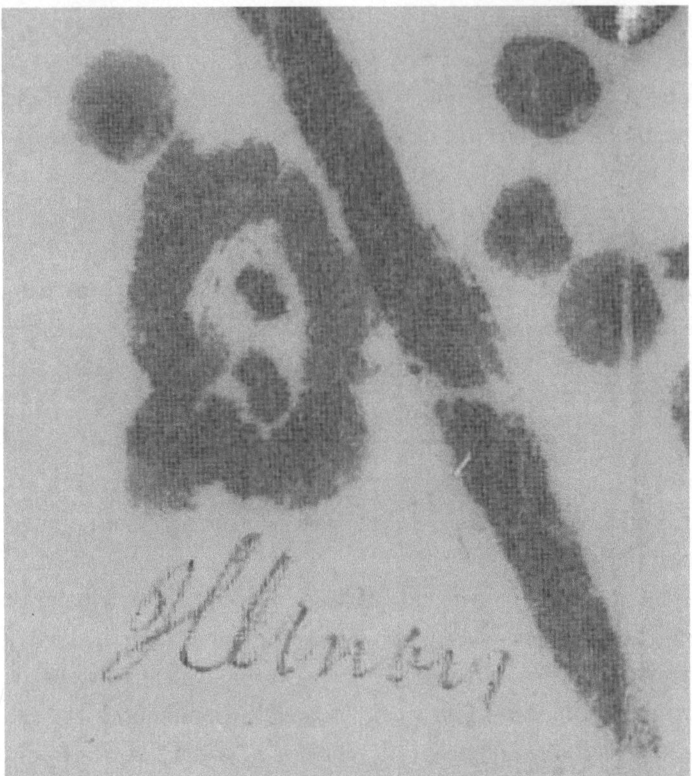

Figure 22. Close-up of the 1837 map showing "Illinois."

ancestral homes and mounds were still visible. The long route connecting Sites L through O therefore records notable journeys to other tribes rather than settlement migrations.[35]

Although this route and the non-Ioway villages might seem irrelevant to the 1837 land claim, they illustrate several important aspects of the Ioway negotiating strategy. First of all, they lent credibility to the Ioway case by illustrating comprehensive historical knowledge. Second, everyone at the council probably knew that in 1811–1812, the Illinois villages had been allied with Tecumseh's Confederacy, had been pro-British, or were otherwise considered threats to the United States. Council participants also knew that despite sympathy among some Ioways toward the British and Tecumseh's movement, from 1815 onward the Ioways (at least the faction requesting and represented at the council) had demonstrated their allegiance to the United States. One council attendee might have paid particular attention to this point: Vice President Richard Mentor Johnson, Tecumseh's reputed killer (see chapter 2, n. 18). With the Ioways adding these sites to the map and referring to their visit to the Kickapoos, they attempted to strengthen their diplomatic position by reminding everyone at the council that they, unlike their neighbors, had remained at peace with the Americans for the previous twenty-plus years.[36]

Site P

Site P is situated on the Des Moines River, opposite and slightly downriver from the mouth of the Raccoon River. This location would place it near downtown Des Moines, Iowa (figure 19). The route connecting it to Iowaville (Site J) suggests Site P might have been the second Des Moines River village of the early nineteenth century, if not the "dry field" then perhaps the "big groove [grove?]." A trading post may have been located at Des Moines before 1830, and Sauk and Meskwaki villages were sited there later, but no archaeological evidence of an Ioway occupation has yet been found in the Des Moines area. Information travelers obtained in 1817 indicated that the Ioways lived 100 or 120 miles up the Des Moines, which would place their village 20–40 miles southeast of Des Moines if they meant air miles, or between Ottumwa and Eddyville if, as is more likely, they meant 100–120 river miles. If these secondhand reports are close to accurate, they (and other indications noted with Site J) would indicate at least some Ioways had moved upriver from Iowaville by 1812–1817. As at Des Moines, later Sauk and Meskwaki villages but no Ioway sites have been recorded in the other upriver locations, although several Ioway-related trading posts were located northwest of Iowaville to about 30 miles southeast of Des Moines.[37]

The route leading from Iowaville to Site P and continuing on to Sites Q, R, and S would appear to be one of the ways Ioways left their Des Moines River village(s). Sauk and American pressure had made continued residence along the Des Moines untenable, so the Ioways returned to the Missouri River in various stages between around 1819 and 1824. One division of the tribe moved back to the Council Bluffs area (Sites Q, R, S) while another settled along tributaries of the lower Missouri River in northern Missouri, even though most of that land was ceded by the treaty of 1824, as discussed under Site T.[38]

Site Q

Site Q is an Ioway village located on the lower Iowa River in southeast Iowa (figure 19). It probably corresponds to the Ioway village Zebulon Pike recorded in 1805. According to Pike, this village was "about 10 miles up" the Iowa River on the river's left bank. The 1837 map shows Site Q just below the fork of the Iowa and Cedar Rivers at Columbus Junction and Fredonia, Iowa, on the left bank of the Iowa about 25 miles upstream from its mouth. Despite the discrepancy in distance from the mouth of the Iowa River (10 versus 25 miles), the 1837 map and Pike's account likely refer to the same site because Pike placed the village below the Iowa-Cedar fork but learned about the site secondhand, as he did not ascend the Iowa himself. Not much is known about the site Pike noted other than that its period of occupation coincided with or overlapped that of the Ioways' Des Moines River village(s), Site J (Iowaville) or Site P.

Archaeological evidence of the village on the lower Iowa River is so far elusive. Many archaeological sites have been recorded in the Iowa-Cedar fork locality, but none has yet been confirmed as a turn-of-the-nineteenth-century Native habitation. In fact, as in the Des Moines area (Site P), all of the recorded historic-era Indian archaeological sites and places along the lower Iowa River in Iowa's Archaeological Site File and Historic Indian Location Database are of unknown or slightly later Sauk or Meskwaki affiliation; none are definitively Ioway. The lower portion of the Iowa River valley has experienced significant channel shifts, erosion, and sedimentation, possibly accounting for the difficulty in locating sites that "ought" to be there such as the village Pike reported.[39]

Sites R and S

These sites are located in the middle to upper portions of the Iowa River drainage (figure 23). Site R is mapped approximately where the South Fork of the Iowa River meets the Iowa main stem, on the right (west) bank of the South Fork. This location would be close to Gifford, Iowa. Several precontact sites, including a chert quarry, have been recorded in that locality, but, again, neither the Iowa Archaeological Site File nor the Historic Indian Location Database show any Ioway or pre-1830s Historic Indian sites there. The latter database does indicate that in 1855, a local Potawatomi leader convened a council of Dakotas and white citizens on the South Fork "near where the town of Gifford now stands" to ward off a feared impending Dakota attack.[40]

Site S is farther up the main stem of the Iowa River, on the right (west or south) bank of the river. However, with no additional reference point, it is difficult to determine even a general location. The site could be located almost anywhere along the Iowa River above Eldora in Hardin, Franklin, or Wright County. No Ioway or pre-1830s Historic Indian sites have been recorded along the Iowa River north of the South Fork.

The route up the Iowa River northwest from Site Q to Site S covers at least 120 overland miles. From Site S, the route turns southwest, leaving the Iowa River valley on an overland return of about 160 miles to the Missouri River at Site I (at or near Council Bluffs). Close inspection of this route's dotted line on figure 18 suggests that the route back to Site I bends back toward Site J (Iowaville), forming a loop. As noted earlier, many Ioways relocated from southeast Iowa to the Missouri

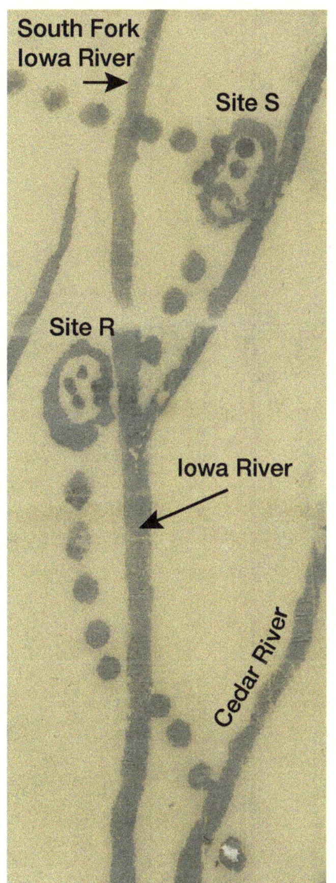

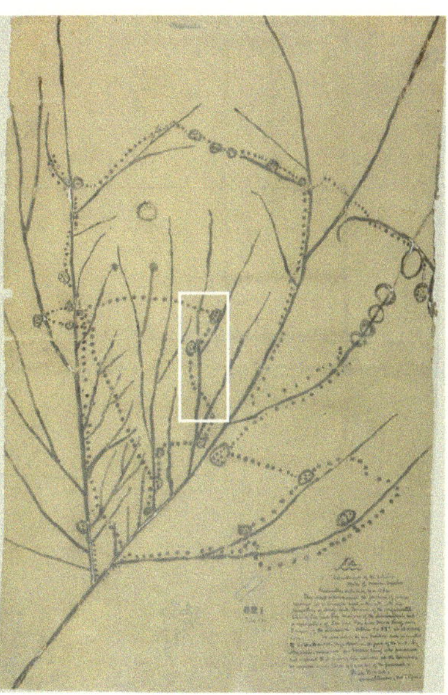

Figure 23.
Sites R and S and vicinity on the 1837 map.

River in several stages around 1819–1824, so the map might indicate multiple moves between the Missouri, Des Moines, and Iowa Rivers associated with this relocation or with other travels. Specific routes and other details of these moves are unknown except for these hints on the 1837 map. Sites R and S probably represent short-term camps occupied during those treks. Ephemeral sites such as these can be challenging to identify archaeologically, especially post-1820 Native sites whose artifact assemblages are generally similar to those of non-Native sites.[41]

Site T

Site T is situated on the right (south) bank of the lower Missouri River opposite the mouth of the Grand River in the vicinity of Miami, Missouri, in the northern part of that state (figure 24). The site is connected to a well-traveled route that mostly parallels the Missouri River and links the Council Bluffs area with the St. Louis area. In the 1837 council, Walking Rain stated, "When we left the Ottoes

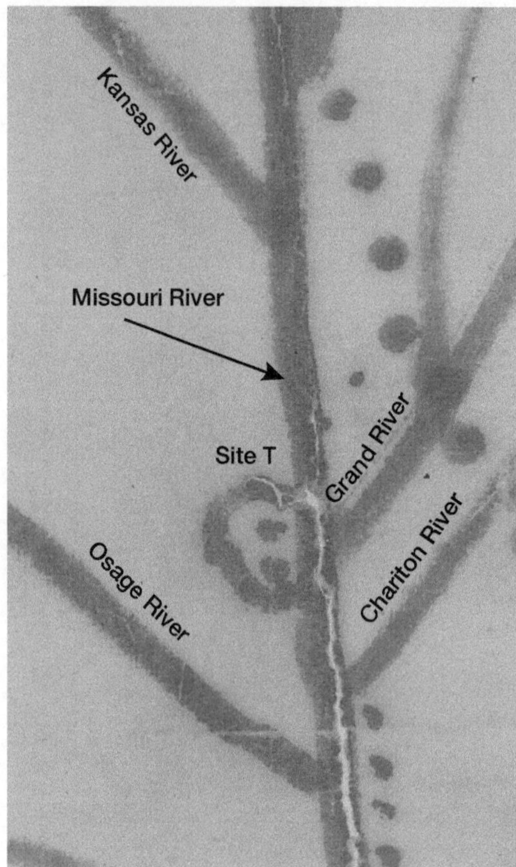

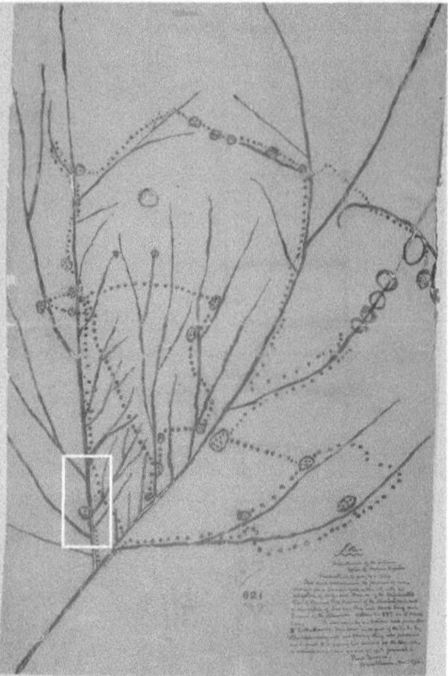

Figure 24.
Site T and vicinity on the 1837 map.

Village we started and travelled on each side of the river Missouri until we arrived at the mouth of Grand river." The Ioways resided with the Otoes in the Platte River and Omaha region in the 1820s (see Sites V, W), indicating the likely frame of this route's usage. While documentary and archaeological records show no Ioway village that corresponds to Site T, trading posts for the Ioways were established near the mouth of the Grand River around 1817. It is likely that the map indicates one of these trading locations rather than an Ioway village. Still, the Grand River drainage had long been an Ioway hunting and wintering ground, and the mapping of Site T plus Walking Rain's remark about the Grand River indicate the importance of that river to the Ioways in the early nineteenth century.[42]

The Grand River valley and nearby parts of northwest Missouri and southwest Iowa contained numerous Ioway habitations during the second through fourth decades of the nineteenth century. These camps and villages were principally associated with the Big Neck (Great Walker) faction of the tribe that resisted attempts to remove them from the portions of Iowa and Missouri that had been ceded in treaties of the 1820s and 1830s. Wawnonqueskoona's 1848 map (see chapter 4) shows one village on the Little Platte River in the area ceded in 1836, and seven villages in the area ceded in 1824: four in the Grand and Chariton River valleys, plus three (that have no corroborating documentation) along the Salt River in northeast Missouri. Occupation along the Grand and Chariton continued past 1826 when Ioways were supposed to have vacated that area. Archaeological evidence is suggestive but not yet definitive of precise site locations. The important point is that—Site T notwithstanding—the 1837 map shows none of these sites. Their absence speaks volumes. In 1837, No Heart and Walking Rain had no wish to revive still-fresh controversies surrounding Ioway settlement in Missouri, an area they were no longer claiming. While they had tried to bolster their case by noting interactions that did not offend U.S. interests with tribes in Illinois, citing the northern Missouri villages that some Ioways were still inhabiting but were located in lands the Ioways had already ceded would have been counterproductive to their case.[43]

Sites U, V, and W

When presenting the map at the 1837 council, No Heart said, "The Ottoes village was the last village passed in going out to our settlement." No Heart's settlement at that time was along the Big Nemaha River near the Kansas-Nebraska border, as ordered by the Platte Purchase treaty of 1836. His statement was true for most Ioways. Prior to their move to that settlement, many among the Ioways' "treaty-abiding" faction had resided with their close linguistic and cultural kin the Otoes, beginning around 1819. This co-residence provided some respite from the turmoil and tensions pervading the Des Moines and Grand River valleys. Still, many Ioways (e.g., the Big Neck faction) continued living in Missouri into early 1837, though once again the 1837 map does not depict their locations for obvious political reasons.[44]

An Otoe named Gero-Schunu-Wy-Ha made a map in 1825 that shows Ioway, Otoe, Omaha, and Pawnee villages in Nebraska, as well as the original Council Bluff location west of the Missouri River. It also shows villages of other tribes and locations of councils far up the Missouri into North Dakota, as well as routes of travel up the Platte River into the Rocky Mountains. Most importantly for present purposes, the 1825 Otoe map depicts an Ioway village on the Missouri River slightly north of the mouth of the Platte and some distance south of Council Bluff (Nebraska). The Ioway village is shown as quite a bit smaller than the Otoe and Pawnee villages on the Platte River and the Omaha village on the Elkhorn River. The Ioway site might have been located approximately at present-day Bellevue or Omaha, Nebraska.[45]

Site U might match the Ioway village shown on the Otoe map. But while the 1837 map locates Site U on the Missouri River north of the mouth of the Platte, as the 1825 map does, the 1837 map shows Site U north of the mouth of the Boyer River (figure 18). Again, as discussed with Site I, when the villages were added to the map, the Little Sioux River apparently was misunderstood to be the Boyer River, meaning that the Boyer River was probably misunderstood to be the Nishnabotna River (see figures 9, 18). In view of these errors, Site U would be located in the general Omaha area. Its location slightly downriver from Site I suggests that it could correspond to an early nineteenth-century Otoe village (archaeological site 25DO167) situated under what is now downtown Omaha. Site U connects to the route Walking Rain identified as one the Ioways used to travel down the Missouri after leaving the Otoe village. Walking Rain's statement implies that the Ioways had already been residing with the Otoes, either at this site or Site V. Along with the Otoe map, Walking Rain's testimony supports assignment of this site to the 1820s.[46]

Site V corresponds to the Otoe village known as the Yutan site (25SD1). The Yutan site is situated on high ground bordering the right (west) bank of the Platte River about 20 miles west of Omaha and about 40 miles above the Platte's confluence with the Missouri River. The site and the nearby modern community of Yutan are named for the Otoe Chief Ietan. The Yutan site appears as a large village on the 1825 Otoe map and was the principal Otoe settlement from the 1770s into the 1830s. Too-Né's 1805–1806 Arikara map identifies this site as a Missouria village; by that time, the Missourias had joined the Otoes, at least in this location. The village as it looked in 1820 appears in a watercolor painted by Titian Ramsay Peale of the Stephen Long Scientific Expedition. As that image shows, and as the Long Expedition journal states, the village was "composed of large dirt lodges, similar to those of the Konzas [Kansa] and Omawhaws [Omaha]." These circular lodges look much like the large conical burial mounds of northeast Iowa (see the 1836 Ioway petition in appendix 1 and chapter 3, n. 7). Several of the Yutan site's circular lodge foundations and other features have been excavated but not yet reported in detail. The Yutan site is listed on the National Register of Historic Places.[47]

Site W is the final one of the series of sites marked on the 1837 map. It is located on the right (west) bank of the Missouri River nearly opposite Site I and the mouth of the Boyer River, mistakenly mapped as the Little Sioux River (figure 18). Site W might be an Otoe village in light of No Heart's statement that an Otoe village was the last one they passed before arriving at their current (1837) settlement. The location of Site W coincides with Council Bluff (of Nebraska) and several nearby sites, including the trading post founded by Manuel Lisa (1812–1823), the Long Expedition's Engineer Cantonment (1819–1820), Fort Atkinson (1820–1827), and Cabannés Post (1822–1840). No Otoe village is known in that location, but Ioways participated in councils and made extended visits at these places, notably in 1819. The 1825 Otoe map depicts an overland trail connecting the Yutan village with Council Bluff; the 1837 Ioway map shows the identical route connecting Sites V and W.[48]

So ends the chronicle of Ioway settlement history as No Heart and Walking Rain narrated with the aid of their map. In chapter 5, I explore the map's accuracy and historicity and the types of information the Ioways in 1837 would have used to make the map and retell their history. At this juncture, though, we can already appreciate the many connections—some specific, some general—between the 1837 oral and cartographic testimony on one hand and numerous settlements, travel routes, and events known through independent historical and archaeological evidence on the other. It must have been extremely frustrating for the Ioway delegation to have had their historical account and supporting exhibit not only disregarded but also derided as mere evidence of their weakness. And one can only wonder what they might have felt—anger? resignation?—if they knew nobody would pay serious attention to the map for the next 140 years.

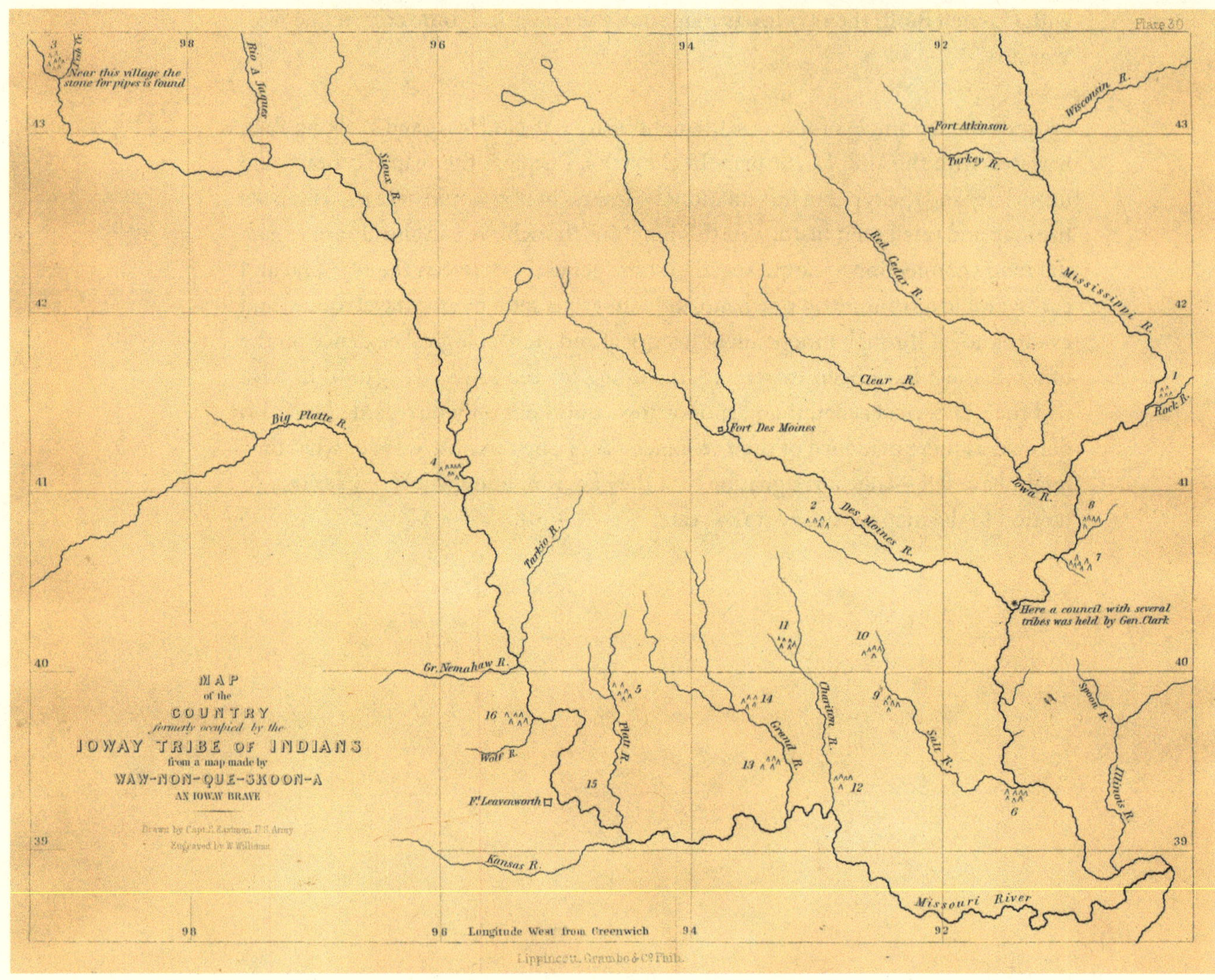

Figure 25. Wawnonqueskoona's map. From Henry R. Schoolcraft, *Information Respecting the History, Condition and Prospects of the Indian Tribes of the United States*, Part 3, 1853.

CHAPTER FOUR

Wawnonqueskoona's Map

UNTIL 1976, there was only one published and widely known nineteenth-century Ioway map, and it was not the 1837 map: It was the map made in 1847 or 1848 by an Ioway man named Wawnonqueskoona, as mentioned in the discussions of Sites K and T in chapter 3 (figure 25). Henry R. Schoolcraft published a redrafted version in 1853 in volume 3 of his definitive (for its time) book series about Native Americans, *Information Respecting the History, Condition and Prospects of the Indian Tribes of the United States.* That map and the accompanying interpretation were the only published sources about Ioway mapping for more than 120 years. Several authors cited and reprinted it in their discussions about Ioway history. We will see here and in chapters 5 and 6 not only that its accuracy is suspect but also that it was even once mistaken for the 1837 map.[1]

The map's title is: "Map of the country formerly occupied by the Iowa tribe of Indians from a map made by Waw-non-que-skoon-a an Ioway brave. Drawn by Capt. S. Eastman, U.S. Army, Engraved by W. Williams." In Schoolcraft's book, the map was published as a full page in a section Schoolcraft wrote titled "Migration of the Iowas [With a Map.]" (brackets in original). That section preceded a lengthy chapter written by missionaries Samuel Irvin and William Hamilton titled "History of the Iowa and Sac Tribes," which consists of their responses to a government questionnaire meant to elicit information about various tribes.[2]

Who was Wawnonqueskoona? The name "Winauguscconey" (glossed as "The Man Who Is Not Afraid to Travel") was one of several applied to Great Walker or Big Neck, the Ioway leader known for his repudiation of the 1824 treaty, insistence on living on ceded land in Missouri, and arrest and trial for the "Big Neck Affair."[3] One of the signers of the 1830 treaty in Prairie du Chien was "Wa-nau-quash-coonie," glossed as "without fear"; this person could have been Great Walker (Big Neck), who had been released from prison in St. Louis in March of that year. But he was killed in a battle in 1831, so the individual known by that name in later years was almost certainly a son or nephew. An 1838 treaty signer was "Wah nun gua schoo ny (Wanugwaskuni)," or "He that has no fear."[4] Tabulations of goods received by

Ioways in 1842, 1844, and 1848 list him as "Wy nun co sku na," "Wy non cus koo na," and "Wa nun ques scoo na."[5] Unfortunately, we know nothing more about him.

Captain S. Eastman was Seth Eastman (1808–1875), an Army mapmaker and artist. His artistic career is well documented, and his paintings and other works can be found in numerous museums. His association with Schoolcraft, which began in 1850, led him to create hundreds of illustrations for Schoolcraft's books about Native Americans.[6]

Wawnonqueskoona apparently drafted his map in the winter of 1847–1848. By February 1848, Samuel Irvin had prepared a bundle of manuscripts and some printed material to send to the U.S. Indian Commissioner in Washington that included the map and the responses to the standard series of questions.[7] After Eastman joined Schoolcraft's publishing project in 1850, he transformed Wawnonqueskoona's original map into the Cartesian-coordinate version that appeared in Schoolcraft's 1853 volume. Schoolcraft described the map's preparation and purpose as follows:

> The original outlines of the Indian map which is herewith exhibited, (Plate 30,) is due to those gentlemen [Irvin and Hamilton], and is a singularly interesting document in Iowa history. It was drawn in the rough, by Waw-non-que-skoon-a, with a black-lead-pencil, on a large sheet of white paper, furnished at the mission-house, and has been reduced in size, and its rigid lines adapted to the surveys of the public lands on the Missouri and Mississippi. It furnishes a practical and affirmative reply to query No. 31, on the capacity of the Indians to execute geographical charts. The original is retained in the Indian Bureau.
>
> The object of Waw-non-que-skoon-a was to denote the places where the Iowas had lived during the sixteen migrations which preceded their residence at their present location, the Missouri; and, in truth, it nearly exhausts their history.[8]

The original map's "rigid lines" probably were straight-line depictions of rivers, as on the 1837 map and most Native American maps of that era. Schoolcraft explained that the tipi-like ("lodge") symbols on the published map denoted the Ioways' "fixed residences." Each settlement had a unique number, 1 through 16, accounting for the migrations Schoolcraft mentioned and indicating their relative chronological positions, each settlement presumably representing the endpoint of an individual migration. Schoolcraft created a chronicle of Ioway movement between these settlements, but he had access to information about only the sequence—not the dates—of occupations. Furthermore, all he knew about the village locations was based on their plotting on the original map and on Eastman's transcription. Apparently, no Ioway narrative accompanied the map, and Hamilton and Irvin offered little in the way of tribal history, merely Ioways' recollections of events such as battles and disease outbreaks that occurred only as far back as around 1802. Tribal members also recalled experiencing the 1811 tremors later known as the New Madrid earthquakes. With no other historical information from the Ioways, Schoolcraft could offer no discussion about the settlements and movements shown on the map other than to surmise that Ioway migrations "were probably determined by the facility of procuring food." Schoolcraft recognized that the map did not depict some well-documented early Ioway villages such as those in northeast Iowa, so he concluded that the migrations shown on the map were "all of quite modern date, not exceeding the probable period to which well-known tradition could reach." Estimating that villages were occupied for no more than an average of 12 years and assuming that only one village was occupied at a time, Schoolcraft concluded that the map depicted Ioway settlements spanning no more than 180 years "before their arrival at their present place."[9]

In fact, Wawnonqueskoona's map does not accurately show even half the time span Schoolcraft estimated (figure 26). Site 1, the earliest site, might be Saukenuk, or it might represent any number of ancestral villages east of the Mississippi River. No date or time range can be assigned to it. Site 2 is a slightly misplaced Iowaville on the Des Moines River, founded no earlier than 1765 (Site J on the 1837 map). The label for Site 3—"Near this village the stone for pipes is found"—would indicate Blood Run or another site close to Minnesota's catlinite quarry. However, Site 3 is not only out of sequence (Ioways occupied the Blood Run and pipestone area at least sixty years before Iowaville) but also misplaced high up the Missouri River, past the mouth of "Fish Creek," now Platte Creek. This location is in the general vicinity of the early eighteenth-century Ioway settlements near the mouth of the White River or Bow Creek in South Dakota (see Site G on the 1837 map). Site 4 near the mouth of the Platte River returns to the actual historic sequence, representing the general location of the return of most Ioways to the Omaha–Council Bluffs area (probably Site U on the 1837 map) after having departed Iowaville around 1819–1824.

Sites 5–6 and 9–15 on Wawnonqueskoona's map represent settlements in northern Missouri that probably date between about 1820 and 1837. It is significant that none of these sites appear on the 1837 map (figure 26). If Wawnonqueskoona was Big Neck's son or nephew, he very likely lived in northern Missouri in the 1820s and 1830s and knew many of the area's villages firsthand. Big Neck, probably born around 1780 at Iowaville or elsewhere on the Des Moines River (or in western Illinois), would have told his sons and nephews about his early life, but he would have had no firsthand experience of pre-Iowaville sites such as Sites 1 and 3 on Wawnonqueskoona's map.[10]

Sites 7 and 8 are located on the east side of the Mississippi River in western Illinois, between the mouths of the Iowa and Des Moines Rivers near Henderson Creek and another small stream, possibly Honey Creek or Ellison Creek. These

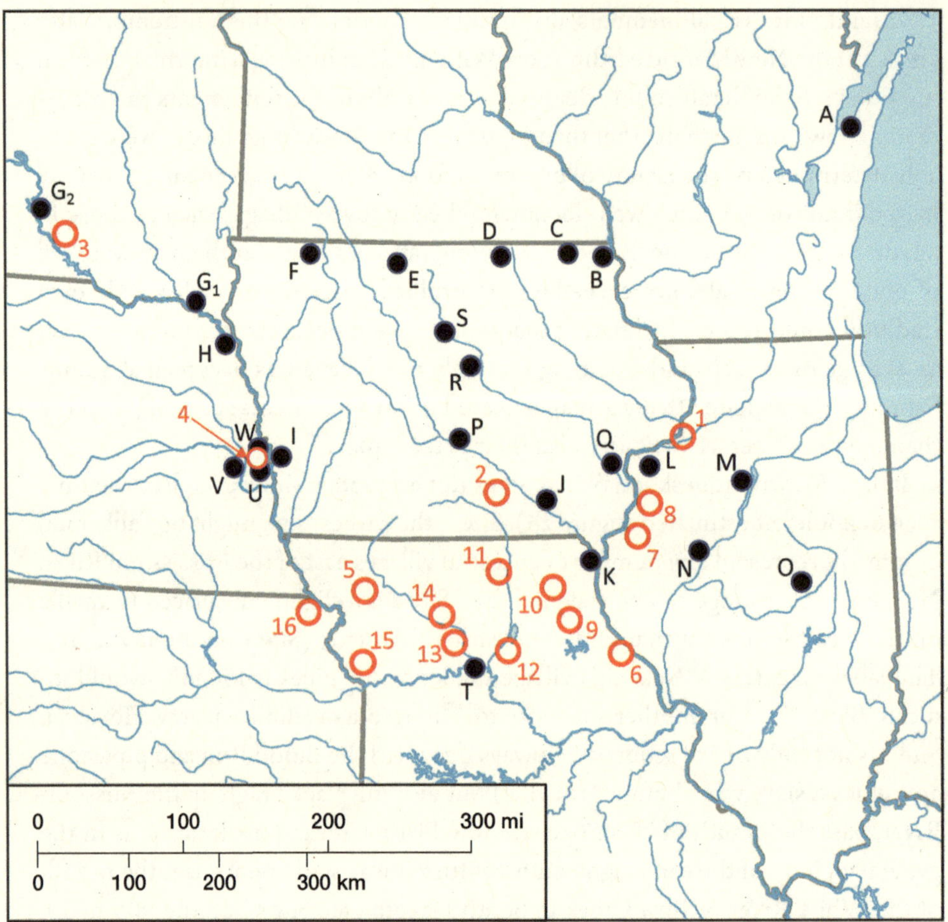

Figure 26. Estimated locations of settlements depicted on Wawnonqueskoona's map (open red circles) and on the 1837 map (solid black circles). Base map from the *National Atlas of the United States of America*, U.S. Geological Survey 2024.

locations match, in a general sense, the two Iowa Towns Hutchins mapped in the 1770s, although if Site 7 is Lower Iowa Town, it should be south rather than north of the mouth of the Des Moines River (figure 21). As noted in the discussion of Site L on the 1837 map, Hutchins's 1778 map is the principal—really, the only—source on the locations and sizes of those Illinois settlements, with McKenney and Hall also conveying a report that some Ioways lived in Illinois around 1779. Wawnonqueskoona's map adds an intriguing twist to this information. If Sites 7 and 8 postdate or are contemporaneous with Iowaville and belong to the sequence of northern Missouri villages (Sites 5–6 and 9–15), their apparent omission from the 1837 map makes sense: They would have belonged to the Big Neck faction rather than the "official" White Cloud–No Heart–Walking Rain segment of the tribe. Post-Hutchins maps that show the two Iowa Towns in Illinois might attest to site occupations around the turn of the nineteenth century, although their appearance on those maps might simply be unverified carryovers from the 1778 map. The Iowa Towns in Illinois will remain mysteries until new historical or archaeological evidence emerges.

Wawnonqueskoona's Site 16 is the Great Nemaha community, where he lived when he made his map.

Wawnonqueskoona's original map has not been located. It is the holy grail of Ioway historical cartography, its location or disposition another mystery awaiting resolution. Still, although the published version is a copy and exhibits shallow time depth and limited geographic accuracy, it augments the 1837 map by providing information about places occupied during the decades just prior to the Ioways' removal west of the Missouri River and by offering insight into the settlement strategies of the tribe's Big Neck faction.

CHAPTER FIVE

Historicity

HOW ACCURATE IS THE 1837 MAP? That is, how well do the locations of the depicted rivers, lakes, villages, and routes conform to their locations according to independent lines of evidence? How well does the timeline match with chronologies established through documentary and archaeological records? Having assessed the map's accuracy, how can it help in understanding Ioway diplomacy, history, and culture?

Sources

Before addressing these questions, it is important to consider the sources of information the Ioways used in drafting their map. Consider first the physical features. Ioway leaders would have been familiar through lived experience with most of the rivers and lakes the map depicts, especially those in Iowa and Missouri. Still, by 1837, numerous published maps and atlases identified all of the rivers shown on the Ioway map. It is therefore not necessary to attribute depiction of those physical features to Ioway experience or historical memory. Conceivably, the delegation could have begun creating the map by referring to, or tracing from, a printed Euclidean map. But doing so would have departed from familiar and traditional topological mapping practices. It would not have been an Ioway creation.[1] Moreover, Ioway geographic knowledge and experience are reflected in certain details of the rivers and lakes that do not derive from published sources. The clearest example is the mapping of Blackhawk Lake and its connections to both the Raccoon and Boyer Rivers (figure 17). Apparently, the earliest printed map that shows Blackhawk Lake is David H. Burr's map of 1839, so the lake's presence on the 1837 map likely derives from other-than-published sources. Ioways were familiar with the Boyer River valley long before the 1830s. Therefore, while some depicted physical features might derive from published sources, the Ioway map incorporates landscape information from the delegates' own knowledge and experience.[2]

Likewise, some of the cultural features shown on the Ioway map—several Ioway, Omaha, Otoe, Sauk, and Kickapoo villages—appear on printed maps available in 1837, but several site locations on the Ioway map appear on no printed sources then available and can only derive from oral tradition and historical memory. The principal examples are Site A (the origin at Green Bay), Site H (likely Aowa Creek), Site P (upriver from Iowaville along the Des Moines River), and sites R and S (as yet unidentified sites along the Iowa River on the return route from southeast Iowa to the Council Bluffs area). This is not to say that any of the other sites necessarily derive from printed sources: The Ioways had access to maps that showed those sites, but those places also figured in their own traditions.[3]

How were traditions and tribal history conveyed prior to the institution of literacy among Prairie-Plains peoples? Orally, through stories and other forms of instruction, and through material culture such as bundles. The Orator "was told [of Ioway settlement history] by his father, who derived it through eight preceding ancestors." In 1912, an Omaha elder, 90-year-old Jesse Morris (In sta na za we), explained how he was able to recount a lengthy series of events and village movements: "The old men told the younger children of old times and old events. They were told to remember these things because they belonged to the Tribe and we would have to depend on ourselves when they were gone." These stories and chronicles formed a rich oral literature. But also, especially in negotiations and diplomacy in postcontact times, Ioways made maps.[4]

Locations on the 1837 map that match most precisely with sites corroborated by independent evidence are primarily those at which the delegation members themselves or their fathers or uncles had resided or visited. No Heart and Walking Rain were both born around 1797 and the Orator was born around 1786. All had lived at Iowaville (Site J) and, later, at one or more of the Omaha-area sites that were occupied after around 1819 (Sites U, V, W). No Heart's brother White Cloud I (born around 1784), who represented the Ioway at important councils such as the 1824 treaty council in Washington, or their father the Wounding Arrow (Mahaga or Mauhawgaw, also a principal chief) were probably among the Ioway representatives at councils with the Sauk and Kickapoo in Illinois around 1811–1812. Therefore, Sites J through W represent places familiar to the 1836 petitioners and 1837 council delegates through their lived experiences or those of their fathers or uncles. And because the 1836 petition mentions visiting sites at the mouth of the Upper Iowa River, Site B was also a place known to Ioway leaders through personal experience.[5]

The Wounding Arrow was probably born around 1760 at Site I or nearby in the Council Bluffs vicinity.[6] He was quite young when the Ioways relocated to the Des Moines or Mississippi River around 1765, so he would have been able to convey little personal experience-based knowledge of the Council Bluffs–area village(s) to his sons White Cloud and No Heart. He would have known general information about those villages, other villages, and travels his parents and grandparents had experienced and learned of, and he would have passed that knowledge along to his sons just as his elders had to him. Sites A through I on the 1837 map belong to this category: They are places not directly experienced by the Ioway delegates or the preceding generation but were known on the basis of having been conveyed by grandparents and earlier generations. (Site B is an exception, having been confirmed by a recent visit.) The locations of Sites A and C through I are generally concordant with independent evidence but lack the specific locational data associated with Sites J through W (except Sites P, R, and S, which so far lack independent confirmation).

Ioway residence at Site I and the Wounding Arrow's birth there occurred around 75–80 years prior to the 1837 council. Site I and its period of occupation can be considered a pivot point in the Ioway historical record. For most of the previously occupied sites and Site I itself, the council testimony and the 1836 petition supply only general locational information ("a village on some river running into the Missouri"; "spotted in various places with their ancient Towns and Villages"). In contrast, subsequently occupied sites and routes are more specifically located, named, and dated ("the Ottoes village was the last village passed in going out to our settlement"; "the dry field on the desmoine river another place called the big groove, it was ours at the time the Spanish & French came into the Country"; "when we left the Ottoes village we started and travelled on each side of the river Missouri until we arrived at the mouth of Grand river"; "village on the Desmoines . . . which place the Ioways only left about 25 years ago"). The starting point (Site A) also has an extensive amount of associated information in tribal origin traditions, and the map clearly identifies that place as situated on the east shore of Green Bay, even though there was confusion between Green Bay and Lake Pepin (see Site A discussion, chapter 3). The sites thus fall into three categories. The most recently occupied sites (Sites J–W) are primarily based on personal accounts; most of the earlier sites (Sites C–I) are based on group accounts derived from cultural memory; and Site A reflects an account of origin.[7]

Lance Foster explains the attenuation of Ioway historical consciousness:

> In our oral tradition we have a pretty good record from the 1800s onwards[;] before that time there's bits and pieces, and I'd say right around the 1600s it almost goes right into mythological time. It's hard; you've got time working against you, you've got the fact that we've suffered catastrophic population loss, with all the loss of memory that goes along with that, and also I would say there's another factor in that in our warrior tradition, you remember when you win battles, more than when you lose them.[8]

“Mythological time” is an important concept. Accounts of origin are often unfortunately termed myths—unfortunate because a myth is “a widely held but false belief or idea.” But that is the secondary definition. The primary definition of myth tracks with how anthropologists and historians conceive of it: “a traditional story, especially one concerning the early history of a people or explaining some natural or social phenomenon.” The term “legendary history” conforms to what we mean by myths or accounts of origins.[9] Accordingly, Malcolm Lewis offers this insightful observation about many maps made and used by Indigenous North Americans: “They were based on a combination of personal experience and oral traditions that might incorporate myth. Native Americans did not find it necessary to segregate geography, cosmography, and mythography. Indeed, they would often combine them graphically.”[10]

Orality and Historicity

Overall, the Ioway testimony illustrates the tenets of oral tradition as history, as elucidated by the historian Jan Vansina:

> Accounts of origin, group accounts, and personal accounts are all different manifestations of the same process in different stages. When the whole body of such accounts is taken together there typically appears a three-tiered whole. For recent times there is plenty of information which tapers off as one moves back through time. For earlier periods one finds either a hiatus or just one or a few names, given with some hesitation. There is a gap in the accounts, which I will call the floating gap. For still earlier periods one finds again a wealth of information and one deals here with traditions of origin. The gap is not often very evident to people in the communities involved, but it is usually unmistakable to the researchers. . . .
>
> There are many accounts for very recent times, tapering off as one goes farther back until one reaches times of origin for which, once again, there are many accounts. This profile has been compared to an hourglass. At the junction of times of origin and the very sparse subsequent records, there usually is a chronological gap. It is called “floating” because over time it tends to advance towards the present, that is, the oldest accounts of later times tend to be forgotten or else amalgamated with later or earlier materials.[11]

The 1837 map reflects these three tiers and the floating gap between the lower (older) two (figure 27). Site A, the oldest place, is indeed associated with a wealth of accounts pertaining to Ioway tribal and clan origins, occurring in a timeless past. A gap of unknown length—Vansina’s floating gap—separates it from Sites B–I. Those sites epitomize Vansina’s middle category: group accounts of places having few names and uncertain locations but known through cultural memories and occupied, in the Ioway case, as far as 200 years in the past—around eight generations as in Vansina's study, as the Orator related, and as determined by the current study.[12] Sites J–W, the most recent sites, in the uppermost part of the hourglass, are associated with extensive historical information derived from personal memories (oral history rather than oral tradition) or obtained firsthand from people who had experienced or witnessed those places or events. The diminution in cultural memory between those two sets of sites above the floating gap is significant. Ioways in the 1830s could provide basic information but little detail about villages prior to the establishment of Site J (Iowaville), that is, before the 1760s, or about seventy-five years—three generations—prior to the 1837 council. Details continued to be lost: Already by 1848, Wawnonqueskoona, who could accurately map villages occupied in the 1820s and 1830s in Missouri, evinced difficulty and imprecision regarding any sites earlier than Iowaville, omitting or mislocating pre-1765 villages that had been mapped more accurately only ten years earlier.[13]

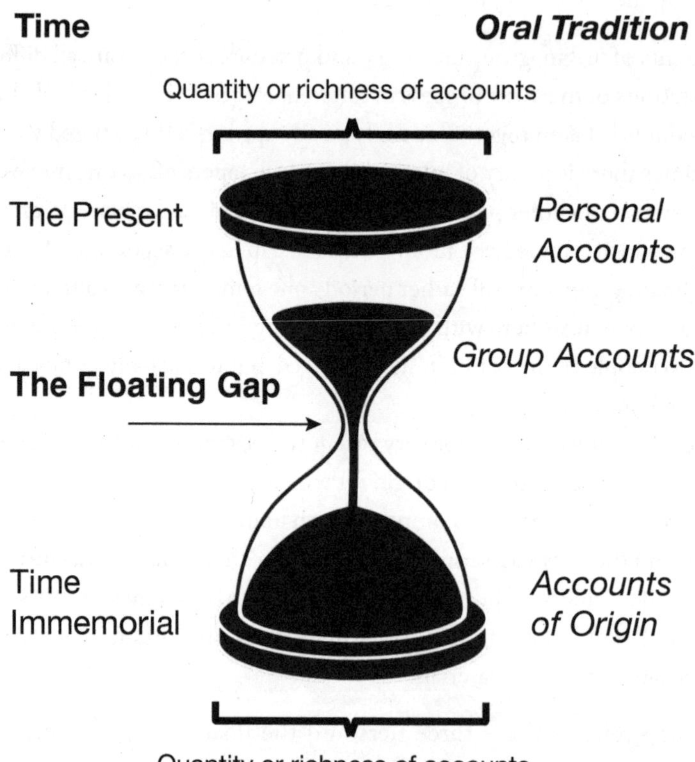

Figure 27. The hourglass model of oral tradition, illustrating the diminution of oral tradition's historicity over time, as discussed by Jan Vansina. Illustration by William Green.

Oral traditions have been characterized as exhibiting "achronicity," retelling of a timeless past that is not necessarily preoccupied with "chronology, temporal linearity, sequentiality, causality, or narrative consistency." Some scholars claim that "achronicity is one of the concomitants of an oral non-calendrical society." Yet societies like the Ioway had long been encountering and negotiating with Europeans and Americans as well as other Indigenous nations. Cultural memories of places and movement fostered effective defense of group interests as the tribe navigated the complex postcontact political and economic landscape. In the postcontact era, at least, Ioway oral tradition was not at all achronological. Like other oral traditions, Ioway "transgenerational group memories" built event sequences as experienced within physical and social environments. Illustrating such a sequence, the 1837 map is a flow map or itinerary map, a map that describes the direction of movements of people over time. Even if the associated narrative (as translated and transcribed) is choppy and untethered to firm dates before about 1812, the map epitomizes temporal as well as spatial consciousness. For the period above the floating gap, the map exhibits chronology, albeit one without exact dates: "to use an analogy with a common archaeological contrast, orally communicated history"—as the Ioways employed—"relies on a relative rather than an absolute time scale."[14]

The (relative) historicity of the 1837 Ioway map and its accompanying narrative is akin to other Native American "event-dominated" art forms and artifacts—"mnemographic records"—that also recorded various events. While "such documents cannot be unequivocally 'read' without the knowledge of an associated oral tradition," narratives and other information can often assist in interpretation. Several early Native American maps in addition to the Ioway map depict a temporal as well as spatial dimension. More common chronicles of events, especially in the Great Plains, are record-keeping media such as calendars and winter counts. These accounts offer Indigenous perspectives on important occurrences, in some cases covering more than 100 years. Also, the Biographic tradition of Great Plains rock art, which attained its florescence in the protohistoric and postcontact eras, featured representational and narrative storytelling "depicting everyday occurrences and recording historical events," in contrast to earlier, nonnarrative rock art traditions. Increasing warfare and other pressures apparently fostered a need to record events more permanently and prominently than before. Similarly, for the Ioways, oral records and maps of settlement locations and movements, and of antagonisms, alliances, and agreements with other groups, became useful in the turbulent contact era, to try to blunt the power literate societies wielded in their efforts to control, colonize, and dispossess Indigenous people.[15]

As a chronicle of movement and migration, and one that adheres to Western notions of linear time, the map had to have both an origin point and an end point. The end point was fairly obvious: it was the "last village passed" before the Ioways arrived at their current settlement. The choice of an origin point was not as obvious. It could have been the earliest known or recalled site in Iowa (Site B), or it could have been one or more of the traditional origin locales such as Red Banks (Green Bay) or Lake Pepin. The Ioway leaders chose to depict Green Bay as the origin on the map, while the accompanying narrative mentioned both Green Bay and Lake Pepin. Those origin loci and their legendary histories, while outside the territory at issue in 1837, anchor the entire narrative in deep time and with the genesis of the Ioway people.[16]

On the basis of this analysis of the historicity of the 1837 map and the associated oral traditions and cultural memory, it is possible to address the issue raised earlier about whether the Ioway mapmakers referred to printed maps that depicted old Ioway villages. As one follows the 1837 map's villages back in time, the generally diminishing geographic detail and accuracy suggest that the depicted village locations did not derive from printed maps. Had the delegates used printed maps such as those cited in this chapter, note 2, they could easily have mapped more villages and mapped them more precisely. Or they could have simply brought those printed maps to the council. That they did neither might indicate they lacked access to such maps or, more likely, decided that their case would be stronger using their own map based on their own oral history, traditions, and cultural memory.

The 1837 map depicts Ioway settlements and migrations over tens of thousands of square miles, graphically indicating the vastness of the territory claimed by this relatively small tribe. The 1836 petition and 1837 council testimony assert Ioway historic occupation throughout what is now Iowa, northern Missouri, and southern Minnesota. As we saw in chapter 2, William Clark concurred with the Ioways' territorial claim, writing that when he arrived in the area in 1803, the Ioways possessed unquestioned historical and current claims to that "immense tract of country." The territory that the Ioways of the 1830s considered their ancestral lands constituted much of the area Oneota people had occupied from the twelfth through the seventeenth centuries. Oneota regional "group continuities," consisting of closely related or sequentially occupied villages, resided in numerous river valleys throughout the Prairie Peninsula. Inhabitants of the different localities and regions traveled widely, interacted both peacefully and violently, and moved periodically. Because Oneota people had become familiar with this vast area over at least 500 years, it is not surprising that their descendants would have known and utilized it as well. Understanding this lengthy history permits us to appreciate the seemingly dizzying movement of the Ioways: They were not simply being pushed around but were occupying and reoccupying familiar places and regions that had been ancestral territory for twenty generations or longer.[17]

Movement

How did it happen that the Ioways occupied and moved between so many settlements throughout such a large area? Several factors apparently were at play. The Orator attributed the "migratory character of the people" to "the will of the Great Spirit that they should not be stationary, but travel from place to place, cultivating different ground; and they believe that they will only continue to have good crops and healthy children so long as they obey this law of their nature." The 1836 petition states that the Ioways left their Des Moines River village around 1812 "on search of Game on other parts of their land, but never intended to abandon their claim to the Same or the bones of their fathers, which are yet to be seen there." Tellingly, the petition added, "the Country has never been taken from them by Conquest." Yet, as noted in chapter 3, Dakota Sioux attacks in the early 1700s apparently had driven the Ioways and Omahas from the Big Sioux River valley and the pipestone region onto the Missouri River.[18]

A more recent conquest formed the focus of the Sauk leader Keokuk's retort to the Ioway claims, as noted in chapter 2. Keokuk argued that the Ioways occupied and moved often between so many villages because the Sac and Fox "always pushed them before us," fighting and driving them off. The fighting was mostly in the form of small-scale raids and ambushes. Meskwaki chief Wapello, also quoted in chapter 2, claimed (or feigned) surprise at the Ioway claims, attributing the Ioways' dissatisfaction to white people's influence. If Wapello was not being disingenuous, he might simply have been reflecting the belief, more bluntly stated by Keokuk, that one's land claim vanishes or becomes irrelevant once the next group occupies the "vacated" region, a sentiment that surely resonated with U.S. government functionaries at the height of the Indian removal era.[19]

Additional factors probably contributed to the Ioway propensity to move frequently, at least during the postcontact era. Native people of the Prairie Peninsula moved seasonally, often shifting between summer agricultural villages and winter camps, even in precontact times. Village locations moved periodically to allow local resources to replenish, as the Orator suggested. But movement apparently accelerated in the seventeenth and early eighteenth centuries. Expanded interest in bison and other western prairie resources drew Oneota people and their Ioway descendants farther into the Great Plains. The arrival of the horse among the Ioway, perhaps as early as the mid-seventeenth century, facilitated even greater mobility. Later, improved trading opportunities attracted settlement in economically strategic locations on the Des Moines River (see Site J [Iowaville] discussion, chapter 3) and, subsequently, back on the Missouri River (see Site W discussion). Tragically, smallpox epidemics in the eighteenth and early nineteenth centuries were killing many Ioways, causing the smaller surviving populations to become more susceptible to attack and impelling them to seek more secure village locations. Although "conquests" were rare, repeated raids and skirmishes with neighboring tribes continued to wear on the Ioways throughout the time reflected on the 1837 map. But it was settler pressure, not intertribal conflicts or other factors, to which Ioways attributed their later village movements. Ioway elder Frank Kent (Nawanoway, 1841–1956) explained that the Ioways had to move from place to place because "we were driven out of our villages and land where we made our home by white people with guns. That was the reason we had to move." Overall, Ioway movements were long-standing practices, but imperial and colonial forces steadily reduced the Ioways' control over where and how frequently to move.[20]

In light of all of the factors that might have contributed to these movements, it is fair to characterize the Ioways of the 1830s as diasporic, as Lance Foster indicates in the foreword. Ioway communities reflect the criteria for diasporas offered by Sarah Trabert and colleagues: They were "made up of a dispersed population that chose to or [were] forced to leave their homeland"; the people retained "a nostalgia or longing for their homeland that shape[d] their identity and [was] reflected in collective memories of their homeland and a desire to return there at some point in the future"; and they remained "separate and distinct from their host communities resisting assimilation" as far as was possible or advisable. In diasporic communities, "boundaries and identities are . . . remade as perceptions and connections to homelands shift and change" over time. The Ioways' desire to restore their Des Moines River villages dissipated after they were forced to cede the land, which had become settled by Sauks, Meskwakis, and Americans. Although individual and collective memories of Iowa faded as the people who had lived there passed on and as their descendants had to make a living elsewhere, the Ioways did not forget their homelands. As when most ethnic groups are separated from their homelands, an association remained between the people and the territory. "This association itself becomes an essential part of the collective memory and identity of the community"—strengthened in this case by the shared name for both the people and the territory.[21]

Places and Placemaking

The analysis in chapter 3 attempted to identify locations depicted on the 1837 map and match them with places known through independent historical or archaeological evidence. The map and related Ioway testimony recognize places, spaces, and events dating from time immemorial (Site A) to around 1830 (Site W), while omitting several places and events the Ioways considered irrelevant or potentially damaging to their case. Some matches between mapped locations and known sites are close while others are less certain, and some mapped places do not correspond to any known sites. Overall, the map's temporality and historicity conform to the hourglass model of oral tradition as history: The specificity of depicted places declines with their age until the "floating gap" is reached at about 200 years. Below that gap, that is, before the 1630s, events and places are so uncertain that they become parts of origin stories or myths, better termed legendary history. Similarities in those origin stories to those of the linguistically related Ho-Chunk and Otoe-Missouria people are consistent with these tribes' common heritage.[22]

The Ioway map is a multidimensional representation of collective spatial and historical consciousness as of 1837. It depicts not only physical and cultural features (rivers, lakes, settlements) but also an explicit temporal component. Most of the routes between settlements are directional and represent migrations or visits to other groups, and probably duplicate ancient travel routes as well. Similar routes and trail systems have been characterized as "Indigenous infrastructure" in recognition of their significance and longevity. Several other nineteenth-century Native American maps incorporate time and flows, but few as clearly and with as much time depth and corroborating evidence. While the map is first and foremost a political document, it is as faithful a depiction of up to ten generations of Ioway places—"center[s] of meaning constructed by experience"—as oral tradition can produce. Furthermore, the map and its supporting narratives presented Ioway "place-stories," augmenting these places with references to "the landscape found at [those locations] and the meanings which people assign to that landscape through the process of living in it." Ioway movements over long spans of time in fact were entwined with placemaking, and the map shows that the Ioways explicitly "temporalized the landscape," belying the apparently static nature of most maps and concepts of territory. Temporalizing places and landscapes is a cultural statement as well as a political argument, as it embodies cultural memory and the links between events and places, territory and identity. Such is the power of maps: presenting "the accumulated thought and labor of the past" while working, in this case, as a negotiating tool to claim land rights.[23]

CHAPTER SIX

The Life of the Map

OBJECTS, LIKE PEOPLE, LIVE—in a sense. An object's life is not necessarily animate, but it can be just as eventful as a person's. Also like people, objects can sleep and die. The Ioway map, as a physical object, was born in 1837, served an important purpose when it was young, then lay dormant for decades. It wasn't until the 1970s, when it was nearly 140 years old, that the map once again attracted attention.

In this chapter, I discuss the life history of the Ioway map. I try to understand how and where it was made, what happened to it and with it during the long period when it was essentially ignored, and how people have been treating it since its awakening almost fifty years ago. In effect, this is the map's biography.

In anthropology and material culture studies, object biographies and life histories aid in understanding relationships between objects, people, and social and historical contexts. Object biographers examine an object's creation, its uses over time, its disposition(s), and the implications of the ways it has been used or not used. In the field of Native American cartography, Carolyn Gilman and G. Malcolm Lewis applied the method to an eighteenth-century, probably Miami, map that depicts most of the present states of Illinois and Indiana.[1]

Writing a biography of an inanimate object can be a daunting task, especially if the object was made nearly 200 years ago. Researchers must carefully scrutinize any associated documentation as well as the object itself. As we saw in chapters 3 and 5, details provided in Ioway testimony and close inspection of the map—along with various forms of independent evidence—helped to identify many places shown on the map and their approximate dates of occupation. Now, what can we learn about the map's own history, and what can its life and activities—its itineraries and uses—tell us?

Who Made the Map, Where and When?

Although the 1837 Ioway map is often referred to as No Heart's Map, the 1837 council transcript indicates simply that the map was "executed by an Indian." There is no reason to doubt this general attribution. In most respects, the map's symbology adheres to well-documented Native American traditions. The use of straight or slightly curved lines to represent rivers is standard on early Native American maps, whereas non-Native explorers and cartographers used wavy or undulating lines for rivers. Circles represent lakes on the Ioway map, as on other Native maps. Dot-filled circles represent villages on the Ioway map, as on many Native American maps, while non-Native maps often used triangles (stylized tipis) to indicate Indian villages. The Ioway map's use of dotted lines to represent routes of movement adheres to Native mapping standards of the era, though contemporary non-Native maps also used the same symbol for trails or routes. The Ioways had described their former territorial boundaries in their 1836 petition, but the map is unframed and unbounded as in most Native cartographic traditions. One researcher believes the map employs Euro-American cartographic conventions by using a constant rather than shifting scale—a Euclidean "perspective from above" as is familiar to most modern map users instead of a shifting scale based on one's point of view—but scale is actually variable in different portions of the map (figure 28).[2]

The map was Native—and certainly Ioway—made, but we don't know precisely where, when, or by whom. It is most likely that No Heart, Walking Rain, and perhaps the Orator were its principal drafters. No Heart, as the "village" or "peace" chief and the brother of the late principal chief White Cloud I, had been part of Ioway leadership for many years and was among the most knowledgeable individuals regarding tribal history. Walking Rain was the nephew of the U.S.-designated chief Hard Heart and had signed the 1836 petition with its geographic and historical information. The Orator was knowledgeable about Ioway history and had signed and may have authored much of the 1836 petition. It is also possible that White Cloud II assisted in drafting the map, given his late father's leadership position.

The Ioways may have created the map in Washington shortly before the 1837 council began, perhaps even on October 6 as suggested in chapter 2. But the delegation could have made the map at an early stage of their journey, perhaps at Fort Leavenworth or in St. Louis. If the map was made in September, it would have been necessary to protect it during the four-week journey down the Missouri and Mississippi Rivers, up the Ohio River, and across the Appalachians to Washington. Letters routinely made that trip, folded to fit into a pouch. The map shows evidence of having been folded: One line, apparently the initial fold, extends lengthwise through the center of the map, and smaller fold lines and broad, dark outlines of once-exposed edges suggest that the map was folded to a rectangle of about 4 by 8 inches (approximately 10 by 20 centimeters). Some ink is missing at the folds, indicating the map was folded after it was made. Whether it was folded before or after the delegation's arrival in Washington is uncertain. Many documents were

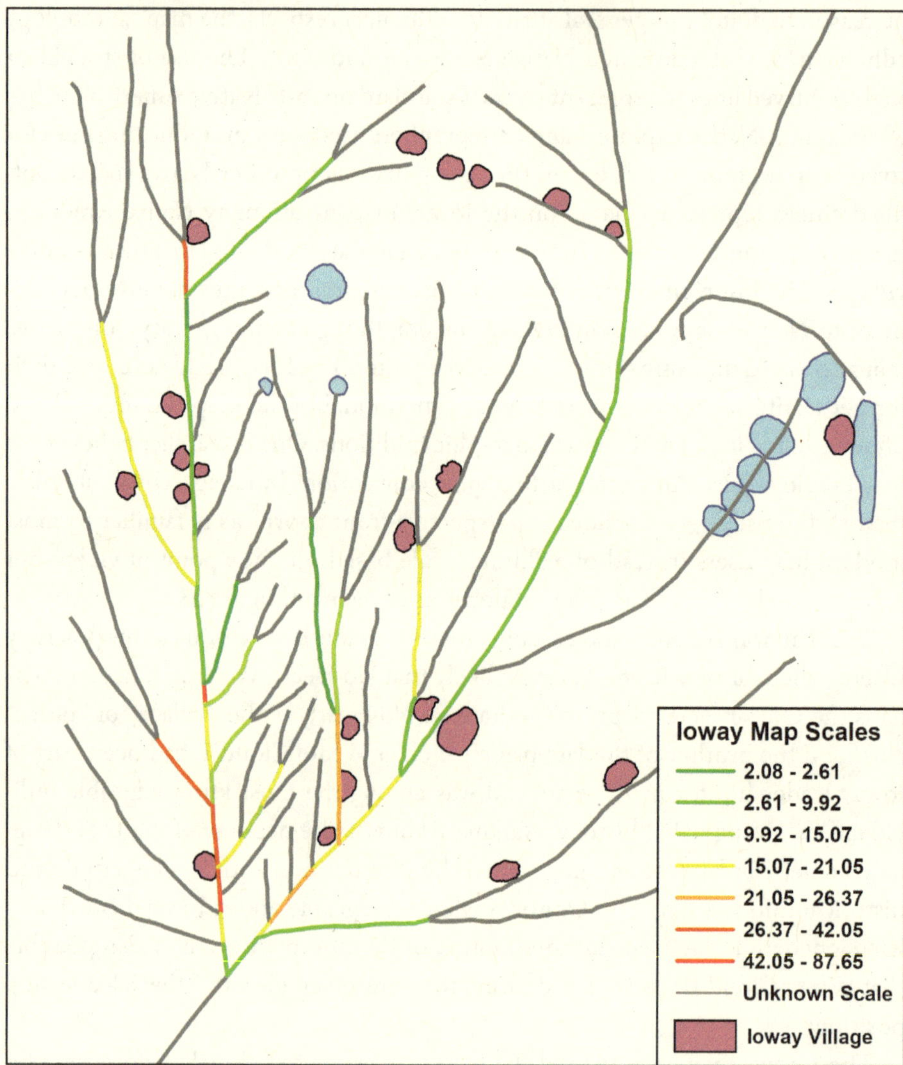

Figure 28. Variety of map scales identified on the 1837 Ioway map. Courtesy of Mary Whelan (2003).

delivered to and filed at the Indian Office in approximately 4-by-8-inch folded form (the Journal of Proceedings, for one).[3]

Faint reverse "ghosts" of solid and dotted lines—rivers and routes—appear on the map in the area south of the large circle representing one or more northern Iowa lakes and Storm Lake and in the headwaters of the North Raccoon, Des Moines, and Iowa Rivers. These appear to be faint transfers of ink that occurred when the map was folded.

Because the map was encapsulated in Mylar before physical analysis of the paper, ink, or adhesive could be conducted, we know little about its composition.

As noted in chapter 3, the map measures 69 by 104 centimeters (27 by 41 inches). Two large sheets of light to medium brown paper were joined with an adhesive. Attaching the sheets created an approximately 4-centimeter (1½–2 inch) band of overlap between them through the center of the map. Each sheet would have measured about 56 by 69 centimeters (22 by 27 inches). Dark brown-black ink was applied with a broad-tipped tool, perhaps a large quill or a brush. Some ink losses appear at folds, as just mentioned, and in a few other places. On the basis of an examination in April 2001, Susan Page, senior paper conservator at the National Archives and Records Administration (NARA), suggested that "the ink was a type of iron gall ink which is known to be highly acidic, thus the breaks and losses along the heavily inked lines." Iron gall ink was the standard ink used in Europe and North America for hundreds of years, well into the twentieth century.[4]

Then What Happened to (and with) the Map?

The Indian Affairs office retained the Ioway map after the 1837 council concluded. The map's physical location over the next few years is not certain, but it was probably filed with other records of the 1837 council. A label casually written in green pencil or a narrow crayon on the lower central part of the map (when viewed in portrait orientation) reads:

FILE

B-402
O. I. A. Mis.
Feb. 20 – 1838

This label was added with the map in a landscape orientation, just as the map had been presented (see chapter 3, Sites A and N). "O. I. A." is the Office of Indian Affairs, "Mis." is Miscellaneous, and B-402 is an identifier.[5] February 20, 1838, was the date when Secretary Chauncey Bush transmitted copies of the Journal of Proceedings of the 1837 council to Commissioner Carey Harris. The following day, Wednesday, February 21, was the proclamation date for several treaties that were concluded in 1837, that is, the date on which they became law. Bush's February 20 cover letter indicates the enclosed material was "Miscellaneous, B-402/1838," confirming the association between the map and the Journal. The label on the map simply provides catalog information, where the map should be filed, and when it was transmitted rather than the date it was actually inscribed.[6]

On the map, "Iowa" was scrawled near the "File" label, using the same or a similar green pencil or crayon, though oriented in the portrait rather than landscape direction. And the same hand might have added the label "821" that appears below

"Iowa," 821 being the map's catalog number within the Central Map File of Record Group 75. It is not known when that number was assigned. One other green pencil or crayon mark is present that might have been made at that time: At the top of the map (in portrait orientation), three bold lines cross out the notation "806," which had been written in light pencil in Chauncey Bush's handwriting, consistent with a crossed-out "806" in an inscription on the cover of the Journal of Proceedings that reads:

821
For Map See Sec Draughtsman's No. ~~806~~

This inscription might date to the 1880s.

About five years after the 1837 council, on May 28, 1842, Thomas Hartley Crawford, Carey Harris's successor as Indian commissioner, wrote a 6,500-word letter to Secretary of War John C. Spencer addressing the issue of whether "Indian title," and particularly any legitimate Ioway claims, persisted in Iowa Territory. After reviewing the Ioway and Sac and Fox treaties from the previous two decades, Crawford read through the Journal of Proceedings and looked at the 1837 map—"the Indian Map referred to is before me." He believed that the Ioways' presentations and "the rude map they exhibited" were intended to deny all Sac and Fox right to Iowa "and to supplant their claim to such right." He concluded that the Ioway map and testimony did not refute the premise of the earlier treaties: that both tribes held an undivided interest in the territory, despite the Ioways having lived there longer (though recently departed) and the Sac and Fox having recently arrived. He also concluded that the Sac and Fox still held title to a portion of the territory, which became a factor leading to the October 1842 treaty that forced their (temporary, for some) exile to Kansas.[7]

I know of only one other nineteenth-century use of the map. Paul Brodie, a draftsman in the Office of Indian Affairs, added this label to the lower right-hand corner of the map when viewed in portrait orientation:[8]

Note.
Department of the Interior
Office of Indian Affairs
Washington, D.C. July 4, 1884

This map accompanied the Journal of Proceedings at a Council held in this city with a delegation of Chiefs and Braves of the Confederated Tribes of the Sac and Fox Indians of the Mississippi, and a delegation of Sac and Fox and Iowa Chiefs and Braves of the Missouri October 7–1837 at 10 o'clock A.M. It was made by an Indian and presented to C.A. Harris, Esq., Comr. on the part of the U.S.

> by "Non-chi-ning-ga" an Ioway Chief who produced and referred to it during his address at the Council, as appears upon pages 46 and 47 of the Journal.
>
> Paul Brodie,
>
> Draughtsman, Ind. Office.

It is not known what occasioned the addition of this label to the 1837 map. The placement of the note guaranteed that most future uses of the map would orient it in portrait mode, although the lightly penciled Lake Pepin, Green Bay, and Illinois labels indicate its original presentation was in landscape orientation. Also added to the map in Brodie's handwriting was "Tube 520" just above the penciled "821." The map's storage in a tube for an unknown length of time likely protected it from excessive handling. And finally, perhaps also in the nineteenth century, a stamped "821" label was added near the "Tube 520" inscription.

On a cover sheet of the Journal of Proceedings labeled "Miscell. B.402, 1838," Brodie added this reference to the map: "Mem. The Map referred to in pages 46 and 47 of this Journal is numbered 821 and on file with the Draughtsman. See his Index of Maps." Brodie also might have been responsible for the "draughtsman's" note with the crossed-out 806, although that note's handwriting differs from Brodie's in the labels just noted.

In sum, the map was active in 1837, briefly received attention again in 1838 and 1842, received a few cataloging and filing notations at unknown dates, and was inscribed with a lengthy descriptor in 1884.[9]

Since 1884

I find no mention of the Ioway map in archival or published sources between 1884 and 1976, with the exception of a few notes made in the 1950s in relation to Indian Claims Commission cases, discussed in the next section. It is not even certain when the map was transferred from the Bureau of Indian Affairs to the National Archives. In response to queries about the map's history, NARA Reference Branch archivist Rose Buchanan reported there were

> two significant transfers of cartographic material in the late 1930s. In 1938, NARA brought in roughly 18 cubic feet of maps, mostly printed maps of Indian reservations, General Land Office maps of public land States, and township plats of lands in and near Indian reservations. In 1939, NARA brought in roughly 6,000 cubic feet of maps and related material, such as survey descriptions; this amounted to over 17,000 maps covering a variety of topics, from original surveys to allotments to rights-of-way across reservations. The accessioning paperwork does not in either case include an itemized list of the maps that were transferred to NARA nor indicate, of course, which series the maps ultimately ended up in. But the

accessioning paperwork does confirm that a significant number of BIA maps were with NARA by the 1950s.[10]

The existence of the Ioway map's catalog card in the NARA Cartographic Branch (see this chapter, n. 5) indicates that the map probably was part of the 1930s transfers. Cartographic Branch supervisory archivist Brandi Oswald reported that "the card index was created in the late 1930s" and that "the initial conservation, processing, and indexing was completed on the Central Map File records in the late 1930s."[11]

Since 1976, the map has received attention from historians, anthropologists, and tribal members. It has been exhibited in several high-profile venues and received treatments of varying depth in scholarly and popular books, articles, websites, and even art projects. Here, I review the most notable activities associated with the map in order to understand this second active phase of its life history.

The map owes its reactivation to the historian Herman Viola, whose Smithsonian Institution career included positions as director of the National Anthropological Archives and curator at the National Museum of American History; he was also an archivist at the National Archives. Viola's 1976 book, *The Indian Legacy of Charles Bird King,* was the first publication to include an image of the 1837 map. King's portraits of Native Americans are among the most detailed and highest quality of the era, and they received wide distribution as illustrations in McKenney and Hall's *History of the Indian Tribes of North America.* King made his paintings during tribal visits to Washington between 1821 and 1842, and Viola provides accounts of those visits based mostly on newspaper reports and official records. His discussion of the 1837 council includes a black-and-white image of the Ioway map along with black-and-white and color images of King's portrait of No Heart, plus a later daguerreotype of No Heart. Viola wrote that No Heart "presented a remarkably accurate map of the Mississippi River valley, drawn by one of his delegates, pointing out the territory his small and peaceful tribe had already lost to Sac and Fox encroachment." It is unclear how Viola determined that the map was "remarkably accurate." His caption for the map reads, "map used by No Heart in his confrontation with Keokuk in Washington. Now in the Cartographic Archives Division of the National Archives," followed by Brodie's 1884 inscription. Viola's next book, *Diplomats in Buckskins* (1981), which focused on the Native American delegations that visited Washington, also mentions and illustrates the Ioway map—the illustration this time being a full page (8-by-10-inch) figure—and includes a different daguerreotype of No Heart. Viola's 1981 text is identical to that in his 1976 book.[12]

We have cited Martha Royce Blaine's comprehensive book on the Ioway people frequently. It was first published in 1979, then reprinted with a new preface but no other changes in 1995. Using the Journal of Proceedings, Blaine summarized

No Heart's presentation as follows: "He said that the Ioways prepared a map showing the villages of the new nation in all the lands that they claimed or had inhabited in their remembered history. He pointed first to the earliest villages near Lake Pepin and Green Bay. He then indicated the villages near the Otoes and Omahas on the Missouri and noted the places along the Des Moines where they had lived when the French and Spanish were in the area."[13]

It is unclear what Blaine intended with "the new nation"—perhaps she had meant to write "the Ioway nation." Blaine went on to mention other salient parts of No Heart's and Walking Rain's presentations, and she provided Keokuk's response verbatim. She did not include an image of the map or discuss its possible significance.

Also appearing in 1979 was the first in a series of important works that discuss the Ioway map by the British geographer G. Malcolm Lewis. Over a forty-year career, mostly at the University of Sheffield, where he established the Amerindian and Inuit Maps and Mapping Programme, Lewis became the acknowledged expert on historic Native American maps. As mentioned in this chapter, note 9, he examined the map during a 1994 visit to NARA, and he probably viewed it earlier, too. Lewis's 1979 article, "The Indigenous Maps and Mapping of North American Indians," was published in the *Map Collector*, a UK quarterly that ran from 1977 to 1996 and was an important periodical on the history of cartography. In that article, he wrote:

> Even more representational [than Ojibwe birch bark scrolls that depict migrations and recognizable places] is a map done boldly, perhaps with a stick or finger, in ink on paper and presented by an Iowa Chief in 1837 as evidence in a dispute over land at a council between Indians of the upper Mississippi and middle Missouri valleys respectively. It depicts, quite recognizably, the drainage systems of the Mississippi and Missouri Rivers and their tributaries above St. Louis, settlements and a complex network of migration routes between Green Bay, Wisconsin, and the middle Missouri valley. There is no key but the journal of the council proceedings makes it quite clear that the route depicted the migration of the Chief's forefathers and that the settlements are some of the sites occupied en route, of which the Chief admitted that he could not tell the total.[14]

Lewis was the first author to attempt to identify the rivers and lakes the map depicts, and he redrafted the map's hydrographic features into a modern cartographic representation. This allowed readers to see the rivers and lakes in a more familiar form and to appreciate the scale of the territory represented (see figure 11). In his 1984 article in an issue of *Great Plains Quarterly* devoted to the topic of "Mapping the North American Plains," Lewis suggested that "ethnologists might discover more about the functions of certain art and artifacts if they had greater awareness of the ability of Indians to make maps and of the characteristics and functions of the maps. . . . Evidence presented by Iowa Indians in the course of nineteenth-century treaty negotiations suggests that maps (both mental and artifact) were used as a means of preserving important information about the history of the tribe's migrations."[15]

To illustrate this point, Lewis once again included a black-and-white image of the 1837 map and the hydrographic map he had published in 1979. Republication of Lewis's 1984 article and others from the *Great Plains Quarterly* mapping issue in a 1987 book not only provided broader dissemination but also printing of the maps in a larger (8¼-by-11-inch) format.[16] Then, in his 1998 magnum opus, "Maps, Mapmaking, and Map Use by Native North Americans," Lewis again published the 1837 map along with his modern hydrographic interpretation, and he added some historical context about the 1830 and 1838 treaties. He also indicated that the map depicts "routes of the Iowas' late prehistoric migrations" and stated No Heart was the "maker of the map."[17] I noted in chapter 3 that most of the routes between villages depict postcontact rather than prehistoric migrations, and earlier in this chapter I pointed out that No Heart may well have been the mapmaker but this is not certain. These quibbles aside, Lewis's work complemented Viola's and Blaine's historical discussions by providing specific geographical contexts and placing the 1837 map in the broader corpus of Native American cartography.[18]

Lewis's work on the 1837 map was influential among geographers. In 1981, the German historical geographer Rainer Vollmar, a professor in the John F. Kennedy Institute for North American Studies at the Free University of Berlin, published a monograph about the Indian-made maps of North America. The book contained images, information, and discussions about dozens of maps of Native American origin. Vollmar based his work on research he had conducted in numerous U.S. archives in 1977 and on information Lewis had shared with him in 1976, including a draft cartobibliography of North American Indian maps and mapping that was later fleshed out in Lewis's 1998 publications. Vollmar accurately described his own book, which appeared after Lewis's 1979 article but before Lewis's wider-ranging surveys, as "the first comprehensive treatment of [these] previously neglected ethnocartographic representations and influences."[19] Some Anglophone scholars cited Vollmar's German-language work (it has a 1½-page English summary), but the book was mostly ignored even as interest in Native American maps grew. Vollmar included an image of the 1837 Ioway map as a full-page black-and-white figure. He described the map's features but incorrectly suggested it was presumably "executed using charcoal." In English, Vollmar added part of No Heart's presentation from the Journal of Proceedings as well as Brodie's 1884 note, and he included a copy of Charles Bird King's 1837 portrait of No Heart, captioned (in German), "No Heart (Notchimine), the author of this sketch of the Iowa Territory on the upper

Mississippi, from a painting by Charles Bird King, 1837." Vollmar did not indicate the map's size, and his suggestion that the map was drafted in charcoal suggests he did not view it in person.[20]

David Turnbull's 1989 book, *Maps Are Territories, Science Is an Atlas,* was prepared for a course called Nature and Human Nature at Deakin University in Australia. Turnbull, a science and technology studies scholar, offered multiple perspectives on the cultural meanings and uses of maps and presented a worldwide cartographic sampling. Like Vollmar, Turnbull was informed in part by Malcolm Lewis's work. Turnbull's book presents an image of the Ioway map, captioned "Manuscript map of the upper Mississippi and lower Missouri presented by Non Chi Ning Ga, an Iowa Indian chief, as part of a land claim in Washington, 1837." The map's size is not given. The book also includes Lewis's hydrographic identification maps, with the caption "Contemporary Western interpretation of Non Chi Ning Ga's map." Turnbull's brief text claims that "Non Chi Ning Ga's Missouri map is an American Indian map which differs from a modern map [referring to Lewis's maps] of the same area only in the details." The "Missouri" misuse aside, Turnbull's argument that Indigenous maps were important and sophisticated attracted attention and gained a wide audience when the University of Chicago Press republished his book in 1993. Native American studies scholar Gerald Vizenor, whom we met in chapter 1, quoted Turnbull's description of the Ioway map in 1998 to illustrate the significance and power of Native maps as elements of "transmotion" and sovereignty.[21]

A 1992–93 NARA exhibit, *Western Ways,* featured 127 maps, images, and documents that depicted the Native and non-Native people and landscapes of the trans-Mississippi West.[22] The Ioway map was subjected to some conservation treatment in preparation for the exhibit. Following close examination of the map and associated documentation in April 2001, NARA senior paper conservator Susan Page (cited earlier about the ink used on the map) reported that some conservation work had already been done on the map prior to 1992. It had been laminated, probably in the 1950s or 1960s, with cellulose acetate film and reinforced with a cloth fabric. Ms. Page noted this

> was a common and widespread preservation treatment for items of value prior to the introduction of polyester film encapsulation. . . . The fabric was a plain weave cotton. Cellulose acetate film was applied to both the front and back with heat and pressure. No additional adhesive was used. This was a very common preservation practice and may have substantially contributed to retaining several of the fragmented and fragile sections of the map.[23]

Condition reports generally were not done at the time, and none exists for this early treatment of the map. In January 1992, prior to the October opening of *Western Ways* in the National Archives Building, the NARA conservation lab undertook "minor treatment and encapsulation." The lab staff mended tears with methylcellulose, a standard, well-tested, reversible material for paper repair, and they flattened the map prior to encapsulating it in 4-mil Mylar, again a standard means of preserving fragile paper. It is unknown whether the map was deacidified prior to encapsulation, but the acid content of pre–Civil War paper is low and generally does not pose preservation problems. Still, the map is fragile, and some edges were fragmented.[24]

Encapsulating the map prior to the *Western Ways* exhibition was a wise decision because the map was displayed for more than a year. The exhibition, inspired in part by Patricia Limerick's landmark book, *The Legacy of Conquest*, was timed for the Columbian Quincentenary: October 9, 1992–October 17, 1993. The *Western Ways* catalog illustrates the Ioway map, published as before in black and white and again with no size indicated. The caption reads "Map of the Mississippi River Valley drawn by Iowa Chief No Heart, 1837. This map was drawn in conjunction with treaty negotiations with the Iowas in 1837. It depicts trails, villages, rivers, streams, and tribal boundaries." Attribution to No Heart as the map's creator, not just its presenter, had solidified.[25]

The pace of research and publications about the 1837 map increased in the 1990s. Inspired by Lewis's 1987 book chapter, I began researching the map and presenting papers about it at regional and national archaeology and history conferences. I gave presentations at the Iowa Tribe of Kansas and Nebraska's annual business meeting and Báxoje Fall Encampment and Powwow in 1997. I made a few nearly full-size black-and-white copies of the map, mounted on poster board, and gave one to the Iowa Tribe of Kansas and Nebraska and, later, one to the Iowa Tribe of Oklahoma. My work on the map in the 1990s culminated in a description of it for a historical atlas published by the Illinois State Museum in 2001, which included the first attempt at identifying the settlements shown on the map and their occupation dates. Chapter 3 in this book is an expanded and updated version of that description.[26]

Also in the 1990s, Sona Andrews and Mark Warhus at the University of Wisconsin–Milwaukee were compiling an extensive image collection and database of Native American maps. While the compilation was not completed until 2023,[27] Warhus began developing exhibitions about Native American maps and researching and writing what turned out to be a popular and well-reviewed book about those maps. The first exhibition Warhus curated—with Malcolm Lewis as its assistant director—was titled *Cartographic Encounters: An Exhibition of Native American Maps from Central Mexico to the Arctic*. The Newberry Library in Chicago showed the exhibit from June 16 to August 5, 1993, in conjunction with the both the Fifteenth International Conference on the History of Cartography and the library's

Kenneth Nebenzahl Jr. Lectures in the History of Cartography, the latter of which Lewis organized and published. The exhibition utilized facsimiles of more than sixty maps, including the Ioway map. The exhibition also included King's portrait of No Heart, but unlike Viola, Warhus was uncertain whether the No Heart King painted was the same No Heart who had presented the map. The Ioway map's exhibit label, published in the catalog, identified the map as "a picture of both space and time." The story depicted on the map "begins before European contact" on the Great Lakes and continues with migrations across the prairies and into the Great Plains. In terms of its broader significance, "Non chi ning ga's map provides a glimpse of the conflicting concepts of land use and land ownership that existed between American Indian nations and the expanding United States."[28]

A version of this exhibition without the Mesoamerican maps, titled *Another America: An Exhibition of Native American Maps,* traveled to museums and libraries throughout North America between 1995 and 2001. Temporal coverage was from the colonial era to the present. The main themes were Native American maps as cultural, historical, and geographic documents as well as stories of individuals and people. At the conclusion of its tour, the exhibition material was housed in the American Geographical Society Library at the University of Wisconsin–Milwaukee.[29]

Warhus's *Another America: Native American Maps and the History of Our Land,* published in 1997, was the first book about Native American maps to reach a broad, English-speaking audience. It contains depictions of more than sixty maps, including a sepia-toned full-page image of the Ioway map, titled "Notchininga's Map." Warhus's two-page discussion about the map and its associated historical contexts draws from works by several authors, including Blaine, Viola, and Lewis, and quotes brief passages from the Journal of Proceedings. Warhus wrote, "Notchininga's map goes back to the very beginnings of his people; the point, both geographically and historically, at which the Iowas became a separate tribe," and he noted, "Like most Native American maps, it is in the light of the Iowas' oral traditions and cultural history that the map is best seen." Augmenting the discussion are King's portrait and a daguerreotype of No Heart, plus Wawnonqueskoona's map as published by Schoolcraft. By this time, Warhus was certain the No Heart whose portrait King painted was the same No Heart who had presented the map.[30]

A spate of studies utilizing the Ioway map, many of which are cited in earlier chapters, followed in the late 1990s into the early 2000s. Timothy Roberts and Christy Rickers employed the map in their attempt to locate Ioway sites in the Grand River basin of Missouri and southern Iowa. Mary Whelan reviewed the map's historical and political contexts and meanings, and she applied GIS technology to better understand the map's scale and internal logic and to help make it more intelligible to a modern audience. Her 2003 thesis is the most comprehensive work on the map that is freely available online: As of July 2024, it had been downloaded more than 1,500 times. Whelan's innovative GIS approach (figure 28) informed several subsequent projects and led Lewis to enthuse, "The richness of this map's content and its archaeological significance are such that the Ioway map is probably the first historical First Nations map to have been subjected to Geographic Information Systems analysis"—a process that has been dubbed "indigitization."[31]

The historian Greg Olson pictured and discussed the map in his 2008 and 2016 books about Ioway history. While one book focused on the Ioway in Missouri and the other on the period from 1837 to 1860, both noted the importance of the 1837 map. Regarding the map's use in the treaty council, he stated that No Heart "produced this map to document that the Ioway had lived on the disputed land for the previous two centuries" but noted that their 1837 St. Louis treaty relinquished their rights to "a huge section of land between the Des Moines and Missouri Rivers, in what is now western Iowa."[32]

The historian David Bernstein also pictured and discussed the Ioway map in his examinations of the geopolitical strategies Ioways and other Native American nations used in the nineteenth century. The map is a focus of discussion in his 2003 master's thesis, 2007 journal article, 2011 dissertation, 2012 book chapter, and 2018 book. As noted in chapter 3, Bernstein argued that the map constituted an important element of Ioway diplomacy. He also suggested that the map represents a blending of Native and Euro-American cartographic conventions. While he was mistaken in attributing a consistent (Euro-American) scale to the map (see this chapter, n. 2 and figure 28), he was correct in noting that the map's creation and use involved "creative geopolitical tactics," as discussed in chapter 5.[33]

American studies scholar Frank Kelderman also focused on the 1837 map as an element of nineteenth-century Ioway diplomacy. He contrasted Ioway negotiating strategies with the oratory and writings of other tribes, especially the Sauk as represented by Keokuk. He also devoted an entire article to the Ioway map, arguing that it could be seen as "a form of indigenous writing that was legible within colonial settings, but [was] nevertheless disregarded because it did not align with settler-colonial projects of indigenous dispossession."[34] Referring to Bernstein's 2018 book but nicely summing up the significance of his own work as well, Kelderman noted that "the mapping of indigenous geographies emerged from moments of geopolitical negotiation and contestation," and therefore that "both U.S. colonialism and Native agency" are key elements of their narratives. Material culture studies echo this cartographic-diplomatic perspective, exemplified by Saul Schwartz's and my studies of Iowaville, in which we argue that Ioways and their neighbors employed both "Middle Ground" and "Native Ground" strategies—at times accommodationist, in other circumstances resistive—as elements of survivance.[35]

Several exhibitions in the early 2000s included the Ioway map, in these cases the actual map rather than facsimiles. The first time the map traveled to Iowa—perhaps the first time it left NARA—was for an exhibition titled *The History of Iowa in the Art of Maps* at the University of Iowa Museum of Art. Education professor and map collector H. D. Hoover curated the exhibition, which was shown from October 2004 through January 2005 and included thirty-five maps. With coverage ranging from early sixteenth-century maps of North America to a 2004 state highway map, the exhibition's purpose was to "trace the changing perception of the Midwest and Iowa through historic maps." Hoover was especially pleased to include the Ioway map, which he considered the centerpiece of the exhibition, not only for its depiction of Iowa waterways but also because of its significance as a "historical document, showing the homes and movements of the Ioway Indians over a period of more than 200 years." Several Ioway tribal members traveled from Kansas to view the map, probably the first time any Ioways had seen the map since 1837. Accompanying the Ioway map was one I drafted that showed the approximate dates of occupation for the depicted settlements, indicating, according to the gallery guide, "that the Ioway lived along what are now Iowa's borders and over much of the interior, making it clear why our state should be named 'Iowa.'"[36]

The map made a second trip to Iowa three years later. In September and October 2007, NARA again loaned the map to the University of Iowa, this time to the Museum of Natural History. The museum exhibited it along with archaeological material from Oneota sites and Iowaville as well as "historic photographs, biographies, and artistic expressions of Ioway descendants." The display and associated lectures and films were some of the many Iowa Archaeology Month programs presented statewide under the theme of "Maps, Material Culture, and Memory: On the Trail of the Ioway." The 1837 map anchored the programming, with thirteen events held on the topic of the map and the Ioway people, many of which involved tribal members as presenters or panelists. The Archaeology Month poster, still accessible online, contains discussions of the map as well as Ioway history and archaeology in general.[37]

Another highlight of Iowa Archaeology Month 2007 programming was the premiere of the documentary film *Lost Nation: The Ioway.* Held at the State Historical Museum in Des Moines, the event drew about 200 Ioway tribal members, the largest number of Ioways gathered in one place in the state since the 1830s. Segments of the film—which ultimately became part 1 of a three-part series about Ioway history and culture—feature the map and my discussion of its significance. While in Des Moines, tribal members witnessed Iowa Governor Chet Culver's declaration of October 7–13 as Native Ioway History Week, and they presented several gifts to the state, including a framed print of King's portrait of No Heart. Tribal representative Mae Murray Sine described No Heart as a leader who possessed the "innate perception, intelligence and wisdom to negotiate the treaties for millions of acres of aboriginal title to land the Ioway occupied. One of his most historical achievements is the 1837 hand-drawn map of rivers and Ioway Indian villages. When a delegation of Ioway Chiefs went to Washington in 1837, he presented this extraordinary map to the U.S. Government in his plea for compensation from the government for ancestral lands."[38]

Immediately following this second trip of the 1837 map to Iowa, it traveled to the Field Museum in Chicago. If a map exhibition can be considered a blockbuster, this was one. *Maps: Finding Our Place in the World*, developed by the Newberry Library and Field Museum, featured more than 130 maps and related items. The exhibition was shown at the Field Museum for three months, where between 85,000 and 91,000 people viewed it, before it traveled to Baltimore's Walters Art Museum in early 2008. In both Chicago and Baltimore, the exhibition formed the centerpiece of citywide Festivals of Maps. The exhibit's companion volume included a color image and brief description of the Ioway map, exhibited, according to exhibition cocurator James Akerman, as an example of an "itinerary map" that Native Americans made "to preserve their communal histories." In this case, "Non-Chi-Ning-Ga hoped that the cartographic retelling of his nation's movements would reinforce the historic claim of the Ioway to much of [the upper Mississippi and Missouri River valleys], and defend them against unfavorable treaty settlements."[39]

Sometime before 2017, NARA scanned the Ioway map and posted the scanned image online, allowing anyone to view it at any time. NARA reframed the map in 2017 (it had been framed prior to the 2007 and, probably, 1992 exhibits) and posted a new scan. Then, in 2019, the Nathan B. Leventhal Map and Education Center at the Boston Public Library used one of the NARA scans to print a color image of the map in its exhibition *America Transformed: Mapping the 19th Century, Part 1: The U.S. Pushes Westward 1800–1862*, which ran from May to November 2019. The exhibit and the associated catalog presented the Leventhal Center's curatorial viewpoints as well as perspectives provided by the Akomawt Educational Initiative, a majority Native American–owned group specializing in museum education, one of whose panels read:

> The perspectives of Native populations in the 19th century cannot be properly told in maps, because Native concepts about land are not two-dimensional, and qualifying ownership with a paper document was an imported European concept. During the rapid expansion of the United States, the idea of Native homeland, a multi-layered place giving life, sustenance, language, spiritual communion, and kinship, would change to a theory that land is pre-ordained to be "improved" or "developed" for the purposes of commodification. This was a near universal

Figure 29.
Logo of the Great Plains Action Society's Riverland Native Voter Project. Courtesy of *Riverland Native Voter Zine: An Indigenous Perspective and Guide on Native Voting* (https://www.greatplainsaction.org/files/ugd/b1ee4e0cab4293e570473f85447753 801765ob.pdf). Artists: Shelley Buffalo (Meskwaki) and Sikowis Nobiss (Nehiyaw/Saulteaux), inspired by Lance Foster.

change from Native land management systems that had sustained populations for millennia.[40]

The Ioway map has experienced a variety of additional uses in the twenty-first century. The most widely read work about Iowa archaeology, Lynn Alex's *Iowa's Archaeological Past*, pictures and discusses the map.[41] Iowa Tribe members incorporate the map into publications and presentations about Ioway history as well as current environmental planning efforts.[42] The proliferation of online images increased the map's visibility and facilitated its incorporation into a variety of popular publications and other outlets. Many recent publications about Iowa and Missouri archaeology, history, and natural resources, as well as new atlases of Iowa and Nebraska, contain images and brief descriptions of the map.[43] The map became the centerpiece of a community engagement effort with the Iowa Tribe of Oklahoma and part of a resource guide for Illinois history teachers.[44] Several websites and videos about Ioway, Iowa, and Minnesota history and archaeology feature the map as an educational resource or as an illustration of Indigenous occupancy.[45] The Iowa Department of Natural Resources Water Trails Program employs the map in its publications and website to emphasize the historic and cultural importance of rivers, and newspaper articles about Iowa rivers also feature the map.[46] For some observers, the map's depiction of river systems recalls (or presages) the schematic but functional and easily comprehended style of subway system route maps.[47] The map has been used for the logo of a political activism project (figure 29) and was the theme of a University of Iowa book-arts project.[48] Community groups in Iowa can host a lecture about the map from the Office of the State Archaeologist.[49]

A Significant Silence

How and why was the Ioway map essentially unnoticed and unused until 1976, and what resulted from its absence? While these questions have no easy answers, one span of time within the map's long dormancy deserves particular attention: the era of the Indian Claims Commission, 1946–1978.

As we have seen, the earliest published mentions of the 1837 Ioway map came from Herman Viola, G. Malcolm Lewis, Martha Royce Blaine, Rainer Vollmar, and David Turnbull in the late 1970s–early 1980s. All mentioned the map briefly within broader discussions of Native American maps and treaty councils or, in Blaine's case, in a history of the Ioways. Except for Blaine's book, which devoted three sentences to the map, no pre-1990s historical or anthropological study by twentieth-century scholars of the Ioways (Alanson Skinner, Mildred Mott Wedel, Zachary Gussow, David Stout, Anthony F. C. Wallace, Duane Anderson, Dale Henning, and others) mentioned the map. Nor did any of the nineteenth-century writers who discussed Ioway history and culture (Henry R. Schoolcraft, J. Owen Dorsey, Lewis Henry Morgan, and Thomas Foster). The missionaries Samuel Irvin and William Hamilton, who resided among the Ioways for many years beginning in 1837, would not have had access to the map and never wrote about it; still, they were well acquainted with No Heart and Walking Rain and supplied Schoolcraft not only with detailed information about Ioway history and culture but also with Wawnonqueskoona's map.

The 1837 map's near-absence from pre-1990s Ioway scholarship is especially striking in light of the enormous amount of research anthropologists and historians conducted in the 1950s about Ioway settlement history for the Indian Claims Commission (ICC). The ICC "was a quasi-judicial branch of Congress created in 1946 to deal *finally* with the long-standing claims of Native Americans against the Federal Government." The money Congress ultimately allocated to tribes as a result of ICC judgments ameliorated some of the effects of unfair or broken treaties (tribes won awards in 58 percent of their claims), but the ICC could offer no final resolution to the broader political and moral issues inherent in the relationships between the U.S. government and tribal nations. This is especially true because the ICC chose to apply an adversarial approach to settling claims—pitting tribes against the government and often each other—and because it limited the purview of cases to "money damages for injuries against property and breach of contract."[50]

ICC case witnesses, attorneys, and researchers conducted an enormous amount of archival, documentary, and oral-history research, compiled reams of records, wrote lengthy reports, and testified and argued about all facets of the cases. The anthropologists and historians hired as expert witnesses by the tribes and the government were academics, not accustomed to being cross-examined and forced to defend under oath not only their credentials but also every one of their written and oral statements. Witness statements therefore had to be thoroughly and rigorously researched and supported, not least because lawyers and expert witnesses on one side were often tasked with discrediting or impugning the opposing witnesses' expertise, judgment, or veracity.[51]

The two Iowa tribes brought claims against the United States in a total of nine ICC cases, most of which also included the Sac and Fox as coplaintiffs. In keeping with the ICC focus on "injuries against property," the cases turned on two main points: joint versus exclusive and bounded tribal use of the contested lands in the early nineteenth century, and the fair-market value of those lands. After many years of hearings and deliberations, the commission awarded the Iowas nearly $8 million, though attorneys' fees and other expenses reduced the final distribution to tribal members.[52]

The eminent cultural anthropologist and ethnohistorian Anthony F. C. Wallace (1923–2015) served as the principal expert witness for the Iowa Tribe of Kansas and Nebraska and the Iowa Tribe of Oklahoma.[53] The Justice Department called upon three expert witnesses in the Iowa cases. Mildred Mott Wedel (1912–1995), whom we met in chapters 1 and 3, was for many years a research associate at the Smithsonian Institution's National Museum of Natural History and a highly respected ethnohistorian and archaeologist.[54] David B. Stout (1913–1968) was an anthropology professor at the University of Iowa from 1949 to 1959.[55] And Zachary Gussow (1923–1991) was a lay psychoanalyst and, later, a medical anthropologist.[56] Two other anthropologists, Nancy Oestreich Lurie and A. Irving Hallowell, participated briefly in the ICC Iowa cases, both of them on behalf of the plaintiff tribes. Their task was primarily to support Wallace's arguments and rebut (and discredit) Wedel's.[57]

The four principal witnesses expended considerable effort researching, reporting, and testifying about Ioway settlement history. They and their teams' researchers spent hundreds of hours examining primary-source material at the National Archives and elsewhere. Both teams knew well that No Heart and Walking Rain presented a map at the October 7, 1837, council. The Iowa tribes' Exhibit 130 in Docket 135 (identical with their Exhibit 163 in Docket 153) was a typed transcript of the complete Journal of Proceedings. The plaintiff's research file also includes a typewritten synopsis of the council proceedings, quoting portions about the map. Wallace's copy of the Schedule of Exhibits used by the plaintiff's team bears the penciled note "Jnl. I. map" (Journal Iowa map) in his handwriting next to the entry for the Journal of Proceedings. On another copy of the Schedule of Exhibits, next to the entry for "Map by Waw-non-que Skoon-A for Capt. Eastman," Wallace circled "for" and wrote "just re-coppied [*sic*] by him, Drawn for missionaries 1837–48." These notes indicate that Wallace almost certainly knew that the map presented at the 1837 council was not the same map as the one Wawnonqueskoona drafted for Hamilton and Irvin and that Eastman redrafted. Wallace's 1954 ICC report, "The Iowa and Sac-and-Fox Indians in Iowa and Missouri," mentions the map that No Heart presented and distinguishes it from the map Wawnonqueskoona later drafted. Yet neither he nor the plaintiff's research assistants noted the 1837 map's existence in the National Archives, so no copy was entered as an exhibit in the ICC cases, and it was not listed among the maps consulted.[58]

The tribes' Exhibit A was Wawnonqueskoona's map as published by Schoolcraft, which their attorney described as "a map prepared by an aged Indian showing the migration of the Iowas from some sixteen various locations, all of which, except four, lie between the Missouri and the Mississippi Rivers." The plaintiffs proceeded to disparage the historical accuracy and value of this map. Wallace testified, "I do not think it (the Schoolcraft old Indian map) is an extraordinarily accurate description of what these migrations were. . . . Some of the particular locations are difficult to relate to historically known locations and . . . the villages on the—or village on the Des Moines does not appear in the right sequence." But the plaintiffs' attorney then conflated the two maps: "Dr. Wallace did not subscribe to the old Indian map as tracing the migration path of the Iowa Indians correctly. . . . Likewise, all of the references to the Schoolcraft map only show the migration path of the Iowas *as contended by the Indian chief in 1837* when, as Dr. Wallace said, it is evident that the old chief's memory was playing tricks on him" (emphasis added). Among the examples of the Schoolcraft map's inaccurate dating or missing villages, "the record is full of testimony on the part of both Dr. Wallace and Mrs. Wedel that the Iowas had villages in Lake Okoboji—Spirit Lake region—when they were first contacted there by the whites in the 1690s"—and those villages are absent from the Schoolcraft map.[59]

The defense team's arguments likewise employed the Journal of Proceedings with its transcribed record of No Heart's and Walking Rain's 1837 presentation and description of their map. The government took the added step of labeling its Exhibit 25 in Docket 138 as the map No Heart referred to in 1837, but this unwittingly duplicated the plaintiff's attorney's error. Exhibit 25 decidedly is not the 1837 map: It is a photostat from William Harvey Miner's 1911 book, *The Iowa*, and Miner's map is a merely a reprint of Wawnonqueskoona's map as published by Schoolcraft.[60]

Although Wallace knew that the 1837 map and Wawnonqueskoona's map were not the same, the rest of the plaintiff's team as well as the defendants mistakenly conflated the two maps or believed they were essentially the same. Neither side left any record that they examined or analyzed the 1837 map. Wallace apparently was the only participant in the case who even knew it existed as something other than the map Schoolcraft published, yet his team failed to make this distinction in their testimony. When the ICC litigants on both sides referred to the map presented in the 1837 council, they instead exhibited Wawnonqueskoona's map. This oversight and conflation of maps is puzzling and confounding. Was the 1837 map not accessible to ICC researchers in the 1950s? This is highly doubtful. As mentioned earlier, the map was in all likelihood transferred to the National Archives in the 1930s. A card index to the map existed at the National Archives at that time, and NARA staff reports that "a copy of the card index was also provided to the Office (Bureau) of Indian Affairs. Once the initial conservation, processing, and indexing was completed on the Central Map File records in the late 1930s, they should have been accessible to researchers," though NARA has no specific information regarding their availability in the 1950s.[61]

The 1837 map's absence from the ICC cases effectively silenced the Ioways' most forceful and cogent contemporary claims. Why was it ignored? Catalog information about the map—if not the map itself—as well as associated documentation in the council proceedings were accessible at the National Archives, so at this juncture it is inexplicable why Wallace did not obtain a copy of the map. There was no shortage of research help: Among the plaintiff's research assistants was an attorney identified as Mrs. K. O. Smith, who "worked about ½ time for a year, largely going through, copying, and abstracting material in the National Archives." If Smith located the 1837 map, it is implausible that she would have mistaken it for Wawnonqueskoona's original map because of Brodie's annotation indicating the map's 1837 origin and council provenance. It is also a mystery why Mildred Mott Wedel or others on the defendant's team didn't realize the 1837 and Wawnonqueskoona maps were different. Perhaps Wallace's 1954 report, "The Iowa and Sac-and-Fox Indians in Iowa and Missouri," was not shared with the defendants, but the defendants should have known the maps were different even without Wallace's report.[62]

Even more perplexing is the map's absence from Mildred Wedel's post-ICC work on Ioway history. None of her nine publications about the Ioway and the Oneota tradition from 1959 onward mention the map, nor does any mention appear in the drafts of these papers housed in the National Anthropological Archives. It is especially jarring to note that Herman Viola—whose 1976 and 1981 books pictured and discussed the Ioway map—and Waldo and Mildred Mott Wedel were all associated with the Smithsonian Institution's National Museum of Natural History at the same time, Viola as director of the National Anthropological Archives (1972–1989), Mildred Wedel as research associate in anthropology (1974–1990), and Waldo Wedel as curator and senior (later emeritus) archaeologist (1936–1990). All three were active scholars of Native American history, and all worked in the same building. Mildred participated in a 1980 conference honoring Waldo that Viola chaired, and she authored a chapter in the resulting 1982 book Viola coedited. Given her thorough research habits and attention to detail (archaeologist David Gradwohl characterized her as "a demanding perfectionist" in her research), Mildred must have read her colleague Viola's books. Her chapter on the Ioway in the Smithsonian *Handbook of North American Indians* (drafted in 1978 but published, posthumously, in 2001) contains a detailed and accurate map of Ioway settlement locations and migrations (figure 2) whose presentation could have been enriched by noting that the 1837 map shows essentially the same things but from the perspective of Ioway historical memory rather than from written or archaeological records.[63]

It is perhaps a fool's errand to try to determine why the ICC participants conflated the 1837 and 1848/1853 maps. It would be even more fruitless to try to divine how the ICC cases might have proceeded had the plaintiffs or defendant paid attention to the 1837 map. The map does not explicitly indicate tribal boundaries, a key point of debate at the ICC hearings. It depicts only one site in northern Missouri (Site T), which would have been insufficient to demonstrate "continuous use and occupancy" of that area "for a long period of time" prior to 1824, as the tribes had claimed in one of the cases the ICC dismissed.[64] Several villages the 1837 map does show (the Council Bluffs and Des Moines and Iowa River villages, Sites I, J, K, P, Q) were mentioned in documents that had been entered in evidence, both from Ioway sources (notably the 1836 Ioway petition with Clark's accompanying letter and the Journal of Proceedings) and from other records. But it would have made a difference: It would have validated tribal historical memory as chronicled by No Heart and Walking Rain and cast further doubt on the pre-1760s reliability of the Wawnonqueskoona map. For example, the 1837 map's depiction of villages in northern Iowa (Sites B–F) and the Green Bay origin locale (Site A) contrasts with those sites' absence from Wawnonqueskoona's map, belying Wallace's dismissal of Ioway historical cartography.[65] Although the ICC ultimately adjudicated most cases in favor of the Iowa tribes, the 1837 map could have made a material difference in the outcome of the proceedings by confirming exclusive, long-term Ioway occupancy of the claimed lands.

Regardless of ICC outcomes, it is undeniable that understandings of Ioway history and culture would have differed had either the tribes or the government cited the map. Tribal members certainly would have embraced the map if it had attained notice in the 1950s. If tribal members' recent heightened interest in Iowa homelands and frequent reference to No Heart and the 1837 map are any indications, one can only imagine what impacts the map might have had in the 1960s and 1970s: a symbol of identity and persistence during the Red Power movement? A catalyst for research and activism on history and heritage sites? A focal point for conversations between the two Iowa tribes? A spark for an early Land Back movement?[66] The Ioways might well have taken a leading role in the field of Indigenous cartography. Enterprising Ioway and non-Ioway scholars might have developed studies similar to Keith Basso's classic collaborative Apache ethnogeography *Wisdom Sits in Places* or William Meadows's later *Kiowa Ethnogeography*. But counterfactual would-have/could-haves amount to futile hindsight. The map stayed dormant through the ICC years. At least it was eventually resuscitated and is now accessible to the world.[67]

Epilogue: Past and Future

> For hundreds of years we moved along the rivers and streams of Iowa, building bark lodge villages, planting corn, beans, and squash, and hunting deer and buffalo in the woodlands and across the prairies. Our villages moved as garden soils and wood supplies became depleted, or sometimes due to frictions or whim. We moved freely across the lands that would become Iowa, as a man moves freely between the rooms of his house. In 1837, Grandfather No Heart defended our ancestral rights to these lands by producing a hand-drawn map showing our many villages and routes of travel.
> LANCE FOSTER, "A Closing Circle"

> A map organizes the entire narrative. . . . No story without a map.
> RASMUS GRØNFELDT WINTHER, *When Maps Become the World*

MAPS ARE UNIQUELY POWERFUL OBJECTS. They help create, alter, and reify how people understand the world. They can depict spaces and places in innumerable ways and can serve innumerable purposes. Despite their often-objective appearance, maps represent regions and peoples in ways that serve their makers' interests. As Denis Wood writes, a map "selectively brings into being a world that is socially construed." Native American–made maps can be especially powerful and significant because they illuminate Indigenous perspectives and aspects of history and culture that are often absent from documents and narratives produced by or for non-Indians.[1]

Historian Ted Binnema has said about Native American maps, "If maps are historical artifacts, knowledge of the individuals and societies that produced the maps, of the contexts in which the maps were produced, and of the landscapes portrayed in the maps should help us interpret them." This book has explored the life and uses of the 1837 Ioway map, enabling interpretation of the map as a tribal chronicle and offering new insights into culture and history. We have seen that

Ioway oral traditions were commensurable with documentary and archaeological records for a period of around 200 years, though the specificity of recollections faded with time. I have strived for caution in assigning mapped places to locations on the ground, trying to avoid overenthusiastic matching ("site-identification syndrome," per David Henige) and staying cognizant of the "disconnect between what we want the evidence to tell us and what its creators provided." Still, as Henige recommends, I tried carefully to employ primary historical sources and archaeological data, as well as other lines of evidence, and found frequent convergence that permitted identification and dating of likely locales, especially the more recently occupied or visited places.[2]

Like most maps, those drafted by Indigenous people can be viewed as political documents as well as artifacts. Examinations of the 1837 map in this book and in other studies have emphasized the map's importance as a tool of diplomacy during a precarious time for the Ioways. Homelands and associated histories were vital elements of Ioway identity, but both were being threatened and usurped not only by an expansionist colonial enterprise but also by their own neighbors. The Ioway leaders' cartographic gambit in the 1837 treaty council, as well as their 1836 petition, were meant to prove the Ioways' exclusive land rights by virtue of many generations of occupancy throughout the territory. Yet maps do not always exert the power their makers hope for. Notwithstanding the Ioway leaders' demonstration of deep spatial-historical ties, they could not persuade the U.S. government to recognize their territorial and compensatory claims until 1838 when they agreed—under duress—to settle for far less than they had demanded.[3]

But the map told the Ioway story, even if it was ignored for 140 years. Now that the map has been resuscitated, what should the next phases of its life entail? What new opportunities do GIS, StoryMaps, multimedia, crowd-sourcing, artificial intelligence, radiography, and other technologies enable? What are the interests and responsibilities of tribal and nontribal users? There can be a multitude of answers to these questions. The burgeoning field of Indigenous cartography provides especially exciting prospects. Indigenous mapping is not only a notable facet of early American history but is also a growing and dynamic expression of tribal sovereignty. Native nations across North America are making greater use of the power of maps. Tribes employ Indigenous mapping to assert identity, counteract colonial geographies, and defend rights to lands and resources.[4]

Future uses of the Ioway map can take this book as a point of departure but should not be bound by it. In fact, everything discussed here can be further analyzed, augmented, or disputed. If the book spurs new thinking or research about the map, or inspires new approaches to the map or its contexts, then it has succeeded. If it stimulates interest in Ioway or Native history and archaeology, or contributed substantively to historical cartography in general, so much the better.

Regardless of the map's future, we have already seen that it is an outstanding document of historical memory.[5] It has become a symbol of Native occupancy of and ties to the land of Iowa and surrounding states. The map and its stories provide opportunities to appreciate the region's long pre-statehood history, the remarkable cartographic expression of tribal historical memory, and the persistence of sovereign Native nations even though they may no longer be resident in their original homelands. Awareness of the map contributes to wider recognition of Ioway peoplehood.

For the map to have a relevant future, it must have lasting value to Ioway people. As noted in chapter 6, the map is receiving some attention and use by tribal members and Indigenous activists. The Ioways made the map nearly 200 years ago to resist U.S. imperial power, but the map was lost—buried—in the maze of the colonial apparatus. It is well past time to decolonize and Indigenize the Ioway map. What does this mean? The map needs to serve the Ioway people again. How best to do this—how to determine the most appropriate futures and the next phases of the map's life—are for the citizens of the Iowa tribes to decide.

APPENDIX ONE

The 1836 Petition[1]

TO GENERAL ANDREW JACKSON President of the United States, or his Successor in office, as well as to The Senate and House of Representatives of the United States of America in Congress assembled.

The undersigned Chiefs and Braves of the Ioway Nation of Indians residing at present on the north side of the Missouri River—Upper Missouri, for themselves and at the earnest solicitation of the young men, women and children, of their Tribe, do most respectfully ask leave, for they cannot beg, although their Nation is small, to present to your honourable Personages, a plain and true statement of their grief, and the oppression that has been in a most unsparing manner heaped upon them by their Red Brothers the Sacs and Foxes of the Mississippi, and they regret to say that this oppression has been in a good degree fostered and cherished by their White Brothers. But they fondly hope that it has been by oversight or mistake, and not with intention on the part of their Brothers, and Congress to cheat, neglect and defraud them, only because their numbers are small, at this day, and this deduction of their Tribe has been mainly caused by their association with and strict adherence to their white fathers and Brothers to keep their Treaties and the peace with all Nations. It is a notorious fact that they have stood like Squaws, with their Bows unstrung and scalping knives and Tommahawks buried, with the peace pipe in their hands untill they have been killed and destroyed both by White and Red skins. Although once the most powerful and warlike Indians on the Mississippi and Missouri Rivers, they have been cut off and reduced to nothing, a mere handful of that Nation that was once masters of the Land. No Indians of any other tribe [would] dare build his fire or make a mocasin track, between the Mo. and Mississippi Rivers, from the mouth of Missouri, as high north as the head branches of the Calamut [Calumet], upper Ioway and Desmoines Rivers, without first having obtained the consent of the Ioway Nation of Indians. In fact this Country was all theirs, and has been for hundreds of years. And this fact is susceptab[l]e of the clearest proof, even at this late day. Go search at the mouth of the Upper Ioway River, (which has been the name of their Nation time out of mind) there see their dirt Lodges, or Houses, the mounds and remains of which are all plain to be seen, even at this day, and even more, the Country which they have just claim to, is spotted at various places with their ancient Towns and Villages, the existence of which no Nation can deny. And even now their village on the Desmoines is held and occupied by the Sacs—which place the Ioways only left about 25 years ago, on search of Game on other parts of their land, but never intended to abandon their claim to the same or the bones of their fathers, which are yet to be seen there, and the Country has never been taken from them by Conquest.

Your Petitioners would most respectfully represent, that whilst enjoying in peace and in happiness all the blessings and plenty which the great master of life had freely given to them. On the September 11, 1815 their Nation were requested by their great Father the President to meet two of his Commissioners, Genl. Wm. Clarke and Ninian Edwards, to hold a Treaty of peace and perpetual friendship. A Treaty was made, the Ioway Chiefs & Braves agreed to become the Children of their great father the President, who was to protect them as his Children. That on the 4th of August 1824 their Chiefs were called together and Genl. Clarke told them in Council that their great Father wanted to buy from them all the Lands they then held lying within the State of Missouri, Amounting to several millions of acres—and which has been and is worth to the United States several million of Dollars. They listened to the word of their great father and sold the land for $5000, payable on 10 equal anual payments of $500. each. A Blacksmith and farming Utensils & Cattle were then promised to them. The Blacksmith and farmer has been furnished them but the other articles have never been received, which constituted a part of the consideration, for which they were induced and persuaded to sell their Lands, and to part with the Bones of their fathers, but they still hope that ample Justice will be done to them.

For the Treaty referred to (See Book of Indian Treaties Page 288)

Your Petitioners further charge and state that they promptly left the land refered to, and settled and remained in quietness on their Lands west of the Mo River, until the 19th day of Augt. 1825. Previous to this date they had been informed by their friends Genl William Clarke, and the Honorable Lewis Cass, that strife and difficulties and war existed betwixt the Sioux, Winnebagos, Menomines, Chappewas, Otteway, Pottawatomees, Sacs & Foxes, and that with a view to produce peace and settle all the Boundaries of the Contending Parties for Land the aforementioned named gentlemen called and convened your Petitioners Nation and the other Nations at Prairie Du Chein on the last mentioned date, and after a Council a Treaty of Peace was made, in which the Boundries and Division of Land were defined. That at the Treaty your Petitioners gave permission to the Sacs to hunt on their Lands west of the Mississippi, and which permission was placed in the Treaty, in words and language which they did not understand by which the Sacs claim title to all their ancient possessions and Land. Your Petitioners charge that the Sacs never had any previous claim to the Land west of the Mississippi. And by the use of words on the face of the Treaty your Petitioners are only made to stand in the attitude of Copartners as to the ownership of the Land which they had held before ever a white man dare make a moccasin track on that Section of the Continent of North America. But because these things has been done by the hand of power they are willing to rest in quietness provided half way Justice can be done them. But now wronged, as they are, they would beg leave to refer to the 3rd Article of the Treaty referred to, by which a small portion of their claim and rights are held good and recognized.

Your Petitioners charged that since the Treaty aforesaid they have been informed and believe that Treaties have been held without notice to them, or their knowledge or consent, by which Large tracks of valuable Land have been ceded to the United States by the Sacs, to the amount of many Thousands of Dollars. Your Petitioners Pray that your Honourable Bodies will, or by a Committee of Congress may examine to the extent of your Petitioners' claims. And in the end they trust that ample Justice will be done. If not they will have again to appeal to arms, and try to repossess themselves of their ancient possessions.

They have deputed & appointed Frank White Cloud, 1st Chief of the Nation, and their particular friends, Majr. A.G. Morgan and J.V. Hamilton, or either one of them to make and sign all Treaties in their name. We have sent these Agents & delegates at our own proper Costs and Charges.

We also wish to receive in Lieu of our Rations for one year the amount thereof in money, at twelve cents per Ration. We could offer many reasons for this but our Agents will fully explain. When their case shall be fully considered they pray Justice and relief may be granted to them. They ask permission to refer to Genl. Wm. Clarke their father who has always been their friend, and upon his word they are cheerfully willing to place all their complaints and claims, and they will most cheerfully submit to his decision whether it may be for, or against them and for our peaceable and good conduct for many years we ask leave to refer to our agent Genl. Andrew S Hughes.

Justice is all your Petitioners want and this, they fully expect. And your petitioners ever pray &c.—

Watche Money his X mark
Congee his X mark
Nee amoney his X mark
Tarro hongh his mark
Rube doux his X mark
O Kig Water his X mark

I certify that the above was given by the Nation and Signed in my presence

And. S. Hughes
Sub agent, Ind. affairs

State of Missouri
County of Clay

I Abraham Shafer, Clerk of the County Court within and for the County aforesaid certify that Mohasko Roubidoux and On kig wato acknowledged as chiefs of the Ioway Nation the foregoing Power of Attorney in my office before me. In testimony whereof I hereto subscribed my name and affixed the seal of said Court at office in the Town of Liberty this 14th day of December 1836.

Abraham Shafer clerk.

[The handwriting in the main portion of the petition above the clerk's certification is that of Subagent Andrew Hughes, who had been at the Ioway Subagency, located in the northwest corner of Missouri, since 1828.[2]]

APPENDIX TWO

Ioway Testimony at the 1837 Council[1]

AN IOWAY CHIEF made the following address, "Non chi ning ga" or "No Heart"

My Father

You are going to hear me speak and you will hear the truth. My Father you have sent for me. I have come. I am now in the house of the Great Spirit. The Earth and the Sun witnesseth what I say. I hope I will tell you no lie. My Father this is the rout[e] of my forefathers (pointing to a map executed by an Indian which he then presented to the Commissioner). It is the land that we have always claimed from old times. We have the history. We have always owned this land. It is ours. It bears our name. This village (pointing to a few dots on his map) was the residence of our forefathers. If I should try I could not tell you the number of villages our people made. They built one on the bank of Lake Pepin. The Sacs call it Green Bay, we call it Lake Pepin.

I went and settled at Omaha village on the Missouri river. I was told it was the Missouri river. My Father I had forgot one word. The Ottoes village was the last village passed in going out to our settlement. We went around the Illinois to the Kickapoos with the Ioways. My home is in the middle of that country. I have never heard of that country being claimed by any other nation nor have I heard of any other nation living in that country. I should like to know by what right they claim it. Who are the people that I have given this land to. I have heard that it has been sold but I don't know to whom I have sold it. My Father by accepting your invitation to come on here I have met with our friends the Sacs (of Misso[uri]). We are connected. They are our relations. We are friends with the Sioux of the Mississippi. We have not met them for a great while. My Father those people the Sacs and Foxes (of Mississippi) were invited through friendship to come and hunt to eat with us and divide the game but never understood they were to have our lands. The old (Punkin) chief was the man that gave the game but not the lands. My Father when at the treaty at Prairie du Chien we had no Interpreter [but] understood the Sacs & Foxes had an Interpreter. I would ask if that man (pointing at Le Cleare) was not the Interpreter for the Sacs & Foxes at that treaty (Mr. L made no reply). I have understood that the Sacs & Foxes say they now own the land where the big boats run. It is my land. I have the best right to it. It is called after our people. There is a place called the dry field on the des moine river, another place called the big groove. It was ours at the time the Spanish & French came into the Country. I have been there. My Father those people (the Sacs & Foxes) have always taken the advantage of us knowing that we were a small tribe. They steal from us and then sell to you.

I hope soon to return to my friends. We live in bark houses. We are a small tribe. I am told they are my children. They have increased in numbers. Our tribe has decreased. They now improve upon us. I have one of my friends along with me, "White Cloud." He is my nephew but I call him my son.

Neo-Ma-Ni or "the Walking Rain" remarked as follows

My Father

My friend has spoken to you. He has told the truth. When we left this place (pointing to a Village on his map) we crossed the Calumet river, built a Village on some river running into the Missouri. I must explain when we left the Ottoes Village we started and travelled on each side of the river Missouri until we arrived at the mouth of Grand river. As you have been told we met with many different tribes [and] made friends with them. I will explain another proof of our claim to this country. The Ioways named all the rivers. The Sacs have never named any. If so we have never heard of it nor have the whites ever named any of the rivers. My Father at the treaty at Prairie du Chien we had no interpreter, don't think we were understood. The Sacs & Foxes had an interpreter, believe you were the man (pointing to Le clear[e]). My Father after the Sacs have spoken I will say more.

[Parentheses are in the original; brackets are added.]

Notes

Acknowledgments

1. Lewis 1987.

2. Green 2001; G. Malcolm Lewis, personal communication (letter), February 20, 2002.

3. Akerman and Wilkes 2022; see also GMLC.

4. Office of the State Archaeologist 2025.

5. Ioway Cultural Institute 2024a.

Introduction

1. DeMallie 1993:534. Also on the ethnohistorical method, see Wedel and DeMallie 1980. Much has been written about Native American maps, but there is only one other book about an individual historic Native American map: Johnson's (2009) treatise on a late nineteenth-century northern Athabascan map of parts of Alaska and the Yukon. Another lengthy treatment of a single map is the full issue of a Lewis and Clark history magazine that was devoted to a recently rediscovered Arikara map (Jenkinson 2018). Two master's theses focus on single maps, including the Ioway map that is the subject of this book (Whelan 2003; see also Beimers 2022a).

Chapter One

1. Foster 2009:6–9; Iowa Tribe of Kansas and Nebraska 2024a; Iowa Tribe of Oklahoma 2024; Wedel 2001.

2. Mott 1957. For the songs, see Lockard et al. 1921 and Rogers and Hammerstein 1945.

3. For Ioway tribal names, see Wedel 1978, 2001:445–446. "Aiaouez" and "Báxoje" might have denoted two separate groups that later consolidated as the Ioway; see Betts 2019.

4. For Siouan language history, see Parks and Rankin 2001; Rankin 2015; Springer and Witkowski 1982. On the Chiwere–Ho-Chunk connection and possible timing of the split between the languages, see Grimm 1985; Rankin 2021. For the Ho-Chunk as the Ioways' "fathers" or "grandfathers," see Foster 2000, 2010:22.

5. Dorsey 1890; Hamilton and Irvin 1843; Merrill 1835. For Hamilton and Irwin's work among the Ioway, see Anderson 1957, 1958; Gullett 1994; Herring 1987; Plank 1908; Schoolcraft 1853:259–276. The Presbyterian Historical Society in Philadelphia houses the Hamilton and Irvin records (RG 224, AIC). Portions of their correspondence have been transcribed, but much remains unpublished. On Ioway/Chiwere language revitalization, see Goodson 2019; GoodTracks 2024a; GoodTracks et al. 2016; Ioway Cultural Institute 2024b; Schwartz 2018a, 2018b, 2021.

6. On survivance, see Vizenor 2008:1. Several North American archaeological studies employ the survivance concept, e.g., Kretzler and Gonzalez 2023. On peoplehood, see Holm et al. 2003.

7. Blaine 1995; Foster 2009:6–9; Iowa Tribe of Kansas and Nebraska 2024a; Iowa Tribe of Oklahoma 2024; Ioway Cultural Institute 2024a; Olson 2008, 2016; Rundle and Rundle 2007–2013; Wedel 2001.

8. For the Oneota tradition, see Alex 2000:185–210; Gibbon 1982; Green 1995; Henning 1998a, 1998b; Hollinger and Benn 1998; Schermer et al. 2015. For Ioway and Dhegihan terms for the ancestral collective, see Buffalohead 2004; Fletcher and La Flesche 1911:41; Foster 1996, 1999. For the Psinomani complex as ancestral Sioux, see Gibbon 2003:27–46; for the Central Plains tradition as ancestral Arikara-Pawnee-Wichita, see Shield Chief Gover 2024.

9. Keyes 1927:224; McGee 1891:204; Schoolcraft 1845. See also Faldet 2009:5; Hall 1995; McLeod 1997; Vogel 1983:60.

10. For the Ioway/Chiwere–Oneota connection, see Betts 1998, 2015; Griffin 1937; Henning 1992; Mason 2006:197–232; Mott 1938; Wedel 1959. For a contrary view of the Oneota–Ho-Chunk/Chiwere connection, see Lurie and Jung 2009.

11. For Ioway and Ho-Chunk origin traditions, see Foster 1996:3, 2000:143, 2020; Hall 1993; Jung 2018:27–30; Lurie 1978b; Lurie and Jung 2009:106–107; McKenney and Hall 1838b:91; Radin 1923; Skinner 1925:480, 502; Whitman 1938. On the formation of the Oneota tradition, see Green 2014.

12. For early (and what might be termed "proto-") Oneota at Lake Pepin, see Henning and Schirmer 2020. For early Oneota in eastern Wisconsin, see Krus et al. 2022; Overstreet 1995. For the pan-regional spread of the Oneota tradition, see Henning 1998b. For the Prairie Peninsula, see Transeau 1935, and for a recent examination of the importance of the Prairie Peninsula in Native American history, see Morrissey 2022. For Oneota in the La Crosse region and a review of Oneota chronology elsewhere in Wisconsin, see Boszhardt 1998.

13. Wedel 2001.

14. Haury-Artz 2014; Pearce and Green 2014; Skinner 1926; Wedel 1961, 1986, 2001:436.

15. For maps depicting the westward movement of Algonquian groups, see Harris 1987:Plates 35–40.

16. Wedel 2001:433.

17. Anderson 1973a; Blaine 1995:7–138; Dorsey 1886; Dorsey and Thomas 1907; Gussow 1974a, 1974b; Ludwickson et al. 1987:39–48; McKenney and Hall 1838b:91; Olson 2008; Roberts and Rickers 1999; Stout 1974; Thiessen 2004; Anthony F. C. Wallace, The Iowa and Sac-and-Fox Indians in Iowa and Missouri, AFCW; Wedel 2001:432–436.

18. Indian Removal Act, Public Law 21-148. For Ioway history during the removal era, see Anderson 1973b; Blaine 1995:139 ff.; Olson 2014, 2016; Ostler 2019:235–237; Wedel 2001:440–443. For a concise summary of the treaty process and key Ioway treaties, see Iowa Tribe of Kansas and Nebraska 2024b.

19. Etcheson 2004.

20. For the post-1830s history of the Ioways as summarized here, see Blaine 1995:205 ff.; Herring 1990:70–97; Olson 2016:17 ff.

21. Catlin 1852; see also Stevenson 1993, but Stevenson erroneously conflates White Cloud II and his uncle No Heart.

22. Blaine 1995:242–243; Olson 2005:114, 2008:107–109.

23. McKenney and Hall 1838b:59–61.

24. Catlin 1852; McKenney and Hall 1838b:81–82; Stevenson 1993.

25. Kurz 1937:50–52, 62; also Blaine 1995:213.

26. Richardson 1852:71.

Chapter Two

1. Blue 1974:iv; Lepler 2013.

2. Flavin 2024:167; O'Sullivan 1845:5. On Manifest Destiny as it relates to anthropology and indigeneity, see Kehoe 2014a.

3. On Indian treaties and removal, see Bowes 2016; Calloway 2013; DuVal 2024:441–462; Foreman 1972 [1932]; Harjo 2014; Prucha 1995:183–292; Saunt 2020. For Indian councils, see Gamble 2014; Viola 1981.

4. Blue 1974:iv; Smithsonian National Museum of the American Indian 2024.

5. Iowa Tribe of Kansas and Nebraska 2024b; this resource also contains a complete list of Ioway treaties. For discussion and analysis of this typical sequence of treaty making, see Deloria 2008:352–353. For data on all nineteenth-century treaties and associated maps, see Royce 1899.

6. Witgen 2022. On the development and operation of treaty making, see Blackhawk 2023:229 ff. and Calloway 2013. For a discussion of how the treaty system, with its asymmetrical power relations, became an unaccountable weapon in the arsenal of the U.S. government, see Jones 1982:xii.

7. The Ioway dispute was with the branch of the Sauk and Meskwaki known as the Sac and Fox of the Mississippi. In contrast, Ioway relations with the Sauk (Sac and Fox) of the Missouri were cordial. For the division between the Sac and Fox of the Missouri and the Sac and Fox of the Mississippi that originated during the War of 1812, and the distinction between yet close association with the Sauk and Meskwaki tribes, see Green 1983; Gussow 1974a, 1974b; Herring 1990:71; Wallace 1970.

8. Ioway diplomatic encounters with the U.S. throughout the early nineteenth century included appeals to Euro-American norms and values; see Bernstein 2007, 2012; Olson 2005.

9. Because the White Cloud family married into the Roubidoux family (see chapter 1), White Cloud II was also known as Chief White Cloud Robidoux—see Lewis 2004:179; Thorne 1996:127, 131. For the ranking of Ioway chiefs or headmen in 1837, see McKenney and Hall 1838b:91, though recall that Walking Rain, as war chief, was also known as the third chief and orator (see chapter 1). The Orator was the name by which non-Ioways referred to the Ioway headman Watche Mani (Watche Money on the petition; Wač̆h'é Máñi), but his name translates as Killing or Killer (Jimm GoodTtracks, personal communication [written notes], 1997), so McKenney and Hall might have confused his identities with that of Walking Rain. Lance Foster could shed no light on the meaning or identity of On-kig-wato (personal communication, email, 2024).

10. Hamilton was a Fort Leavenworth sutler, a witness at the 1836 Ioway treaty signing, and was appointed Indian Agent at Council Bluffs in 1839—see Mattison 1958; JLC. Regarding Nesouaquoit's grievance, the Sac and Fox of the Missouri took umbrage at the failure of the Sac and Fox of the Mississippi (its leader Keokuk in particular) to share

annuities guaranteed by treaty (Colbert 2008). The U.S. government covered western tribes' expenses for participating in official Indian councils, but White Cloud II's 1836–1837 trip to Washington was not at the government's invitation. He was apparently willing to cover the cost himself, but the journey was financed by a loan Nesouaquoit received from a St. Louis businessman, which Nesouaquoit repaid by arranging for the delivery of furs and hides of equivalent value (Buckley 2008:239–240; McKenney and Hall 1838a:152, 155–156, 161–162). For Clark's letter, see William Clark to J. V. Hamilton, January 5, 1837, Letters Received, M234-362-0610, BIA. Most tribes trusted Clark as an honest broker, but he was not above subterfuge to advance the government's expansionist goals (Lee 2022).

11. Joseph V. Hamilton to Carey A. Harris, February 7, 1837, Letters Received, M234-362-0602, BIA. For the travelers' itinerary and activities, see Willis 1837; for the assurances and promises they reportedly received, see McKenney and Hall 1838a:152, 156. Regarding Charles Bird King, portrait painter of numerous Native Americans, see Ewers 1954; Viola 1976.

12. Blaine 1995:167; Viola 1981:34–36.

13. Blaine 1995:168. William Clark instructed Subagent Andrew Hughes to invite four "of the principal Chiefs of the Ioways" and have them assembled for the journey at Fort Leavenworth by August 15 for a scheduled October 1 arrival in Washington (Clark to Hughes, April 15, 1837, Letters Received, M234-R307-13, BIA). Newspapers also reported that four "chiefs" represented the Ioways, but newspaper articles, portraits painted in Washington, and biographies recorded during their visit indicate the presence of one warrior (Plenty of Meat) in addition to the four headmen (White Cloud II, No Heart, the Orator, and Walking Rain; Niles' National Register, November 11, 1837:167). For reports of the delegation's departures and arrivals, see Daily Commercial Advertiser, September 21, 1837:2; Daily Commercial Bulletin, September 8, 1837:2; Daily Courant, September 28, 1837:2; The Globe, September 28, 1837:3; Viola 1976:101, 1981:34–35. For Black Hawk's 1833 journey, see Black Hawk 1964:144.

14. Viola 1976:92–106, 1981:34–36. For a more recent assessment of Indian visits to Washington, see Genetin-Pilawa 2014.

15. The Globe, October 4, 1837:3; Viola 1976:101.

16. The Journal of Proceedings, as it is referred to hereafter, constitutes the official account of the 1837 council sessions. The Journal is essentially a copy of the transcript prepared by Commissioner Harris's secretary, Chauncey Bush. The Ioway portion of the council on October 7 and 9, 1837, comprises pages 45–52 in "Journal of Proceedings at a council held in the City of Washington D.C. with a delegation of Chiefs & braves of the confederated tribes of the Sacs and Fox Indians of the Mississippi and a delegation of Sac & Fox and Ioway Chiefs and braves of the Missouri" (B-402, Misc. File, 1837, 45–52, BIA), published in U.S. National Archives Microfilm Publication T494, Roll 3. The National Archives scan is online at https://catalog.archives.gov/id/245231852; a more legible copy is online at University of Wisconsin–Madison Libraries, https://search.library.wisc.edu/digital/ANCSAVIL5TZV3D87. Pages 1–32 of the Journal report the opening session of the council with the Santee alone; pages 33–44 cover the dispute between the Sioux and the Sac and Fox of the Mississippi. For the significance of the calumet, see Hall 1997. Numerous newspaper articles contain observations of the council, which provided the basis

for the summaries by Gamble 2014:254–259 and Viola 1976:92–107, 1981:34–36. McKenney and Hall's biographies of Keokuk and other Sac and Fox leaders (1838b:49–51, 78–79) also contain council reportage.

The German artist Ferdinand Pettrich (1798–1872), who had moved to Washington in 1836, made drawings and later produced terra-cotta busts and full-body sculptures of many of the Native delegates, as well as friezes depicting the entire council platform (figure 7); see Aigner and Mapelli 2015:366–385; Dalla Torre 1940; Pettrich 1842; Stahle 1966. For a thorough compilation and analysis of Pettrich's Native American drawings and sculptures, see Nielsen and Edenheiser 2013; also Edenheiser 2015. Kelderman 2019a:106 depicts details of the Sioux–Sac and Fox council session, including Secretary of State Forsyth smoking the calumet, from drawings in the Pettrich sketchbook housed in the Edwin E. Ayer Collection at the Newberry Library, Chicago; see also Gamble 2014:256, 259. Most of Pettrich's Native American busts, sculptures, and friezes are housed at the Anima Mundi, the Vatican Ethnological Museum. Charles Bird King and George Catlin painted many portraits of council participants, including all five Ioways, but only Pettrich produced tableaux of council sessions or three-dimensional images of the participants; unfortunately, his work depicts no Ioways.

17. The Ioway delegation to the 1825 treaty council at Prairie du Chien presented a map made by White Cloud (No Heart's brother, White Cloud II's father). This map, which apparently illustrated the extent of their territory, has not been located, so whether it also depicted historical locations is not known; "Journal of the proceedings that took place, under the commission to Gen. Wm Clark & Governor L. Cass to treat with, and mediate between, the chiefs, head men and other representatives of the . . . bands of Indians to be assembled at Prairie du Chien, August, 1825," NAID 245230421, page 37, BIA; see scan at National Archives Catalog, https://catalog.archives.gov/id/245230421.

18. Journal of Proceedings:45–49, 53; National Intelligencer October 9, 1837:3. Vice President Johnson claimed, plausibly, to have been the soldier who had killed Tecumseh (Sugden 1985:136–167).

19. Daily Courant, October 11, 1837:3.

20. Journal of Proceedings:46–49. No Heart and Walking Rain were the only Ioway delegates who spoke at the council. The spelling of "route" as "rout" as in the transcript of No Heart's address was common in the early nineteenth century (Oxford English Dictionary 1971:839–840). For example, relating to another Native American map, a contemporary account of Too Né's 1806 presentation of his Arikara map referred twice to "his rout" as shown on that map (Dunlap 1930:390–391). The title of the present work uses the current spelling of "route" for the sake of clarity.

21. Regarding permission for other tribes to hunt on Ioway land when requested, see the depositions by Ioway elders in Indian Claims Commission, Docket No. 138, Stipulation and Depositions Taken February 27, 1952, AFCW.

22. Daily Courant, October 11, 1837:3. See also Lappas 2006; McKenney and Hall 1838b:80.

23. Journal of Proceedings:50–51; William Clark to Secretary of War John C. Calhoun, December 8, 1823, Secretary of War Correspondence pertaining to Indian Affairs, Letters Received (Enclosure), BIA.

24. Journal of Proceedings:51.

25. National Intelligencer October 11, 1837:3; Commissioner Carey A. Harris to Maj. Joshua Pilcher, October 27, 1837, Letters Sent, Letter Book No. 22, BIA; Maj. Joshua Pilcher to Superintendent T. Hartley Crawford, April 30, 1839, Letters Received, 1839 Great Nemaha, P-515, BIA; Journal of Proceedings:53.

26. Daily Courant, October 11, 1837:3; The Globe, October 7, 1837:3; Lynchburg Virginian, October 20, 1837:4. Commissioner Harris also believed the council was a failure, at least in its two main purposes: to establish peace between the Sioux and the Sac and Fox of the Mississippi, and to "adjust the conflicting claims to the land claimed by the latter and the Iowas" (Office of Indian Affairs 1837:5).

27. Daily Advertiser, October 31, 1837: 2; Daily Advocate, October 30, 1837:2; McKenney and Hall 1838a:51–52; Public Ledger, October 27, 1837:1; Reddin 1999:18–20; Vermont Mercury, November 3, 1837:3. The declaration that they looked or acted in some respects "like the white men" reflects one way the Ioways portrayed themselves, on occasion, in order to protect their interests in negotiations and interactions with the more powerful Americans. For example, White Cloud I used this phrase at the 1830 treaty council to "show their ability to emulate some aspects of Euro-American society, and in so doing, hope to place themselves above the Sac and the Sioux in the eyes of the American agents" (Bernstein 2007:619; also Bernstein 2012; Olson 2005).

28. Poetry File 1788–1873, Box 70, page 22, HRS. It is possible that the poem's author mistook White Cloud II for No Heart or otherwise conflated the two men. No Heart, about forty years of age at the time, might have been less likely than his nephew White Cloud II (age twenty-seven) to have been called a "young man."

29. Daily Advocate, October 30, 1837:2.

30. Office of Indian Affairs 1837:5–6.

31. The only member of the delegation who did not sign the November 1837 treaty was White Cloud II (Iowa Tribe of Kansas and Nebraska 2024b). For the extra $1,000 offer, see Commissioner Carey A. Harris to Maj. Joshua Pilcher, October 27, 1837, Letters Sent, Letter Book No. 22, BIA. On the Des Moines River homeland, see Far West, June 14, 1838 (copy in Letters Received, 1838—Great Nemaha-D-234 [Enclosure], BIA). Regarding the tactics the government used to compel Ioway agreement to the 1838 treaty, Indian Commissioner Thomas Hartley Crawford commented in 1842 about "the refusal of the Iowas to accede to the terms proposed by the Department relative to their claims on the Des Moines" in 1837, citing what Indian agent Joshua Pilcher wrote on the day after Pilcher had engineered the signing of the 1837 treaty in St. Louis: Pilcher suggested that the government disregard "in future, all complaints and applications" by "these deluded people, the Ioways" and "let them remain as they are until their means under the Treaty of Prairie du Chien are ex[h]austed, and they become fully sensible of their destitute situation, and *then* let the government give *as a donation*, whatever it may think right" (emphasis in original); Thomas Hartley Crawford to J. C. Spencer, May 28, 1842, Letters Sent, Indian Office Report Book 3, BIA; Pilcher to Carey A. Harris, November 24, 1837, Letters Received, BIA; Ratified Treaty no. 229, Documents relating to the negotiation of the treaty of November 23, 1837, with the Iowa Indians, BIA (scan at University of Wisconsin–Madison Libraries, https://search.library.wisc.edu/digital/AXUBDWPEI4VNIF82). Pilcher's letter, which had been the

Iowa Tribes' Exhibit 94 in Indian Claims Commission Docket 153, belies the statement in the commission's May 12, 1969, Findings of Fact: "We find no evidence in the record that the Iowa Nation concluded this Treaty of 1838 under duress"; see 22 Ind. Cl. Comm. 439 at 500, ICC (scan at Oklahoma State University Library, Digital Collections, https://dc.library.okstate.edu/digital/collection/p17279coll10/id/1086/rec/9). For the 1838 treaty text, see Iowa Tribe of Kansas and Nebraska 2024b; signers included White Cloud II, No Heart, and Plenty of Meat.

Chapter Three

1. Previous identifications of settlements, rivers, and lakes represented on the 1837 map, superseded by the present study, appear in Green 2001; Lewis 1979, 1984:94–95, 1987:66–68, 1998c:134–137; Whelan 2003. For the map's diplomatic and political importance, see Bernstein 2007, 2012, 2018:29–42; Kelderman 2019b.

2. Journal of Proceedings:47.

3. G. Malcolm Lewis stated in 1998 that "apparently lacking a beginning or an end, the dotted line zigzags across much of the western Middle West" (Lewis 1998b:13). But after publication of Green 2001, he agreed that the migration had a beginning (the Green Bay region) and an end (the Omaha region), though he still referred to it as "a sequence that involved several thousand miles of zigzagging" (Lewis 2006:14–16).

4. McKenney and Hall 1838b:91.

5. For Ioway families at Green Bay, see Thwaites 1900:203. For Allamakee Trailed pottery at Green Bay, see Hall 1962:1:131–132, 2:110. On the trans-Mississippi villages of the Ioway in the late seventeenth century, see Betts 2019; Thwaites 1900:203–205. For Red Banks as the traditional origin locale of the Ioway and Ho-Chunk, see Foster 1996:3, 2000, 2020; Hall 1993; Indian Claims Commission Docket No. 138, Stipulation and Depositions Taken February 27, 1952, pages 12, 13, AFCW; Lurie 1978b; Radin 1923; Skinner 1925:480, 502; Whitman 1938.

6. For archaeological sites at Red Banks, see Jung 2018:31–33; Lurie and Jung 2009:106–107; Speth 2000. On Oneota ethnogenesis, see Green 2014.

7. For Oneota occupation in the La Crosse locality, see Theler and Boszhardt 2003:157–172. The 1836 petition's reference to Ioway "dirt lodges, or Houses, the Mounds and remains of which are all plain to be seen" at the mouth of the Upper Iowa River is notable. Ioways may well have dwelled in "dirt lodges" (i.e., earth lodges) when they lived along the Missouri River. Their Omaha and Otoe neighbors lived in such houses, which appear from a distance quite like mounds (see the discussion of Site V). But Ioway houses in northeast and northwest Iowa probably were not earth lodges but bark-, mat-, or skin-covered pole dwellings—see Blaine 1995:87–88, 154, 171, 175, 208; Skinner 1926:273–277; Wedel 1986:58–61, 2001:436. The mounds mentioned in the 1836 petition probably were large, 1,000–2,500-year-old Woodland tradition conical burial mounds—easily construed from a distance as abandoned earth lodges—such as those at the Fish Farm and Slinde Mounds state preserves near the mouth of the Upper Iowa River (Herzberg and Pearson 2001:50–52, 148–149).

8. For the Paleozoic Plateau, see Prior 1991:84–97. For Oneota and Ioway occupation of the Upper Iowa River valley, see Gussow 1974a, 1974b; Mott 1938:236–241; Wedel 1959,

1961, 1986. On Oneota (likely ancestral Ioway) occupation of the La Crosse region and the move west of the Mississippi River, see Betts 2006, 2015, 2019; Boszhardt 2000; Gibbon 2012:171–173; Henning 1992, 2003; Hollinger 2015; Stevenson 1994:288.

9. Henning 1992, 2003; Pond 1852.

10. Prior 1991:36–47.

11. For Ioway sites in northern Iowa, see Betts 2019:8–9. For the Wanampito site (the name meaning "blue bead" in the Ioway language, as suggested by Lance Foster in recognition of some of the diagnostic seventeenth-century items found at the site), see Betts 2015:136–137; Whittaker and Anderson 2008:4–5; Whittaker et al. 2015:133–135. For the Iowan Surface, see Prior 1991:68–75.

12. For the Aiaouez and Paouté in northwest Iowa, see Betts 2015; Wedel 1981, 1986, 2001:434. On the Chemin des Voyageurs, see Whittaker 2015; Whittaker and Doershuk 2010.

13. For seventeenth-century sites in northwest Iowa, see Henning and Thiessen 2004a:389–392. For pipestone on northwest Iowa sites, see Fishel et al. 2010. On Pipestone National Monument, see Catton and Krahe 2016; Nieves Zedeño and Basaldú 2004.

14. "The 1000 Lakes" was a mid-nineteenth-century term that referred to the myriad lakes and wetlands that once dotted northwest and north-central Iowa (Barrows 1845).

15. Journal of Proceedings:49. For the Calumet River or Redstone River as the early name of the Big Sioux River, see Burr 1839; Catton and Krahe 2016:31; Determination of the Article 2 Line, 1825 Prairie du Chien Treaty, 13 Ind. Cl. Comm. 25 (1959), ICC (https://dc.library.okstate.edu/digital/api/collection/p17279coll10/id/675/download); Mouton 2024. For the Big Sioux River's appearance as "Riv. à la Pierre Rouge" (Red Stone River) on the 1805–1806 Too Né Arikara map, even though it appears to be misplaced above rather than below the mouth of the Niobrara River ("Riv. L'eau qui Courre"), see DeMallie and Havard 2019:18, 21; O'Briant 2018; Steinke 2014:611; van de Logt 2023:124.

16. Betts 2010, 2019; Bray 2003; Henning and Schnepf 2014; Henning and Thiessen 2004b; Wedel 1976, 1981.

17. Journal of Proceedings:47. For early Ioway and Omaha settlement on the Missouri River, see De L'Isle 1718; Fletcher and La Flesche 1911:35, 85; La Flesche 1884; Ludwickson et al. 1987:184, 188–198; Mott 1938:302; Thiessen 1988, 2004. For the Vermillion Bluff site, see Alex 1994.

18. Blakeslee 1986:14–16; Dorsey 1884:213, 1890:454, 458; Fletcher and La Flesche 1911:91; Ludwickson et al. 1987:184, 188–198; O'Shea and Ludwickson 1992:21, 47.

19. On Native oral histories, see Dorsey 1884:213. On villages in the Council Bluffs area, see Blaine 1995:36, 40; Wedel 2001:434.

20. For details about the Ioway village at Council Bluffs, see Mandel and Winham 1992; Mott 1938:247–249; Moulton 2024; Wedel 1988.

21. River 41 (figure 9) is certainly the Boyer River. The small lake near its head (42) can only be Blackhawk Lake because that lake is the only one with both a direct connection to the Raccoon River (16) and a short portage to the Boyer and its tributaries. The original Council Bluff was a prominent topographic feature on the west side of the Missouri River opposite the mouth of the Boyer River. It attained renown as the place where Lewis and Clark held a council in 1804 with the Otoe and Missouria. Fort Atkinson was built nearby

in 1820; see Carlson 1979. In contrast to Council Bluff in Nebraska, "Council Bluffs" refers to the city on the east side of the Missouri, in Iowa.

22. Schwartz 2012 reviews the multiple factors apparently involved in the Ioways' move from the Council Bluffs area to the Des Moines River.

23. Journal of Proceedings:47. For Iowaville settlement history, see Blaine 1995:113, 165; Foster 1996:4. For Clark's 1814 map, see Lee 2022; Soikkeli 1999. On Ioway pro- and anti-British factions, see Dickey 2004; Olson 2005. On the return of some Ioways to the Des Moines River around 1820, see Thwaites 1905:151.

24. Journal of Proceedings:48. Regarding possible Ioway names of Des Moines River villages, see GoodTracks 2024b; Foster 1996. The Ioway place names can be considered cultural econyms, that is, Indigenous geospatial terms that reflect deep knowledge and experience with landscape, natural environments, and history; see Beck 2022:11, 209; Eades 2017:20–24.

25. For archaeological and historical studies of Iowaville, see Peterson 2014; Schwartz and Green 2013; Straffin 1972. On Ioway hunting, trading, and living in the broader region of southern Iowa and northern Missouri in the early nineteenth century, see Olson 2008; Peterson 2009. On the importance of Creole (mixed-descent) individuals and families in the regional economy, see Foley and Rice 1983; Hoig 2008; Hyde 2022; Lewis 2004; Thorne 1996.

26. On the Peoria village at the mouth of the Des Moines River, see Grantham 1993. For Fort Madison, see Jung 2016; McKusick 2009.

27. Jung 2016; Watkins 2012; also Eugene Watkins, personal communication, April 9, 2024; and Patrick J. Jung, personal communication, April 15, 2024. Quashquame's village is recorded as archaeological site 13LE217 (Whittaker 2008).

28. For the Ioways in Illinois, see Blaine 1995:45–65; McKenney and Hall 1838b:66; Mott 1938:250–251. Thomas Hutchins was, from 1763 to 1780, a British government engineer and surveyor who, after switching allegiance, was appointed Geographer of the United States in 1781; see Hicks 1904:7–51; also Collection 308, THP; and Hutchins 1778. For twentieth-century maps depicting the Iowa Towns in Illinois, see Nolan 1992; Tanner 1986:93; Tucker 1942:9–10.

29. Tanner 1986:98.

30. For attempts to locate the Iowa Towns, see Nolan 1992. By 1805, the Upper Town location was identified as a Sac village on the north side of Henderson Creek, 2½ miles upstream from its mouth, and the Lower Town location was simply labeled "Indian Village" (Coues 1895:13, 19–20, 291; also Blaine 1995:85, 89).

31. Unlike the confusion regarding the Boyer and Little Sioux Rivers (see Site I discussion), there is no doubt about the identifications of the Rock and Iowa Rivers. For Saukenuk and the Crawford Farm site, the principal reference is Wagner et al. 2023; see also Blaine 1995:111; Mansberger 2013; Tanner 1986:various pages. For Site L as the largest village indicated on the 1837 map—consistent with descriptions of the enormity of Saukenuk and its thousands of residents—see Whelan 2003:33–36. In view of Saukenuk's size and importance, its absence from Hutchins's 1778 map is surprising.

32. On early Peoria and vicinity, see Franke 1995; Mazrim 2011:19–27, 151–163. On the Ioways annoying the French, see Mott 1938:251. Regarding Potawatomi and other Algon-

quian villages near Peoria, see Alvord and Carter 1915:293–294; Edmunds 1969; Edwards 1870:96; Tanner 1986:98, 106, 112, 117, 119, 140, 152; Temple 1966:132, 136–137, 147; Tucker 1942:11–13. For Indigenous prairie runners, see Morrissey 2022:64–68. The Ioways were known for being great runners and walkers, as the names of some of their leaders attest; see Foster 1999:185.

33. For villages in the Spoon River area, see Fishel 2017; Harn and McClure 2012:2; Tanner 1986:140; Temple 1966:147.

34. For the Kickapoo villages in the Sangamon River valley, see Berkson 1992; Tanner 1986:106; Tucker 1942:12–13; Wagner 2011. Saukenuk, which U.S. forces burned in 1780 and again in 1831, escaped that fate in 1814 thanks to a successful joint Native-British defense; see Cummings 1927; Espenshade 2014; Whitney 1973:84–85.

35. Journal of Proceedings:47. For Ioway travels and visits east of the Mississippi River in the early nineteenth century, see Blaine 1995:109–115; Carter 1948:164–166, 1949:438–441; Kane et al. 1978:102. Ioway leaders also traveled to Prairie du Chien via St. Louis for the 1825 and 1830 treaty councils.

36. Some Ioways aided the British in the War of 1812, joining other tribes in several raids. The treaty of 1815 reestablished peace and friendship between the Ioways and the U.S.; see Blaine 1995:111–116; Dickey 2004.

37. Journal of Proceedings:48. Regarding a move upriver from Iowaville, see Blaine 1995:86–87; Mott 1938:257; Peterson 2009:19–23; Robeson 1926; Schwartz 2008:69–73; Whittaker 2016.

38. Blaine 1995:121; Mott 1938:257–258.

39. On the Iowa River village noted by Pike, see Blaine 1995:87–89; Coues 1895:23, 292, 339. For lower Iowa River valley archaeological sites, see Anderson 2014; Whittaker 2016. The University of Iowa Office of the State Archaeologist manages the Iowa Archaeological Site File and the Historic Indian Location Database.

40. Marshalltown Evening Times-Republican, June 21, 1918:8. The Potawatomi presence was a legacy of U.S. removal efforts, which briefly envisioned a new Potawatomi home in historical Ioway lands. See Clifton 1977:279–329; Edmunds 1978:250–264; Foster 2009:61–63. Potawatomi settlement in Iowa and northwest Missouri would be incompatible with a continued Ioway presence there, so the government's removal of the Ioways facilitated the forced resettlement of the Potawatomis in 1837.

41. Beaudoin 2022.

42. Journal of Proceedings:49; Roberts and Rickers 1999:9.

43. Blaine 1995:various pages; Caldwell 1970; Olson 2008:various pages; Roberts and Rickers 1999; Schoolcraft 1853:257–258.

44. Blaine 1995:119–121; Journal of Proceedings:47; Olson 2008:118–119.

45. Gero-Schunu-Wy-Ha (1825), Map of Indian Territory, Cartographic Branch, Central Map File 931, BIA, scan at National Archives Catalog, https://catalog.archives.gov/id/102278808. See several discussions of this 53 × 42 cm map: Lewis 1984:98–100, 1987:71–73, 1998c:132–135; Treat 1983; Vollmar 1981:113–114; Warhus 1997:175–178.

46. Journal of Proceedings:49. On the Otoe village under the city of Omaha, I acknowledge Rob Bozell, personal communication (email), May 5, 2024. The route Walking Rain mentioned aligns with the overland route along the north side of the Missouri River that

his uncle Hard Heart showed to U.S. Army soldiers in 1819 to help them travel from Camp Missouri (soon renamed Fort Atkinson) to the Chariton, Missouri, area (near Site T); see Watkins 1913. This route appears on early printed maps, for example, Arrowsmith 1832 (see Brown 2022). The 1837 map's apparent mislocation of sites in the general Omaha/Council Bluffs area (see Site I discussion) applies to Sites U, V, and W. The map shows these sites north of the mouth of the Boyer River, with Site W as far north as opposite the mouth of the Little Sioux River, whereas these villages were actually located south of (or, in the case of Site W, nearly opposite) the mouth of the Boyer.

47. On the Yutan site, see Genoways and Lebedz 2018; Jensen 1971; Kivett 1940; Nebraska Public Media 2024. For the Missouria village on Too-Né's map, see Steinke 2014:612. On the Missourias having joined the Otoes at the Yutan village by 1805, see Edmunds 1976.

48. Benson 1988:113, 125–126; Blaine 1995:126–127; Carlson 1979; Jensen 1998; Olson 2008:72–77; Pepperl and Bozell 2018:28, 30. "The last one passed" might also refer to passing by Site V (the Yutan village) as the Ioways moved to the new reservation in Kansas. The well-traveled route between Sites U and V (Fort Atkinson and Yutan) could have been the first part of this journey, made around 1836.

Chapter Four

1. Schoolcraft 1853:256–257. Later printings and references to the map include Blaine 1995:4–5; Dorsey 1886; Dorsey and Thomas 1907; Miner 1911:24, 36–39. Miner's book, including the portion discussing Wawnonqueskoona's map, consists largely of a reprint of an 1876 report on the Ioway originally published by Thomas Foster in his broadsheet series, *Foster's Indian Record and Historical Data*. Foster referred to the map but did not illustrate it; Miner's book reprinted the map from Schoolcraft as well as the discussion from Foster.

2. Irvin and Hamilton 1853.

3. McKenney and Hall 1838a:156–160; Olson 2014. For the "Big Neck Affair," see chapter 3, n. 43.

4. For the 1830 and 1838 treaties, see Iowa Tribe of Kansas and Nebraska 2024b.

5. Lists of goods, Great Nemaha Agency, March–May 1842, pages 4–5, M234-308-0041, BIA.

6. McDermott 1959. Through his first marriage to a Dakota (Santee Sioux) woman named Stands Sacred, Seth Eastman was the grandfather of Dr. Charles A. Eastman (Ohiyesa), the celebrated Dakota physician, author, and Indian advocate; see Ruoff 2005.

7. S. Irvin to W. Lowrie, Letter 104, February 2 and 10, 1848, RG 224-5-04, AIC.

8. Schoolcraft 1853:256–257.

9. Schoolcraft 1853:257–264. Another reason Schoolcraft believed the map did not depict Ioway settlements dating any earlier than 1673 (i.e., 180 years prior to the publication date of 1853) was the absence from the map of an Ioway village at the mouth of the Des Moines River. Schoolcraft mistakenly believed Jacques Marquette had met the Ioways at the mouth of the Des Moines in 1673. In fact, Marquette visited a Peoria (Iliniwek) village there, not an Ioway settlement (Grantham 1993). Aside from this error, Wawnonqueskoona's (or Eastman's) mapping of the first Ioway settlement at the mouth of the Rock River (at Rock Island, Illinois) has no independent confirmation. The Rock River village

might instead represent the Sauk town and regional meeting place of Saukenuk, just as Site L on the 1837 map likely does.

10. For Great Walker/Big Neck's birth around 1780, see Olson 2014:9.

Chapter Five

1. I am grateful to the late Ronald J. Mason for asking the question that led me to consider possible printed sources for elements on the Ioway map. Among many examples of such sources, Tanner's 1829 *United States of America* map identifies every river that appears on the Ioway map, though not every lake (Blackhawk Lake and the Madison Four Lakes are absent), and Young's 1831 *Map of the United States* shows the Four Lakes and all of the rivers east and north of the Missouri River. On the distinction between Euclidean and topological principles of mapping, see Lewis 1980, and for the differences but permeability between the "two modes of engaging the world" through maps—the scientific/analytic and the Indigenous associative/experiential traditions—see Olshin 2022. While it is reasonable to assume that the Ioways based their map on experience and historical memory rather than printed maps, it is important to examine the relevant evidence.

2. Burr 1839 (Library of Congress, https://www.loc.gov/resource/g3700.rr000060/). Joseph Nicollet's 1842 map and the 1837 Ioway map are perhaps the only maps that show outlets from Blackhawk Lake ("Boyer Lake" on Nicollet's map) to both the Raccoon and Boyer Rivers. The more widely published 1843 version of Nicollet's map (as well as Burr's 1839 map) shows only a Boyer River outlet, though in fact the lake is in the Raccoon, not the Boyer, watershed. For Ioways in the Boyer valley in 1819, 1828, and 1831, see Blaine 1995:121, 200; Olson 2008:95–96.

3. For example, Tanner's 1829 *United States of America* shows two Ioway villages: "Iaway Village" at Iowaville on the Des Moines River and "Old Iaway Village" at the mouth of Mosquito "River" (now Creek) at present-day Council Bluffs, Iowa. In northeast Iowa, Young's 1831 *Map of the United States* shows two Ioway villages along the lower part of the Upper Iowa River and another near Harpers Ferry, Iowa, but there appears to be no other indication of Ioway residence in that region around that time. Aaron Arrowsmith's 1802 map showed villages that originally appeared on eighteenth-century French maps such as the "Ajoues" villages near the Iowa Great Lakes and on the Missouri River as well as the "path" connecting the former village to the mouth of the Wisconsin River, and P. F. Tardieu in 1820, based mostly on Arrowsmith, showed "Ayouas" in two villages, one on the Des Moines River (Iowaville) and one on the lower Iowa River (actually on the Cedar River, just above the Iowa-Cedar fork), approximately where Pike recorded an Ioway village in 1805. Many pre-1837 published maps also show the principal Otoe and Sauk villages of Yutan and Saukenuk, respectively.

4. On Ioway oral traditions, see Foster 2010; McKenney and Hall 1838b:91; Skinner 1925. For the Omaha, see Records Relating to *Omaha Tribe of Indians vs. The United States*, Docket No. 31002, RG 512, U.S. District Court—Nebraska District, Series 4, Box 2, Folder 2 (1912), page 59, NSHS. To facilitate transmission of important information, oral tradition generally is perpetuated within particular "structured social contexts" such as wintertime story sessions; see Minc 1986:44. Regarding Ioway maps, in addition to the 1837 and 1848 maps discussed here, the Ioway delegation to the 1825 treaty council at Prairie du Chien

"presented a map drawn by the White Cloud" (No Heart's brother) that apparently illustrated the extent of their territory; see chapter 2, n. 17.

5. McKenney and Hall 1838b:59–62, 81–93. The absence from the 1837 map of certain recently occupied sites also correlates with the delegates' lived experiences. None of the 1836 petitioners or 1837 council delegates belonged to the Big Neck faction that had lived in northern Missouri (other than the Platte Purchase), nor, as noted here, did they wish to call attention to the recent Ioway occupation of that area. That they were fully aware of northern Missouri's geopolitical significance is indicated by the map's depiction of Site T and the overland route from the Omaha area to the Grand River, which Walking Rain mentioned in his testimony and which was associated with his uncle Hard Heart (see Site U discussion, chapter 3, n. 46). By 1848, the Big Neck–faction Ioway settlements of earlier decades in northern Missouri were no longer political flashpoints, so there was no reason for Wawnonqueskoona to omit them from his map—after all, they were probably part of his lived experience, too.

6. An estimate of 1757–1763 for the Wounding Arrow's birth year is based on a guess that he was twenty-one to twenty-seven years of age when his eldest son White Cloud was born around 1784.

7. Blaine 1995:164–165; Journal of Proceedings:47–49. As noted earlier, Site B received additional attention in the 1836 petition as a place where one could see, at the mouth of the Upper Iowa River, Ioway "dirt lodges or Houses, the Mounds and remains of which are all plain." For accounts of Ioway origins, see chapter 1, n. 11. For cultural memory, see Assmann 1995, 2008.

8. Foster 2019:31. As an example of the loss over time of geographic details and secular historical knowledge, but with retention of key elements of important "mythic" origin stories, Ioway elder Emma Kent (1868–1959) stated in 1952 that she knew nothing of any past conflicts with the Sac and Fox or the Sioux, nor where the Ioways lived before they moved to the Great Nemaha Reservation in 1837, other than that she had learned from her father and grandfather that the Ioways had "covered lots of land" and had history in the northern and northeastern parts of Iowa and along the Mississippi River. Yet she also knew from her elders about the Ioway origin at "Red Hill" (Red Banks, Moka'shutzê; see chapter 3) and about the Ioways' early association with the sacred pipestone source in southwest Minnesota; see Indian Claims Commission, "Docket No. 138, Stipulation and Depositions Taken February 27, 1952," pages 12–13, AFCW. On Emma Kent, see Stillwater News-Press, October 8, 1959:2.

9. For definitions of myths, see Oxford University Press 2024. For "legendary histories," see Kehoe 2007:xxxvi; Lankford 2017. Lankford states, "The legend is not fictional. Just the opposite: Legends are about reality. More precisely, legends are about beliefs about reality" (206).

10. Lewis 2014:344.

11. Vansina 1985:23, 168–169. The hourglass model of oral tradition as history derives from Vansina's observations of colonized societies in Africa. In precolonial times, memories and traditions may well have persisted longer and more intact. Several archaeologists and Native American historians have employed Vansina's insights in their analyses of relationships between oral tradition and archaeology in North America, e.g., Bahr et al.

1994:2–6; Bernardini 2005; Bernardini et al. 2021; Crowell and Howell 2013; Echo-Hawk 2000; Mason 2000, 2006.

12. McKenney and Hall 1838b:91; Vansina 1985:12–13.

13. On the distinction between oral histories (accounts of personal experiences) and oral traditions, see Lankford 2017:207; Vansina 1985:12–13. For Wawnonqueskoona's map, see chapter 4 and Schoolcraft 1853:256–259. Wawnonqueskoona's 1848 map, as published by Schoolcraft, is not directly comparable to the 1837 map because the original version is missing, and errors might have been introduced during the redrafting or engraving; still, his map omits even the eighteenth-century Missouri River villages (Sites G and H on the 1837 map). The missionaries who submitted the 1848 map to Schoolcraft, and who had lived among the Ioways for more than ten years, lamented that by 1848, "little worthy of credit can be gathered with regard to [Ioway] origin and early history. . . . The more honest, and not the less intelligent, agree in saying that the true history of the Iowa is in a great degree lost, and that nothing of their early history is any longer currently known" (Irvin and Hamilton 1853:261)—remarkable comments by men who were well acquainted with No Heart and Walking Rain. The apparent attenuation of cultural memory over just ten years is notable: The corpus of detailed pre-reservation-era geographic knowledge had ceased to remain vital in the face of government and missionary acculturation and assimilation efforts and the exigencies of survival. Also, No Heart and Walking Rain might have seen no upside in once again recounting tribal history to no apparent benefit, leaving the historical account to the less expert Wawnonqueskoona.

In general, the diminution of accuracy over time applies to secular, historical traditions (what Vansina terms "group accounts") rather than accounts of origin or sacred traditions. For secular, historical accounts, "unless specific controls to the contrary are in effect, . . . individual error, elaboration, and/or creativity in the retelling will in the long run produce 'noise' or distortion of information leading to a loss of accuracy," whereas for sacred accounts and origin stories, "a body of sanctified ritual action," including prescribed and correct performance, "promotes accuracy in transmission"; see Minc 1986:44. After three generations, the "absolute temporal referent of past [secular] events will lose meaning as new generations are unable to link such a referent to those of directly experienced events" (Hull 2005:361). Historical knowledge in the hourglass model of oral tradition refers to group accounts of specific dates and events, not to sacred histories (as noted) or to ecological knowledges such as the accumulated knowledge of plant medicine; see Geniusz 2015:19–20. And despite the paucity of the temporal and spatial detail historians crave, Plains tribes' oral traditions concerning the narrow portion of Vansina's hourglass often supply insights, even if speculative, that would otherwise be unavailable and that may be supported by independent lines of evidence; see Shield Chief Gover 2024; van de Logt 2023.

14. For "achronicity," see Henige 1974:14. For transgenerational group memories and the construction of event sequences, see Hull 2005:355; McGlade 1995:123. For flow maps, see Segal and Vannieuwenhuyze 2020; Wigan and Winterer 2020; Zerubavel 2003. As a flow map, the 1837 map reflects the Ioways' integration of spatial, temporal, and cultural dimensions within a single document. For the relative time scale of orally communicated history, see Mason 2006:119–120.

15. For "mnemographic records," see Feest 1997:72. For early Native American maps with a temporal dimension, see, e.g., Lewis 1998c; Warhus 1997. For Plains Indian calendrics and record keeping, see, e.g., Greene 2009; Greene and Thornton 2007. For Biographic rock art, see Keyser and Klassen 2001:224, 253. The Biographic tradition is also expressed in certain Native American maps (Ewers 1977; Sundstrom and Fredlund 1999).

16. The common assumption that Native American cultures see time only as cyclical is simplistic. For southwestern societies, see Fowles 2013:254–255; for a more general review, see Rouse 2012.

17. For Clark's letter, see Blaine 1995:167. For the similarity of Ioway claims and Oneota territory, see Whelan 2003:70–71. On Oneota group continuities, see Henning 1998a:14–15. For the Prairie Peninsula as an interaction area, see Brown 1965, 1991; Morrissey 2022. For Oneota interaction in the Prairie Peninsula, see Brown and Sasso 2001:219–224; Hall 1997:152; Hollinger 2018.

18. Blaine 1995:164–167; Dorsey 1886:219; Journal of Proceedings:49; McKenney and Hall 1838b:91. Game was indeed becoming scarce west of the Mississippi River by the second decade of the nineteenth century; see Bernstein 2007:614. Movement across a large territory helped cement ties to those lands, as with the Mandan and Hidatsa, whose "movement across the landscape both generates and constantly reinforces identities through the fulfillment of social and ceremonial obligations, as well as ownership rights connected to specific physiographic features and natural resources. . . . [As oft-used routes become trails,] they foster connectivity, reinforce the right to move freely about the homeland, and provide a means to organize, delimit, and monitor movement" (Nieves Zedeño et al. 2009:106–108; see also Johnson 2010).

19. Journal of Proceedings:50, 51. For an analysis of Keokuk's riposte and the government's response to the dispute between the Ioway and the Sac and Fox, see Kelderman 2019a:105–109. Nineteenth-century settlers in Iowa related a story about a major Sauk attack on the Ioways' Des Moines River village. However, with no confirming contemporary accounts or oral histories, and with Black Hawk himself reporting only small skirmishes and a peaceful outcome to negotiations with the Ioway, the story is likely apocryphal; see Black Hawk 1964:96–97; Blaine 1995:130.

20. On the attraction of western prairie resources, see Boszhardt 2000; Henning 1992; Ritterbush 2002. On the arrival of horses, see Taylor et al. 2023. On disease epidemics, see Bernstein 2007. For Frank Kent's testimony, see Indian Claims Commission, "Docket No. 138, Stipulation and Depositions Taken February 27, 1952," page 3, AFCW. Federal census records indicate Frank Kent's parents lived in Iowa or Missouri in the 1820s–1830s, where they likely experienced armed settler violence such as described by Olson (2008:98–100) and Caldwell (1970). About Frank Kent, who reputedly lived to the age of 114—earning the sobriquet "oldest Indian Chief in America"—and was the husband of Emma Kent, see the Stillwater Daily News-Press, January 15, 1956:2.

Despite traditions of residential mobility across large areas among the postcontact Ioway and their Oneota forebears, colonial-generated pressures probably made settlement movement more frequent and less predictable than in the precontact era; see Cameron and Bowser 2024:5. Group movements and migrations as survival strategies were not unique to the Ioway: For an account of another tribal nation's efforts to reinvent itself and retain its identity as it moved extensively, see Warren 2014. On migration as well as absorption of refugees as strategies of resilience among small tribes, see Ellis 2022.

21. Trabert et al. 2023. Also on Indigenous diasporas, see Lilley 2006:34–39. For archaeological perspectives on diasporic peoples who had experienced dispossession and forced migration from traditional homelands, see Weik 2019. On the associations between people and territory, see Smith 1986:29.

22. The limits of the Ioway map's historicity are echoed in the temporal schemas of other Native American groups that extend back about 150 years or to the time of initial European contact. In addition to the studies cited by Vansina 1985, see, e.g., Hallowell 1937:666–667; Mason 2006:121–122.

23. For routes and trail networks as Indigenous infrastructure, see Armstrong et al. 2023; Ethridge 2017:62–84. On the significance and anthropological study of routes and narratives of movement, see Snead et al. 2009. For places as centers of meaning constructed by experience, see Nieves Zedeño and Bowser 2009; Tuan 1975. For place-stories—"the conjunction between sites of history and the accounts we make of them"—see Thrush 2017:xiii. For places and landscape, see Ryden 1993:38. On the importance of archaeology in documenting significant places and cultural landscapes, and thereby in constructing social identities, see Kuwanwisiwma and Ferguson 2009. On the entwining of movement, place, and landscape, see Bernardini et al. 2021; Dawson and Johnson 2001; Johnson 2010; Lelièvre and Marshall 2015; Oetelaar and Meyer 2006.

On the concept of cultural landscape and its Anglophone origins with the geographer Carl Sauer, see Denevan and Mathewson 2009; also Rowntree 1996. For Native American case studies of place as defined by space, time, and experience, see Beck 2022:23–45; Laluk 2024; Thornton 2008. For temporalizing landscapes and territories, see Brighenti and Kärrholm 2020; Foster 1996; Ingold 1993. On the power of maps, see Wood 1992:1.

Chapter Six

1. For object biographies, see Gosden and Marshall 1999; Kopytoff 1986. Objects such as maps, though not alive in a biological sense, are still active physically (they deteriorate) and also socially and historically; see Brückner 2017 and the follow-up essays in three volumes of *Material Culture Review* (Beck 2023); for a broader perspective, see Miller and Poh 2022. Because maps and similar objects can be active yet are inanimate, "object itineraries" are useful frameworks for understanding and contextualizing their histories; see Joyce and Gillespie 2015. For the eighteenth-century Miami map, see Gilman 2008; Lewis 1996.

2. Journal of Proceedings:47. G. Malcolm Lewis wrote, "The drainage network as represented on the Ioway map has all the hallmarks of Indian cartography: long straight reaches, acute confluences, and pattern adjusted to fit the medium (in this case paper). I doubt if you would find printed maps with such network characteristics" (personal communication [letter], February 20, 2002). For examples of Native American maps with similar symbology, see Belyea 2007; Lewis 1998c; Vollmar 1981; Warhus 1997. For Native American cartographic conventions, see the aforementioned sources and Belyea 1998:141. There are exceptions: Some Native American maps use wavy lines to depict rivers and triangles to indicate villages, but those maps generally date to the late 1800s. On the use of tipis to symbolize Native habitations, see Caldwell 2023. For the suggestion that the Ioway map

exhibits a constant rather than shifting scale, see Bernstein 2007:621–623, 2012:42–43, 2018:38–39. But figure 28 shows that the Ioway map exhibits variable scales, similar to most early Native American maps; see Lewis 1998c:177–178; Whelan 2003:44–48. In light of the many ways the Ioway map conforms to Native cartographic conventions—variable scale, straight lines for rivers, dot-filled circles for villages, unbound edges—it is unlikely that the map "was drawn up for the Ioway delegates by a draughtsman of the Indian Office" as suggested by Kelderman 2019b:45.

3. Observations of the map are based primarily on my 2001 visit to the National Archives and Records Administration's Cartographic and Architectural Branch at College Park, Maryland.

4. Susan Page, personal communication (email), April 23, 2001.

5. The NARA typed catalog card for the map likewise reads "Iowa, 821, B-402, O.I.A. Mis., Feb. 20—1838." On the handwritten catalog information, other maps from that era in Record Group 75, Central Map File, have similar inscriptions in green pencil or crayon, for example: Nathan Boone, Map of Iowa, 1832, Central Map File 92, BIA (scan at National Archives Catalog, https://catalog.archives.gov/id/221149064).

6. Journal of Proceedings prefatory material. For the 1837 Ioway treaty and its proclamation date of February 21, 1838, see Iowa Tribe of Kansas and Nebraska 2024b.

7. Crawford to Spencer, May 28, 1842, BIA (see chapter 2, n. 31). One could argue the Lake Pepin, Green Bay, and Illinois labels were added in 1842 during Crawford's examination rather than in 1837 at the council. However, those labels match Chauncey Bush's handwriting as on the cover of the Journal of Proceedings and other 1837–1838 documents, and Bush was not involved in any post-1837 treaties (Indian Land Tenure Foundation 2024). For the 1842 Sac and Fox treaty, see State Historical Society of Iowa 1920. For Meskwaki (Fox) persistence in Iowa despite efforts at dispossession, see Zimmer 2024.

8. For examples of Brodie's maps, see Brodie 1885, 1886.

9. G. Malcolm Lewis reported in a personal communication (fax, January 9, 1999) that his examination in 1994 led him to gain the impression that the map was a late nineteenth-century transcript rather than the 1837 original; see also Lewis 2006:15. He based this idea primarily on his observation that "the ink on the map seemed to be the same as that of the '1884 note.'" The ink in portions of both the map lines and the 1884 inscription had "corroded the paper to cause disintegration and fragility on sheets that are otherwise in good condition." Lewis also thought that the sequence of application in one portion of the map was significant: "The four lakes at the head of the Rock R. [he was not convinced those were the Four Lakes of Madison] appear to be earlier (i.e. drawn before) than the route/river line through them. This would be possible for a copy (i.e. transcript) but unlikely for an original artifact" (brackets added; parentheses in original). I disagree for six reasons:

Brodie's note states that *this* map accompanied the Journal of Proceedings.

Brodie's note was probably made with a narrow quill, whereas the mapmaker(s) used a broader-tipped implement (and Brodie was the Indian Office's draftsman, i.e., cartographer, the one who would have drafted a copy).

Highly acidic iron gall ink was in standard use throughout the nineteenth century, and the resulting corrosion is greater in the map lines than in the 1884 inscription.

The Lake Pepin, Green Bay, and Illinois labels are in Chauncey Bush's handwriting.

A later transcriber, even having read No Heart's statement about Lake Pepin and Green Bay, would have had no reason to overwrite Lake Pepin with Green Bay, whereas a contemporary reporter (Bush) would have done just that because No Heart was understood to have preferred Green Bay as the toponym after saying that the Sauks called it Lake Pepin.

The Four Lakes constitute the most distinctive hydrographic feature of southern Wisconsin, so it is understandable that the mapmaker(s) would have depicted them before drawing a stylized Rock River (actually the Yahara River, a tributary of the Rock) through them. The mapmaker actually tried to erase (by scraping ink) what had been the upper one-third of the Rock River because it would have interfered with mapping Lake Winnebago and the Fox River.

Still, further research could assess Lewis's claim. On the back of the map, obscured by its cloth backing and nearly invisible from the front, between the Four Lakes and the Mississippi River, I observed (on March 29, 2001, using a light table and magnifying glass) thin pen or pencil marks that might read "1841" and "Copy." Susan Page of NARA wrote, "the inscription on the back could also be read as 13462 and appears to have been written on the outer portion of the folded map" (personal communication [email], April 23, 2001). Perhaps radiography or some other method can be used to decipher this enigmatic inscription.

10. Rose Buchanan, personal communication (email), September 15, 2023.

11. Brandi Oswald, personal communication (email), July 2, 2024.

12. For Herman Viola's biographical sketch, see Marquette University 2016. For his publications of the Ioway map, see Viola 1976:98, 104–105; 1981:35, 170–171.

13. Blaine 1995:168.

14. Lewis 1979:26–27. Lewis was the first author to publish the map's dimensions, which he reported as 1041 × 687 millimeters, i.e., 41 × 27 inches.

15. Lewis 1984:94–95.

16. Lewis 1987:66–68.

17. Lewis 1998c:134–137.

18. Lewis's work with Native American maps can best be appreciated in two 1998 publications: his chapter in the book he coedited with David Woodward (Lewis 1998c) and his edited volume, *Cartographic Encounters: Perspectives on Native American Mapmaking and Map Use* (Lewis 1998a), which contains five chapters he authored. See also Akerman and Wilkes 2022.

19. Vollmar 1981:7–8, 168, 172. Vollmar also published a journal article about Native American maps (Vollmar 1982) soon after publication of his book. It contains an image of the Ioway map along with a caption similar to that in his book. Like Vollmar, other geographers who discussed the 1837 map also indicated their indebtedness to Lewis; see, e.g., Thrower 1996.

20. Vollmar 1981:118–119, 1982:307.

21. Turnbull 1989:20, 22–23; Vizenor 1998:16, 170, 177–178, 227. By "transmotion," Vizenor means spiritual motion and an active spiritual and visionary presence; see Vizenor 2015:63–75.

22. Bustard 1992.

23. Susan Page, personal communication (email), April 23, 2001.

24. Page, personal communication, April 23, 2001. For methylcellulose in paper conservation, see Brückle 1996. For paper quality in the nineteenth century, see U.S. Congress, Office of Technology Assessment 1988:1–3. One significant loss from fragmentation occurred along the map's right-hand edge, viewing it in portrait mode. Vollmar's 1981 and 1982 images show a fully inked-in portion of Green Bay as well as a solid line continuing along the map's edge beyond the mouth of the Fox River, representing the western shore of Green Bay or Lake Michigan. The images published by Viola in 1976 and 1981 and by Lewis in 1979, 1984, and 1987 trimmed and omitted most of that edge of the map, so Vollmar's are the most complete images of the map prior to its encapsulation. Bustard's 1992 exhibition catalog depicts the map with the damaged edge, exhibiting loss of about half of the line beyond the Fox River and partial loss of ink at Green Bay.

25. Bustard 1992:14, 2015; Limerick 1987.

26. For the 1997 Iowa Tribe presentations, see Kansas Humanities Council 1998. For the 2001 atlas publication, see Green 2001; for a brief summary of the atlas with a color illustration of the Ioway map, plus summaries of the Illinois State Museum's other historical atlases, see Wood 2002.

27. Andrews et al. 2023. A 1993 National Endowment for the Humanities grant supported the development of this archive. This self-published digital collection of 375 map images and associated data on six CDs is housed at the University of Wisconsin–Milwaukee library and at the Native American Rights Fund library in Boulder, Colorado.

28. Warhus 1993:15. For the published versions of the Nebenzahl lectures, see Lewis 1998a.

29. Warhus 1994.

30. Warhus 1997:37–43. A paperback edition of the book was published in 1998.

31. Lewis 2006:15; Roberts and Rickers 1999; Whelan 2003. Whelan's thesis is summarized in a conference paper and posters she and I coauthored; see Whelan 2024. For more recent GIS-based studies of Native American maps and the concept of "indigitization," see Palmer 2016; Palmer et al. 2021. Henry Beimers (author of "Decolonizing the Map," 2022a) posted a summary of his GIS study of Native maps of Minnesota that includes a comparison to the 1837 Ioway map; see Beimers 2022b.

32. Olson 2008:123; see also Olson 2016, 2024.

33. Bernstein 2003, 2007, 2011, 2012, 2018:41.

34. Kelderman 2019a:105–109, 2019b:43.

35. Kelderman 2020; Schwartz 2008; Schwartz and Green 2013. Rosemary Joyce (2019) discusses how Indigenous archives (memories, documents, rock art) and materialities of various forms have constituted practices of survivance in the Americas.

36. Hoover 2004:1, 5.

37. Office of the State Archaeologist 2007a, 2007b.

38. Sine 2008a. Filmmakers Kelly and Tammy Rundle report (personal communication [email], 2024) that *Lost Nation: The Ioway* "garnered several film festival awards including Best Documentary at the International Cherokee Film Festival. It was an Official Selection in the Archaeology Channel's International Film Festival and it won a Bronze Telly

Award®. Since its premiere in 2007, the film has screened in over 70 cities throughout the country, was released nationally on DVD and broadcast on PBS stations. . . . [We] estimate the total for all viewers at 150,000+." English- and Ioway-language versions were produced, and a refreshed, high-definition version is in preparation (Rundle and Rundle 2007–2013).

39. Akerman 2007:11, 59, 61; Akerman et al. 2008; Bernstein 2012:27.

40. Information about scanning and framing the map was provided via personal communication (email) from Brandi Oswald (NARA), July 12, 2024. The pre-2017 scan is online in the National Archives Catalog, https://catalog.archives.gov/id/50926148. The post-2017 scan of the framed map is at https://catalog.archives.gov/id/102278806; unfortunately, the mat obscures features along the map's edges such as Green Bay and its partially lost shoreline (see chapter 6, n. 24) and the uppermost portions of several rivers, including the Wisconsin, Mississippi, and Missouri. For the *America Transformed* exhibition, see Norman B. Leventhal Map and Education Center 2019; for the exhibition's lavish book and full-page color image of the Ioway map, see Grim and Lange 2019:80–81. See also Akomawt Educational Initiative 2024.

41. Alex 2000:218, 223.

42. Foster 1999, 2000:142–150, 2019; Iowa Tribe of Kansas and Nebraska 2023.

43. Archer et al. 2021:xv, xvii; Haury-Artz 2016:20; Iowa Department of Natural Resources 2000:16; Kathryn M. Buder Center for American Indian Studies 2021:18; Shepard et al. 2024:27; Withrow 2012:7.

44. Jackson and Bratta 2020; Danzer 2004.

45. In order of citation: Iowa Tribe of Kansas and Nebraska 2024b; Our Iowa Heritage 2022; Office of the State Archaeologist 2007a, 2021, 2019, 2022; Mason 2023; Worley 2021; Trow and Wendt 2021.

46. For the Water Trails brochure, see Iowa Department of Natural Resources 2024; for a newspaper report about Iowa rivers that incorporates the map, see Kilen 2016.

47. There are at least three published references to the Ioway map's similarity to classic subway system maps:

> Geographer Martin D. Mitchell (2014:4–5) wrote that with its straight lines, the Ioway map is "clear, easy to remember, and serves as a means of easily illustrating the riverine transportation network . . . [resembling] the modern day maps depicting mass transit lines (e.g., city bus routes or subway lines) wherein a quick glance yields lucid spatial messages that can be stored mentally and recalled with ease" (parentheses in original).
>
> A reviewer of the *Maps: Finding Our Place in the World* exhibition wrote that the London Tube map designer "simplified the London underground . . . abandoning scale and geographic accuracy to deliver functionality . . . to help tube riders use the system. [Similarly,] Non-Chi-Ning-Ga, the Ioway chief, simplified his map to help federal officials understand why his tribe deserved a satisfactory treaty settlement" (Henning 2008).
>
> The *Atlas of Nebraska* notes that the 1837 map "provides a schematic rather than a geographically precise view, similar to the well-known New York subway map, and charts with remarkable accuracy nearly fifty geographical features of the

region—the Platte River, the Niobrara River, the Republican River, and so on" (Archer et al. 2021:xv).

The Ioway map is not the only map that evokes these similes. Linear depictions of communication routes and rivers on early Native American maps in general led archaeologist and ethnohistorian Kevin O'Briant to observe that, "Like a modern-day map of an urban transportation network, Indian cartographers also employed straight lines to indicate connections between important places on a map regardless of the linearity of the physical route between them. Combined with the variable scale, the end result is 'schematic' in appearance, but would have been valuable to those who understood them, much as a simplified subway map is understandable to us today in spite of its abstract, regularized appearance" (O'Briant 2018:11). In modern parlance, the map's schematic nature—its apparent simplicity—was a feature, not a bug. As the historian Ted Binnema (2001:210) states about an early nineteenth-century Blackfoot map, it "illustrates the very essence of successful cartography: selectivity." The geographers Mark Monmonier and Denis Wood likewise write, "To avoid hiding critical information in a fog of detail, the map must offer a selective, incomplete view of reality" (Monmonier 1996:1) and "[A] map's *effectiveness* is a consequence of the *selectivity* with which it brings [the] past to bear on the present" (Wood 1992:1; emphases in original). Binnema (2001:210) concludes, "In this way, good cartography is like any other effective communication; the intended audience will find it clear and direct. Good prose is concisely written, Poetry is language distilled. If most Western maps are analogous to prose, Old Swan's [Blackfoot, 1801] is akin to poetry."

48. The political activist group (Great Plains Action Society 2020) said, "We believe in abolishing border imperialism and so instead of focusing on the colonial settler imposed state of Iowa we decided to base our voting initiative on an Ioway made map that depicts their own history between the Missouri and Mississippi Rivers." See also Great Plains Action Society 2021. For the book-arts project, see Maher 2014.

49. Office of the State Archaeologist 2024.

50. Rosenthal 1985:35, 68, emphasis in original.

51. For the ICC experiences of anthropologists and historians, see, e.g., Beals 1985; Lurie 1985; Lurie reported "having been deeply distressed on one occasion to see a fellow anthropologist employed by the Justice Department cut to ribbons by one of 'my' attorneys" (p. 364). Another frustration among some case participants was that the commissioners (i.e., judges) often either had no experience in Native American issues or were strongly biased toward the government; see also Lurie 1978a. And, as Arthur J. Ray (2016:22) noted, "cross-examination certainly is a problematic way to attempt to gain understandings of history. Most of the questions are not aimed at elaborating historical perspectives or furthering discussion. Rather, often their object is intended to undermine a witness's credibility in the eyes of the court and to put forward alternative interpretations that favour the interests of the opposing side. As an expert witness, cross-examination is also very frustrating because you are allowed to answer only the questions that are put to you by opposing counsel, no matter how irrelevant or misleading you may think them to be for gaining understandings of the historical issues before the court."

ICC studies undertaken for plaintiffs (hundreds of tribes, in 852 separate cases) and for the defendant (the U.S. government, represented by the Department of Justice) were so extensive and engaged so many anthropologists and historians that this enterprise essentially created the interdisciplinary academic field of ethnohistory, with its namesake association and journal. "While it remains questionable what Indian people will gain from the Government Indian Claims Commission, scholars have clearly profited from the litigation" (Bieder 1984:346). For ethnohistory's origins, its debt to the ICC, and its subsequent development, see Axtell 1978; Chaves 2008.

52. Blaine 1995:319. For a list of the Iowa Tribes' ICC cases, see Native American Rights Fund 1976; U.S. Indian Claims Commission 1979:50–52. For a discussion of the Iowa ICC cases, see Ray 2016:49–55. For all ICC decisions, see Oklahoma State University Library Digital Collections 2024. The ICC judgment's financial benefit to Iowa tribal members was minimal. If, after attorneys' fees and expenses, the tribes received $4 million, then each of the approximately 2,000 enrolled tribal members at the time (1971) would have received only about $2,000, which arrived nearly twenty years after the claims were first filed. As Pete Fee, an elder of the Iowas of Kansas and Nebraska, recalled, "I was one of the fortunate ones. I did get, I think it was $1800 for my share of the state of Iowa" (Rundle and Rundle 2007–2013). In general, ICC monetary awards to tribes were "appropriated, distributed, spent, and forgotten and did little if anything to overcome the sense of Indian grievance" (Lurie 1985:365). As if the Ioways were not under enough pressure in the ICC era, in 1953–1954 the federal government threatened the Iowa Tribes with termination, fortunately not implemented; see U.S. Congress 1954.

53. Wallace was educated at the University of Pennsylvania, earning his BA in history (1947) and his MA (1949) and PhD (1950) in anthropology. He later taught anthropology at Penn, chaired its anthropology department, and directed its ethnohistory program. His best-known ethnohistorical research focused on Iroquoian tribes and (non-Indian) industrial towns. His studies on such topics as culture and personality, and Native American history, religion, and revitalization movements were seminal works that are still cited frequently. He was elected president of the American Anthropological Association in 1971. See Grumet 1998; Urban 2016.

Wallace served as an expert witness on behalf of the Sac and Fox, Iowa, and other tribes in several cases before the ICC. The Wallace Papers collection (AFCW) at the American Philosophical Society (APS) in Philadelphia includes a comprehensive, well-indexed archive of his ICC activities. During my visit to the APS library in 2023, I reviewed Wallace's research material and ICC testimony regarding the Iowa Tribes. I focused on items related to the 1837 treaty council, maps depicting tribal villages or settlement history, and relationships with other ICC expert witnesses. This material provides insights into the tribes' uses of historical records to support their claims. It also provides glimpses of the adversarial interactions that developed between expert witnesses for the tribes and those for the government. The McCarter and English case files at Princeton University also contain extensive records of Wallace's work on the ICC Iowa and Sac and Fox cases. (The McCarter and English law firm represented the plaintiffs.) The forty-three boxes of case records at Princeton (MER) are accessible and well indexed. Saul Schwartz and I examined that collection in 2005.

54. Mildred Mott Wedel earned her BA (history) from the University of Iowa in 1934 and MA (anthropology) from the University of Chicago in 1938. The links she discerned between archaeological complexes and historically known tribes of Iowa and the Great Plains were pathbreaking and are still widely cited and considered mostly valid. Her numerous publications concerning the Ioway, Otoe, Wichita, and other tribes and their early French visitors are detailed and thoroughly researched, as are her critical reviews of ethnohistorical methods and practice. Her posthumous publication about the Ioways in the Smithsonian *Handbook of North American Indians* (Wedel 2001) distills decades of research. See Gradwohl 1995, 1997; Wedel 1976; Wedel and DeMallie 1980.

In discussing Mildred Wedel's position at the Smithsonian's National Museum of Natural History (NMNH), Joanna Scherer and Thierry Veyrié (2024:50) wrote, "Several fully credentialed female anthropologists who married Smithsonian anthropologists were 'honored' with unpaid research associate positions in the NMNH."

The Waldo R. Wedel and Mildred Mott Wedel Papers at the Smithsonian's National Anthropological Archives (NAA) contain correspondence, research material, and drafts of papers. The collection (MMW) includes correspondence relating to Mildred Wedel's ICC work, but most of her ICC reports and testimony are housed in ICC archives at NARA, APS, and Princeton. The Wedel papers contain correspondence about the anthropologists involved in ICC cases, as well as publication drafts and reports written by other scholars about the Ioway, the ICC, and related topics. I examined the Wedel archives in 2023. Complementing the Wallace records at APS and Princeton, the Wedel ICC-related correspondence at the NAA reflects the tensions that emerged in the 1950s between anthropologists working on opposite sides of ICC cases.

55. David B. Stout received his BA from the University of Wisconsin in 1936 (anthropology, zoology, and geology), his MA from the University of Michigan in 1937 (anthropology), and his PhD from Columbia University in 1946 (anthropology). He supervised Works Progress Administration archaeological excavation crews for the Kentucky Archaeological Survey in 1937–1938 and conducted ethnographic fieldwork in Panama in 1940–1941. Stout's specialties were Central and South American ethnology and art. He was one of many anthropologists who served with the Office of Strategic Services (forerunner of the Central Intelligence Agency) and Office of Naval Intelligence during World War II. See Stout, David B. 1949–1959, UI/FSV; Stout 1953; Trager 1974.

Stout served as a government witness for the ICC beginning in 1956. The records of his ICC work on behalf of the Justice Department are housed at NARA, with portions relevant to the Iowa cases in the Wallace papers at the APS and the McCarter and English case files at Princeton. One of Stout's students, Charles F. O'Neal, wrote a master's thesis about Ioway ethnohistory and ethnohistoric methods in general (O'Neal 1958). O'Neal does not mention the ICC, but it is likely that he served as an assistant during Stout's ICC work and contributed in some way to Stout's research and ICC report on the Ioway.

56. Zachary Gussow received a BA in anthropology from the University of New Mexico (1948) and an MA in anthropology (1951) and PhD (1954) from Columbia University. His dissertation about cultural change in African societies was anthropological (Gussow 1954), but the degree was in political science. In the 1950s, Gussow was a lay psychoanalyst and a Columbia University research assistant on contemporary India. From the 1960s

onward, his professional home was the Department of Psychiatry and Neurology at the Louisiana State University Medical Center, where he specialized in medical anthropology, focusing on public health and the behavioral and social aspects of chronic diseases. See LAGenWeb Archives 2005. For aspects of Gussow's career, see Henry 1959:8 and McInnis 1964:21. Gussow's medical anthropology research and publications culminated in his book *Leprosy, Racism, and Public Health* (1989).

Gussow had conducted research for the Justice Department on ICC cases involving the Cheyenne and Arapaho and reportedly was engaged full time on the Sac and Fox and Iowa cases through much of 1955 and 1956. Documentation is housed in the ICC archives at NARA and APS. Cross-examination of Gussow in an ICC hearing in April 1956 demonstrated that he had "lifted"—plagiarized—material for his reports, notably from Mildred Mott's seminal 1938 article; Sac & Fox/Iowa Tribes v. U.S., Docket 135, page 25, April 1956, AFCW. Gussow apparently conducted no subsequent ICC work.

57. Lurie and Hallowell were cultural anthropologists and ethnohistorians who specialized in Native cultures of central and eastern North America. Lurie (1924–2017) was early in her career in the 1950s, while Hallowell (1892–1974) was well established, having served as president of the American Anthropological Association (AAA) in 1949; he was also Wallace's mentor at Penn. Lurie served as an ICC expert witness for several tribal plaintiffs, notably the Winnebago (Ho-Chunk), and wrote extensively about the ICC; she would be elected president of the AAA in 1984. For Lurie's and Hallowell's testimony and its repercussions among anthropologists in the 1950s, see correspondence and transcripts in the Wallace Papers at APS (AFCW) and the Wedel Papers at the NAA (MMW); see also Ray 2016:50. See also Lurie 1978a, 1985.

58. Schedule of Documentary Evidence to Be Entered on Behalf of Petitioners . . . Sauk-Fox/Iowa v. U.S.—Docket 135 & 153, Series IX.A., AFCW; Bibliographic Note Cards, Miami and Ohio, Sac and Fox and Iowa, Series III, Box 6, AFCW; Wallace, The Iowa and Sac-and-Fox Indians in Iowa and Missouri, pages 25, 88–89, Bibliography, AFCW.

59. Transcript of December 7, 1954, session of the Indian Claims Commission, Docket 138, AFCW; Before the Indian Claims Commission, Docket No. 138, the Iowa Tribe . . . vs. the United States . . . Objections by the Iowa Petitioners, Box S-000313, Folder 14, pages 2–3, MER. Wallace erroneously believed that Wawnonqueskoona drafted his map around 1838, rather than 1848, and his team's "aged Indian" and "old Indian" descriptors for Wawnonqueskoona do not appear in Schoolcraft's work or in the information Schoolcraft obtained from the missionaries Hamilton and Irvin. Wallace (The Iowa and Sac-and-Fox Indians in Iowa and Missouri, page 89, AFCW) refers to Wawnonqueskoona as an "old warrior," attributing that description to Schoolcraft, yet the only reference to elder Ioways in Schoolcraft's work is Hamilton and Irvin's statement, "There are a few aged persons who pretend to be able to state their traditions with great accuracy; but we find it is not the most pretending that is the most correct, or to be relied on" (Irvin and Hamilton 1853:266). We have no information regarding Wawnonqueskoona's age when he drafted the map or if he was one of the persons Hamilton and Irvin considered as "aged." Similar to characterizing Wawnonqueskoona as "an aged Indian," dubbing No Heart as "the old chief" whose "memory was playing tricks on him" has no factual basis and could only have been meant to further disparage the usefulness of his—actually Wawnonqueskoona's—map. No Heart

was only about forty years old in 1837 and was held in high regard by Ioways as well as every non-Ioway who knew him, including the "young lady" who penned the poem addressed "to a young Iowa Chief called No Heart" (see chapter 2).

60. Defendant's Request for Findings of Fact Requested by Petitioners, and Brief, page 102, Series IX.A., Sauk-Fox/Iowa v. U.S.—Docket 138, AFCW; Docket 138, Def. Ex. 25 (Entry A1 11A), ICC; Miner 1911:24, 36–39 (see chapter 4, n. 1).

61. The report about the NARA card index was provided by Brandi Oswald, personal communication, July 2, 2024.

62. Wallace, The Iowa and Sac-and-Fox Indians in Iowa and Missouri, page 1, AFCW. Mrs. K. O. Smith worked in the Washington office of the firm of Riegelman, Strasser, Schwarz, and Spiegelman. The head of that office from its founding in 1949 until 1953 was Felix S. Cohen, pioneer in the field of federal Indian law; see Kehoe 2014b.

63. MMW. See Gradwohl 1995:402; Wedel 1982. The eminent ethnohistorian Raymond DeMallie named Mildred Wedel as one of his mentors; see Scherer and Veyrié 2024.

64. 22 Ind. Cl. Comm 232, at 328, ICC.

65. It is ironic that Wallace did not examine or use the 1837 map in his ICC work and failed to credit the historical value of Ioway cartography. In one of his late publications, he compared the experience of time to a "series of maps," noting that "all societies produce and maintain maps of time, historical . . . frames of reference . . . generally beginning in the past with a creation myth, providing chronicles of relatively recent histories of significant events. . . . And each individual plants his own personal memory in his version of his own community's map of time" (Wallace 2005:5). One wonders what Wallace might have written about the 1837 map had he actually looked at it and applied this insightful perspective. Historians of cartography concur with Wallace's 2005 position and echo Vansina's and Lewis's points about accounts of origin: "It is well known that indigenous peoples, far from relying on instinct, have developed elaborate and exacting, usually ritualistic, mechanisms to ensure the dissemination of the most valued knowledge within their society and its transmission from one generation to another. Such cartographic skills as these peoples have are not instinctive but are as much acquired and learned as those of members of modern societies" (Delano-Smith 1987:48).

66. Ioway interests in the state of Iowa are varied and have been increasing since the 1990s. Part of the interest is official: government-to-government relationships are required between the tribal nations as sovereign entities and the agencies that represent state and federal governments. State and federal laws mandate consultation in such matters as burial site protection, repatriation of cultural items, and environmental impact studies; see, for example, the National Historic Preservation Act (16 U.S.C. ch. 1A, subch. II), the Native American Graves Protection and Repatriation Act (25 U.S.C. ch. 32, §3001–3013), the National Environmental Policy Act (42 U.S.C. ch. 55), Executive Order 13175 (November 6, 2000), and the ancient remains and cemetery provisions of the Iowa State Archaeologist statute (Ch. 216A.167 and 263B.7–9).

Lance Foster (2000:146–148) reviews several late twentieth-century Ioway personal and group returns to Iowa. Ioway traditions about ancestral sites in northeast Iowa continue into the twenty-first century; see Zimmerman and Makes Strong Move 2008:190–211. Other connections include tribal involvement in the Iowaville (Site J) archaeological project (Peterson 2014); tribal visits to other archaeological sites in Iowa (Green and Schermer 2015:4); the *Lost Nation* film premiere and associated events (see chapter 6, n. 38); the sister park agreement between Effigy Mounds National Monument and the Ioway Tribal National Park of the Iowa Tribe of Kansas and Nebraska, forged by Lance Foster (National Park Service 2022); and the donation of seven acres of woodlands and prairie overlooking the Iowa River to the Iowa Tribe of Kansas and Nebraska (Shillcock 2022), about which Lance Foster said, "It's symbolically a spiritually significant thing for us after almost 200 years to own a little piece of the land. . . . It is a place to stand and look out over the river that was named after your people, which is a very significant and sacred thing" (KCCI 2022).

In 2008, a statue of No Heart was dedicated in Perkins, Oklahoma, a joint effort of the city of Perkins, the Perkins Community Foundation, and the Iowa Tribe of Oklahoma; for its dedication, Ioway elder Mae Murray Sine highlighted the 1837 map and lauded No Heart as "a visionary leader who contributed to the sovereignty of the Ioway Nations" (Sine 2008b). Of course, these initiatives and Ioway interest in the state of Iowa are not due solely to heightened awareness of the 1837 map, but the map and its presentation are acknowledged and significant elements in many of the current relationships between the Iowa Tribes and the state of Iowa and in tribal members' historical consciousness. For the Land Back movement, see Pieratos et al. 2021.

67. Basso 1996; Meadows 2008.

Epilogue

1. On the power of maps, see American Philosophical Society 2021; Harley 2001; Wood 1992:20. On the study and uses of maps to elucidate socially constructed worlds, see Barber and Berdan 1998:226–246; Wood 1990:95–101. On the historical and cultural significance of Native American maps, see, e.g., Belyea 2007; Bernstein 2018; Cole and Sutton 2014; Gartner 2011; Lewis 1998a, 1998c; Short 2009; Vollmar 1981; Warhus 1997.

2. Binnema 2001:208. On the use of archaeology in understanding Native American maps, see Waselkov 1989; Wood 1990. On oral tradition and archaeology, see references in chapter 5, note 11, as well as Whiteley 2002. On the "site-identification syndrome" and the need for caution in correlating dots on maps with physical locations, see Henige 2007.

3. On maps as political documents, see Marchitello 1994. On the disappointing (to the Ioways) outcome of the 1837 council despite the map presentation, see Kelderman 2019a:105–109.

4. See StoryMaps 2024. A vast literature has developed about Indigenous mapping, Indigenous cartographies, decolonial mapping, and anticolonial mapping, e.g.: Anker 2018; Chapin et al. 2005; Cole and Sutton 2014; de Leeuw and Hunt 2018; Eades 2015; Indigenous Mapping Collective 2024; Johnson 2010; Louis et al. 2012; Rose-Redwood et al. 2020; Sletto 2009; Pearce and Louis 2008; Taylor et al. 2021; Willow 2013. Community engagement is a key element of Indigenous countermapping projects—examples include the Zuni Map Art Project led by Jim Enote as described and filmed by Steinauer-Scudder et al. (2018), the Penobscot place-names project (Pearce 2014), and the mural-size maps of Ho-Chunk and Miami tribal removal histories installed in the Field Museum's permanent exhibit *Native Truths: Our Voices, Our Stories* (Studio1:1 2023). Several Native nations have

produced historical atlases, e.g., Carlson 2001; Ferguson and Hart 1985; Nelson 2018. Indigenous scholars also interweave cartography with other material and literary media; see Wigginton 2022.

5. G. Malcolm Lewis observed in 2002 that although cosmographical maps such as Ojibwe migration scrolls depict long traditions, he knew of "no other native geographical map representing changes over a period of more than 200 years," personal communication (letter), February 20, 2002. For Ojibwe migration scrolls, see Dewdney 1975; Hisatake 1986.

Appendix One

1. Petition of the Ioway Indians, Letters Received 1837, Great Nemaha Agency, Document A, M234-362-0603–0609, BIA (parentheses in original). This transcription was made directly from the microfilm. For an earlier transcription, see Blaine 1995:164–167.

2. For the Ioway Subagency, see Hill 1974:81–82.

Appendix Two

1. Journal of Proceedings:46–49. This transcription was made directly from the microfilm (U.S. National Archives Microfilm Publication T494, Roll 3) and the online scan (University of Wisconsin–Madison Libraries, https://search.library.wisc.edu/digital/ANCSAVIL5TZV3D87).

Bibliography

Abbreviations for Archives

AFCW—Anthony F. C. Wallace Papers, Mss.Ms.Coll.64a., Series IX, Indian Claims. American Philosophical Society, Philadelphia. https://as.amphilsoc.org/repositories/2/resources/2900.

AIC—American Indian Collection: The Presbyterian Historical Society Collection of Missionaries' Letters. Presbyterian Historical Society, Philadelphia. https://www.history.pcusa.org/collections/research-tools/guides-archival-collections/rg-224.

BIA—Records of the Bureau of Indian Affairs, Record Group 75. National Archives and Records Administration, Washington, DC. https://www.archives.gov/research/native-americans/bia-guide.

GMLC—G. Malcolm Lewis Collection of Cartographic Activities of the North American Indian and Inuit Peoples, Library of Congress, Washington, DC. https://hdl.loc.gov/loc.gmd/eadgmd.gm024002.

HRS—Henry Rowe Schoolcraft Papers, 1788–1941. Manuscript Division, Library of Congress, Washington, DC. https://hdl.loc.gov/loc.mss/eadmss.ms000003.

ICC—Records of the Indian Claims Commission, Record Group 279. National Archives and Records Administration, Washington, DC. https://www.archives.gov/research/native-americans/indian-claims-commission.

JLC—John Lee and Company Trade Ledgers. St. Louis Mercantile Library, University of Missouri–St. Louis. https://www.umsl.edu/mercantile/pott/collections_2/pott090.html.

MER—McCarter and English Records on U.S. Indian Claims Cases, 1958–1970, WC030. Seeley G. Mudd Manuscript Library, Princeton University, Princeton, NJ. https://findingaids.princeton.edu/catalog/WC030.

MMW—Waldo Rudolph Wedel and Mildred Mott Wedel Papers, 1893–1994. National Anthropological Archives, Smithsonian Institution, Suitland, MD. https://sova.si.edu/record/NAA.1990-20.

NSHS—Nebraska State Historical Society, Lincoln.

THP—Thomas Hutchins Papers. Historical Society of Pennsylvania, Philadelphia. https://hsp.org/sites/default/files/mss/finding_aid_0308_hutchins.pdf.

UI/FSV—Faculty and Staff Vertical Files. University of Iowa Libraries, Special Collections and University Archives, Iowa City.

UI/WHJ—William Henry Jackson Photographs Collection, MsC 539. University of Iowa Libraries, Special Collections and University Archives, Iowa City.

Aigner, Katherine, and Nicola Mapelli. 2015. *The Americas: Collections from the Vatican Ethnological Museum*. Edizioni Musei Vaticani, Vatican City.

Akerman, James R. 2007. Finding Our Way. In *Maps: Finding Our Place in the World*, edited by James R. Akerman and Robert W. Karrow Jr., pp. 19–63. University of Chicago Press, Chicago.

Akerman, James R., Robert W. Karrow Jr., and David Buiserret. 2008. Festival of Maps, Chicago: Some Personal Views. *Imago Mundi* 60(2):223–226.

Akerman, James R., and Margaret Wilkes. 2022. G. Malcolm Lewis (1930–2022). *Imago Mundi* 74(2):302–305.

Akomawt Educational Initiative. 2024. About Us. https://www.akomawt.org/.

Alex, Lynn M. 1994. Oneota and the Olivet Phase, South Dakota. *Newsletter of the South Dakota Archaeological Society* 24(1):1–4.

Alex, Lynn M. 2000. *Iowa's Archaeological Past*. University of Iowa Press, Iowa City.

Alvord, Clarence Walworth, and Clarence Edwin Carter, eds. 1915. *The Critical Period, 1763–1765*. Collections of the Illinois State Historical Library Vol. 10. Springfield.

American Philosophical Society, ed. 2021. *The Power of Maps and the Politics of Borders*. Transactions of the American Philosophical Society Vol. 110, Part 4. American Philosophical Society Press, Philadelphia.

Anderson, Charles A. 1957. Letters of William Hamilton, 1811–1891. *Journal of the Presbyterian Historical Society* 35(3):157–170.

Anderson, Charles A. 1958. More Letters of William Hamilton, 1811–1891. *Journal of the Presbyterian Historical Society* 36(1):53–65.

Anderson, Duane C. 1973a. Ioway Ethnohistory: A Review, Part I. *Annals of Iowa* 41(8):1228–1241.

Anderson, Duane C. 1973b. Ioway Ethnohistory: A Review, Part II. *Annals of Iowa* 42(1):41–59.

Anderson, Mark L. 2014. *Phase IA Cultural Resource Reconnaissance of the Iowa River and Lake Odessa Water Trails Corridor through Portions of Johnson, Louisa, and Washington Counties, Iowa*. Contract Completion Report 2065. Office of the State Archaeologist, University of Iowa, Iowa City.

Andrews, Sona, Mark Warhus, and Beth Schaefer. 2023. *Archive of North American Indian and Inuit Maps*. Self-published digital collection (six CDs) on file, University of Wisconsin–Milwaukee library.

Anker, Kirsten. 2018. Aboriginal Title and Alternative Cartographies. *Erasmus Law Review* 2018:1, ELR.000098.

Archer, J. Clark, Richard Edwards, Leslie M. Howard, Fred M. Shelley, Donald A. Wilhite, and David J. Wishart. 2021. *Atlas of Nebraska*. University of Nebraska Press, Lincoln.

Armstrong, Chelsey Geralda, Anne Spice, Mike Ridsdale, and John R. Welch. 2023. Liberating Trails and Travel Routes in Gitxsan and Wet'suwet'en Territories from the Tyrannies of Heritage Resource Management Regimes. *American Anthropologist* 125(2):361–376.

Arrowsmith, Aaron. 1802. *A Map Exhibiting All the New Discoveries in the Interior Parts of North America*. A. Arrowsmith, London.

Arrowsmith, J. 1832. *Mexico*. J. Arrowsmith, London.

Assmann, Jan. 1995. Collective Memory and Cultural Identity. *New German Critique* 65:125–133. Originally published in 1988 as Kollektives Gedächtnis und kulturelle Identität. In *Kultur und Gedächtnis*, edited by Jan Assmann and Tonio Hölscher, pp. 9–19. Suhrkamp, Frankfurt am Main, West Germany.

Assmann, Jan. 2008. Communicative and Cultural Memory. In *Cultural Memory Studies: An International and Interdisciplinary Handbook*, edited by Astrid Eril and Ansgar Nünning, pp. 109–118. Walter de Gruyter, Berlin, Germany.

Axtell, James. 1978. The Ethnohistory of Early America: A Review Essay. *William and Mary Quarterly* 35(1):110–144.

Bahr, Donald, Juan Smith, William Smith Allison, and Julian Hayden. 1994. *The Short, Swift Time of Gods on Earth: The Hohokam Chronicles*. University of California Press, Berkeley.

Barber, Russell J., and Frances F. Berdan. 1998. *The Emperor's Mirror: Understanding Cultures through Primary Sources*. University of Arizona Press, Tucson.

Barrows, Willard. 1845. *A New Map of Iowa with Notes by W. Barrows*. Doolittle and Munson, Cincinnati.

Basso, Keith. 1996. *Wisdom Sits in Places: Landscape and Language among the Western Apache*. University of New Mexico Press, Albuquerque.

Beals, Ralph L. 1985. The Anthropologist as Expert Witness: Illustrations from the California Indian Land Claims Case. In *Irredeemable America: The Indians' Estate and Land Claims*, edited by Imre Sutton, pp. 139–155. University of New Mexico Press, Albuquerque.

Beaudoin, Matthew A. 2022. The Struggle to Identify Nineteenth-Century Indigenous Sites in Cultural Resource Management. In *Archaeologies of Indigenous Presence*, edited by Tsim D. Schneider and Lee M. Panich, pp. 109–125. University Press of Florida, Gainesville.

Beck, Lauren. 2022. *Canada's Place Names and How to Change Them*. Concordia University Press, Montreal.

Beck, Lauren. 2023. Introduction to *The Social Lives of Maps*, Vol. 3. *Material Culture Review* 95(1):1–7.

Beimers, Henry Osborne. 2022a. Decolonizing the Map: Indigenous Maps and GIS. Master's thesis, Department of Geography, Minnesota State University, Mankato.

Beimers, Henry. 2022b. Indigenous Maps as Territorial Contestations. March 4. https://storymaps.arcgis.com/stories/2d4149498eee4016bc89835879081b7a.

Belyea, Barbara. 1998. Inland Journeys, Native Maps. In *Cartographic Encounters: Perspectives on Native American Mapmaking and Map Use*, edited by G. Malcolm Lewis, pp. 135–155. University of Chicago Press, Chicago.

Belyea, Barbara. 2007. *Dark Storm Moving West*. University of Calgary Press, Calgary.

Benson, Maxine, ed. 1988. *From Pittsburgh to the Rocky Mountains: Major Stephen Long's Expedition 1819–1820*. Fulcrum, Golden, CO.

Berkson, Alice. 1992. Cultural Resistance of the Prairie Kickapoo at the Grand Village, McLean County, Illinois. *Illinois Archaeology* 4(2):107–205.

Bernardini, Wesley. 2005. *Hopi Oral Tradition and the Archaeology of Identity*. University of Arizona Press, Tucson.

Bernardini, Wesley, Stewart B. Koyiyumptewa, Gregson Schachner, and Leigh Kuwanwisiwma. 2021. *Becoming Hopi: A History*. University of Arizona Press, Tucson.

Bernstein, David. 2003. Towards a More Stable Agricultural Future: The Political and Economic Strategies of the Iowa Indians, 1803–1846. Master's thesis, Department of History, University of Wisconsin–Madison.

Bernstein, David. 2007. "We Are Not Now as We Once Were": Iowa Indians' Political and Economic Adaptations during U.S. Incorporation. *Ethnohistory* 54(4):605–637.

Bernstein, David. 2011. How the West Was Drawn: Mapping, Indians, and the Construction of the Trans-Mississippi West. PhD dissertation, Department of History, University of Wisconsin–Madison. ProQuest UMI 3501290.

Bernstein, David. 2012. Looking Like a White Man: Geopolitical Strategies of the Iowa Indians during American Incorporation. In *Indigenous Knowledge and the Environment in Africa and North America*, edited by David Gordon and Shepard Krech III, pp. 18–52. Ohio University Press, Athens.

Bernstein, David. 2018. *How the West Was Drawn: Mapping, Indians, and the Construction of the Trans-Mississippi West*. University of Nebraska Press, Lincoln.

Betts, Colin M. 1998. The Oneota Orr Phase: Space, Time, and Ethnicity. *Wisconsin Archeologist* 79(2):227–237.

Betts, Colin M. 2006. Pots and Pox: The Identification of Protohistoric Epidemics in the Upper Mississippi Valley. *American Antiquity* 71(2):233–259.

Betts, Colin M. 2010. Oneota Mound Construction: An Early Revitalization Movement. *Plains Anthropologist* 55(214):97–110.

Betts, Colin M. 2015. A Twenty-First-Century Perspective on Oneota Cultural Affiliations. In *Oneota Historical Connections: Working Together in Iowa*, edited by Shirley J. Schermer, William Green, Larry J. Zimmerman, Linda Forman, and Robin M. Lillie, pp. 103–112. Report 24. Office of the State Archaeologist, University of Iowa, Iowa City.

Betts, Colin M. 2019. *Paouté* and *Aiaouez*: A New Perspective on Late Seventeenth-Century Chiwere-Siouan Identity. *Midcontinental Journal of Archaeology* 44(1):94–112.

Bieder, Robert E. 1984. Review of *American Indian Ethnohistory: Chippewa Indians I–VII, Winnebago Indians; Sac, Fox and Iowa Indians I–III*. *Ethnohistory* 31(4):346–350.

Binnema, Theodore. 2001. How Does a Map Mean? Old Swan's Map of 1801 and the Blackfoot World. In *From Rupert's Land to Canada: Essays in Honour of John E. Foster*, edited by Theodore Binnema, Gerhard J. Ens, and R. C. Macleod, pp. 201–224. University of Alberta Press, Edmonton.

Black Hawk. 1964. *Black Hawk: An Autobiography*, edited by Donald Jackson. University of Illinois Press, Urbana.

Blackhawk, Ned. 2023. *The Rediscovery of America: Native Peoples and the Unmaking of U.S. History.* Yale University Press, New Haven, CT.

Blaine, Martha Royce. 1979. *The Ioway Indians*. University of Oklahoma Press, Norman.

Blaine, Martha Royce. 1995. *The Ioway Indians*, 2nd ed. University of Oklahoma Press, Norman.

Blakeslee, Donald J. 1981. The Origin and Spread of the Calumet Ceremony. *American Antiquity* 46(4):759–768.

Blakeslee, Donald J. 1986. *Dixon County Archaeological Survey 1985*. Archaeology Laboratories, Wichita State University, Wichita, KS.

Blue, Brantley. 1974. Foreword. In *The Indian Removals,* Vol. 1, pp. iii–v. AMS Press, New York.

Boszhardt, Robert F. 1994. Oneota Group Continuity at La Crosse: The Brice Prairie, Pammel Creek, and Valley View Phases. *Wisconsin Archeologist* 75(3–4):173–236.

Boszhardt, Robert F. 1998. Oneota Horizons: A La Crosse Perspective. *Wisconsin Archeologist* 79(2):196–226.

Boszhardt, Robert F. 2000. Turquoise, Rasps, and Heartlines: The Oneota Bison Pull. In *Mounds, Modoc, and Mesoamerica: Papers in Honor of Melvin L. Fowler,* edited by Steven R. Ahler, pp. 361–373. Scientific Papers Vol. 28. Illinois State Museum, Springfield.

Bowes, John P. 2016. *Land Too Good for Indians: Northern Indian Removal.* University of Oklahoma Press, Norman.

Bray, Kingsley M. 2003. Omaha Rendezvous: Ethnogenesis and Warfare at a Plains Indian Trade Center. In *The People of the Buffalo,* Vol. 1. *The Plains Indians of North America: Military Art, Warfare and Change, Essays in Honor of John C. Ewers,* edited by Colin F. Taylor and Hugh A. Dempsey, pp. 40–52. Tatanka Press, Wyk auf Föhr, Germany.

Brighenti, Andrea Mubi, and Mattias Kärrholm. 2020. *Animated Lands: Studies in Territoriology*. University of Nebraska Press, Lincoln.

Brodie, Paul. 1885. *Indian Reservations within the Limits of the United States and Territories.* Office of Indian Affairs, Washington, DC.

Brodie, Paul. 1886. *Map of the Navajo Indian Reservation*. Office of Indian Affairs, Santa Fe, New Mexico Territory.

Brown, James A. 1965. The Prairie Peninsula: An Interaction Area in the Eastern United States. PhD dissertation, Department of Anthropology, University of Chicago.

Brown, James A. 1991. *Aboriginal Cultural Adaptations in the Midwestern Prairies*. Garland, New York.

Brown, James A., and Robert F. Sasso. 2001. Prelude to History on the Eastern Prairies. In *Societies in Eclipse: Archaeology of the Eastern Woodlands Indians, A.D. 1400–1700,* edited by David S. Brose, C. Wesley Cowan, and Robert C. Mainfort Jr., pp. 205–228. University of Alabama Press, Tuscaloosa.

Brown, Wesley A. 2022. John Arrowsmith's Maps of 1832: A Little-Known Breakthrough in the Cartography of Western North America. *The Portolan* 114:7–21.

Brückle, Irene. 1996. Update: Remoistenable Lining with Methyl Cellulose Adhesive Preparation. *Book and Paper Group Annual* 15:25–26.

Brückner, Martin. 2017. *The Social Lives of Maps in America, 1750–1860*. University of North Carolina Press, Chapel Hill.

Buckley, Jay. 2008. *William Clark, Indian Diplomat.* University of Oklahoma Press, Norman.

Buffalohead, Eric. 2004. Dhegihan History: A Personal Journey. In *Dhegihan and Chiwere Siouans in the Plains: Historical and Archaeological Perspectives*, edited by Dale R. Henning and Thomas D. Thiessen, pp. 327–343. *Plains Anthropologist* 49, Memoir 36.

Burr, David M. 1839. *Map of the United States of North America with Parts of the Adjacent Countries*. John Arrowsmith, London.

Bustard, Bruce I. 1992. *Western Ways: Images of the American West*. National Archives and Records Administration, Washington, DC.

Bustard, Bruce I., and Eric Rhodes. 2015. Transcript of National Archives History Office Oral History Interview. December 11. National Archives and Records Administration, Washington, DC. https://www.archives.gov/files/about/history/bruce-bustard-12-11-15.pdf.

Caldwell, Dorothy J. 1970. The Big Neck Affair: Tragedy and Farce on the Missouri Frontier. *Missouri Historical Review* 64(4):391–412.

Caldwell, Robert B., Jr. 2023. The Iconic Tipi: Spanish Mapping of Texas, the Greater Gulf, and the Southwest. *Texas Gulf Historical and Biographical Record* 59(2):4–28.

Calloway, Colin G. 2013. *Pen and Ink Witchcraft: Treaties and Treaty Making in American Indian History*. Oxford University Press, New York.

Cameron, Catherine M., and Brenda J. Bowser. 2024. Introduction. In *Landscapes of Movement and Predation: Perspectives from Archaeology, History, and Anthropology*, edited by Brenda J. Bowser and Catherine M. Cameron, pp. 3–22. University of Arizona Press, Tucson.

Carlson, Gayle F. 1979. *Archeological Investigations at Fort Atkinson (25WN9), Washington County, Nebraska 1956–1971*. Publications in Anthropology No. 8. Nebraska State Historical Society, Lincoln.

Carlson, Keith, ed. 2001. *A Stó:lō–Coast Salish Historical Atlas*. University of Washington Press, Seattle.

Carter, Clarence Edwin, ed. 1948. *The Territory of Illinois, 1809–1814*. Territorial Papers of the United States, Vol. 16. Government Printing Office, Washington, DC.

Carter, Clarence Edwin, ed. 1949. *The Territory of Louisiana-Missouri 1806–1814*. Territorial Papers of the United States, Vol. 14. Government Printing Office, Washington, DC.

Catlin, George. 1852. *Adventures of the Ojibbeway and Ioway Indians in England, France, and Belgium*, 3rd ed. 2 vols. George Catlin, London.

Catton, Theodore, and Diane L. Krahe. 2016. *The Blood of the People: Historic Resource Study, Pipestone National Monument, Minnesota*. National Park Service, Washington, DC.

Chapin, Mac, Zachary Lamb, and Bill Threlkeld. 2005. Mapping Indigenous Lands. *Annual Review of Anthropology* 34:619–638.

Chaves, Kelly K. 2008. Ethnohistory: From Inception to Postmodernism and Beyond. *The Historian* 70(3):486–513.

Clifton, James A. 1977. *The Prairie People: Continuity and Change in Potawatomi Indian Culture 1665–1965*. Regents Press of Kansas, Lawrence.

Colbert, Thomas Burnell. 2008. "The Hinge on Which All Affairs of the Sauk and Fox Indians Turn": Keokuk and the United States Government. In *Enduring Nations:*

Native Americans in the Midwest, edited by R. David Edmunds, pp. 54–71. University of Illinois Press, Urbana.
Cole, David G., and Imre Sutton, eds. 2014. *Mapping Native America: Cartographic Interactions between Indigenous Peoples, Government, and Academia*, Vols. 1–3. Privately published, San Bernardino, CA.
Coues, Elliott, ed. 1895. *The Expeditions of Zebulon Montgomery Pike*. Harper, New York.
Crowell, Aron L., and Wayne K. Howell. 2013. Time, Oral Tradition, and Archaeology at Xakwnoowú, a Little Ice Age Fort in Southeastern Alaska. *American Antiquity* 78(1):3–23.
Cummings, J. E. 1927. The Burning of Sauk-E-Nuk, the Westernmost Battle of the Revolution. *Journal of the Illinois State Historical Society* 20(1):49–62.
Daily Advertiser [Boston]. 1837. The Indian Delegation. October 31:2.
Daily Advocate [Boston]. 1837. The Indian Chiefs. October 30:2.
Daily Commercial Advertiser [Buffalo, New York]. 1837. Arrival of Indian Delegation in Cincinnati. September 21:2.
Daily Commercial Bulletin [St. Louis, Missouri]. 1837. Departure of Maj. Pilcher from St. Louis with Indian Delegation. September 8:2.
Daily Courant [Hartford, Connecticut]. 1837a. Correspondence of the N.Y. Commercial Advertiser. October 11:3.
Daily Courant [Hartford, Connecticut]. 1837b. Deputation of Indians. September 28:2.
Dalla Torre, Paolo. 1940. La Plastiche a Soggetto Indigeno Nordamericano del Pettrich nel Pontifico Museo Missionario Etnologico. *Annali Lateranensi* 4:9–96.
Danzer, Gerald A. 2004. Maps from Illinois History: Resources for Teachers. *Illinois History Teacher* 11(2):1–106.
Dawson, Andrew, and Mark Johnson. 2001. Migration, Exile and Landscapes of the Imagination. In *Contested Landscapes: Movement, Exile and Place*, edited by Barbara Bender and Margaret Winer, pp. 319–332. Berg, Oxford, England.
de Leeuw, Sarah, and Sara Hunt. 2018. Unsettling Decolonizing Geographies. *Geography Compass* 12(7):e12376. https://doi.org/10.1111/gec3.12376.
De L'Isle, Guillaume. 1718. *Carte de la Louisiane et du Cours du Mississipi*. Paris.
Delano-Smith, Catherine. 1987. Prehistoric Maps and the History of Cartography: An Introduction. In *Cartography in Prehistoric, Ancient, and Medieval Europe and the Mediterranean: The History of Cartography*, Vol. 1, edited by J. B. Harley and David Woodward, pp. 45–49. University of Chicago Press, Chicago.
Deloria, Philip J. 2008. From Nation to Neighborhood: Land, Policy, Culture, Colonialism, and Empire in U.S.-Indian Relations. In *The Cultural Turn in U.S. History: Past, Present, and Future*, edited by James W. Cook, Lawrence B. Glickman, and Michael O'Malley, pp. 343–382. University of Chicago Press, Chicago.
DeMallie, Raymond J. 1993. "These Have No Ears": Narrative and the Ethnohistorical Method. *Ethnohistory* 40(4):515–538.
DeMallie, Raymond J., and Gilles Havard. 2019. Writing the History of North America from Indian Country: The View from the North-Central Plains. *Journal de la Société des Américanistes* 105(1):13–40.

Denevan, William M., and Kent Mathewson, eds. 2009. *Carl Sauer on Culture and Landscape: Readings and Commentaries.* Louisiana State University Press, Baton Rouge.

Dewdney, Selwyn. 1975. *The Sacred Scrolls of the Southern Ojibway.* University of Toronto Press, Toronto.

Dickey, Michael. 2004. The Ioway Indians: Britain's Ally in the West? https://ioway.nativeweb.org/history/ioway_indians_britain_allies.htm.

Dorsey, J. Owen. 1884. Omaha Sociology. In *Third Annual Report of the Bureau of Ethnology, 1881–1882*, pp. 205–370. Smithsonian Institution, Washington, DC.

Dorsey, J. Owen. 1886. Migrations of Siouan Tribes. *American Naturalist* 20(3):211–222.

Dorsey, J. Owen. 1890. *The Ȼegiha Language.* Contributions to North American Ethnology Vol. 6. U.S. Geographical and Geological Survey of the Rocky Mountain Region, Washington, DC.

Dorsey, J. Owen, and Cyrus Thomas. 1907. Iowa. In *Handbook of American Indians North of Mexico*, Part I, edited by Frederick Webb Hodge, pp. 612–614. Bulletin No. 30. Bureau of American Ethnology, Smithsonian Institution, Washington, DC.

Dunlap, William. 1930. *Diary of William Dunlap (1766–1839): The Memoirs of a Dramatist, Theatrical Manager, Painter, Critic, Novelist, and Historian*, Vol. 2. New York Historical Society, New York.

DuVal, Kathleen. 2024. *Native Nations: A Millennium in North America.* Random House, New York.

Eades, Gwilym Lucas. 2015. *Maps and Memes: Redrawing Culture, Place, and Identity in Indigenous Communities.* McGill-Queen's University Press, Montreal.

Eades, Gwilym Lucas. 2017. *The Geography of Names: Indigenous to Post-Foundational.* Routledge, New York.

Echo-Hawk, Roger C. 2000. Ancient History in the New World: Integrating Oral Traditions and the Archaeological Record. *American Antiquity* 65(2):267–290.

Edenheiser, Iris. 2015. In-Between. Zum Grenzgang zwischen ethnologischen und kunsthistorischen Konventionen in der Ausstellungspraxis. Oder: Don't Represent—Create a Presence. In *Quo Vadis, Völkerkundemuseum? Aktuelle Debaten zu ethnologischen Sammlungen in Museen und Universitäten*, edited by Michael Kraus and Karoline Noack, pp. 257–276. Transcript, Bielefeld, Germany.

Edmunds, R. David. 1969. The Illinois River Potawatomi in the War of 1812. *Journal of the Illinois State Historical Society* 62(4):341–362.

Edmunds, R. David. 1976. *The Otoe-Missouria People.* Indian Tribal Series, Phoenix, AZ.

Edmunds, R. David. 1978. *The Potawatomis: Keepers of the Fire.* University of Oklahoma Press, Norman.

Edwards, Ninian W. 1870. *History of Illinois, from 1778 to 1833; and Life and Times of Ninian Edwards.* Illinois State Journal Company, Springfield.

Ellis, Elizabeth N. 2022. *The Great Power of Small Nations: Indigenous Diplomacy in the Gulf South.* University of Pennsylvania Press, Philadelphia.

Espenshade, Christopher T. 2014. Landscape of Battle: Military Terrain Analysis of the Battle of Credit Island. In *Archaeology of the War of 1812*, edited by Michael T. Lucas and Julie M. Schablitsky, pp. 229–251. Left Coast Press, Walnut Creek, CA.

Etcheson, Nicole. 2004. *Bleeding Kansas: Contested Liberty in the Civil War Era.* University Press of Kansas, Lawrence.

Ethridge, Robbie. 2017. Navigating the Mississippian World: Infrastructure in the Sixteenth-Century Native South. In *Forging Southeastern Identities: Social Archaeology, Ethnohistory, and Folklore of the Mississippian to Early History South*, edited by Gregory A. Waselkov and Marvin T. Smith, pp. 62–84. University of Alabama Press, Tuscaloosa.

Ewers, John C. 1954. Charles Bird King, Painter of Indian Visitors to the Nation's Capital. In *Annual Report of the Board of Regents of the Smithsonian Institution for 1953*, pp. 463–473. Smithsonian Institution, Washington, DC.

Ewers, John C. 1977. The Making and Uses of Maps by Plains Indian Warriors. *By Valor and Arms: The Journal of American Military History* 3(1):36–43. Reprinted in *Plains Indian History and Culture: Essays on Continuity and Change*, by John C. Ewers, pp. 180–190. University of Oklahoma Press, Norman, 1997.

Faldet, David S. 2009. *Oneota Flow: The Upper Iowa River and Its People.* University of Iowa Press, Iowa City.

Far West [Liberty, Missouri]. 1838. Treaty with the Ioway Indians. June 14.

Feest, Christian. 1997. On Some Uses of the Past in Native American Art and Art History. In *Present Is Past: Some Uses of Tradition in Native Societies*, edited by Marie Mauzé, pp. 65–79. University Press of America, Lanham, MD.

Ferguson, T. J., and E. Richard Hart. 1985. *A Zuni Atlas.* University of Oklahoma Press, Norman.

Fishel, Richard L. 2017. The Historic Indian Artifact Assemblage at Buckman Flats, Knox County, Illinois. *Illinois Archaeology* 29:381–398.

Fishel, Richard L., Sarah U. Wisseman, Randall E. Hughes, and Thomas E. Emerson. 2010. Sourcing Red Pipestone Artifacts from Oneota Villages in the Little Sioux Valley of Northwest Iowa. *Midcontinental Journal of Archaeology* 35(2):167–198.

Flavin, Francis. 2024. Paradigms and Poetry: John G. Neihardt's *Cycle of the West.* In *Great Plains Ethnohistory: New Interdisciplinary Approaches*, edited by Rani-Henrik Andersson, Logan Sutton, and Thierry Veyrié, pp. 165–190. University of Nebraska Press, Lincoln.

Fletcher, Alice C., and Francis La Flesche. 1911. The Omaha Tribe. In *Twenty-Seventh Annual Report of the Bureau of American Ethnology, 1905–1906*, pp. 17–672. Smithsonian Institution, Washington, DC.

Foley, William E., and C. David Rice. 1983. *The First Chouteaus: River Barons of Early St. Louis.* University of Illinois Press, Urbana.

Foreman, Grant. 1972 [1932]. *Indian Removal: The Emigration of the Five Civilized Tribes of Indians.* University of Oklahoma Press, Norman.

Foster, Lance M. 1996. The Ioway and the Landscape of Southeast Iowa. *Journal of the Iowa Archeological Society* 43:1–5.

Foster, Lance M. 1999. *Tanji na Che*: Recovering the Landscape of the Ioway. In *Recovering the Prairie*, edited by Robert F. Sayre, pp. 178–190. University of Wisconsin Press, Madison. Reprinted in *The Tallgrass Prairie Reader*, edited by John T. Price, pp. 269–281, University of Iowa Press, Iowa City, 2014.

Foster, Lance M. 2000. A Closing Circle: Musings on the Ioway Indians in Iowa. In *The Worlds between Two Rivers: Perspectives on American Indians in Iowa, an Expanded Edition*, edited by Gretchen M. Bataille, David Mayer Gradwohl, and Charles L. P. Silet, pp. 142–150. University of Iowa Press, Iowa City.

Foster, Lance M. 2009. *The Indians of Iowa*. University of Iowa Press, Iowa City.

Foster, Lance M. 2010. *Sacred Bundles of the Ioway Indians*. Privately published, Helena, MT.

Foster, Lance M. 2019. Ioway. In *Meskonsing-Kansan*, by Rozalinda Borcilă and Nicholas Brown, pp. 28–49. Field Guides to the Anthropocene Drift No. 1. Haus der Kulturen der Welt, Berlin, Germany. https://regionalrelationships.org/anthrodrift/bookletPDFs/MeskonsingKansan.pdf.

Foster, Lance. 2020. Ioway Oral Traditions Concerning Tribal Origins and Identifying a Homeland. https://history.nebraska.gov/wp-content/uploads/2020/07/doc_Nebraska-Archeology-Section-3-Lance-Foster-Supplement-.pdf.

Foster, Thomas. 1876. The Ioway Monograph. *Foster's Indian Record and Historical Data* 1(1):1, 1(2):3–4, 1(3):4.

Fowles, Severin. 2013. *An Archaeology of Doings: Secularism and the Study of Pueblo Religion.* School for Advanced Research Press, Santa Fe, NM.

Franke, Judith A. 1995. *French Peoria and the Illinois Country 1673–1846*. Popular Science Series Vol. 12. Illinois State Museum, Springfield.

Gamble, Stephanie L. 2014. Capital Negotiations: Native Diplomats in the American Capital, 1789–1837. PhD dissertation, Department of History, Johns Hopkins University, Baltimore, MD.

Gartner, William Gustav. 2011. "An Image to Carry the World within It": Performance Cartography and the Skidi Star Chart. In *Early American Cartographies*, edited by Martin Brückner, pp. 169–247. University of North Carolina Press, Chapel Hill.

Genetin-Pilawa, C. Joseph. 2014. The Indians' Capitol City: Diplomatic Visits, Place, and Two-Worlds Discourse in Nineteenth-Century Washington, D.C. In *Beyond Two Worlds: Critical Conversations on Language and Power in Native North America*, edited by James Joseph Buss and C. Joseph Genetin-Pilawa, pp. 117–135. State University of New York Press, Albany.

Geniusz, Mary Siisip. 2015. *Plants Have So Much to Give Us, All We Have to Do Is Ask: Anishinaabe Botanical Teachings*, edited by Wendy Makoons Geniusz. University of Minnesota Press, Minneapolis.

Genoways, Hugh H., and Thomas E. Lebedz. 2018. An Engineer Cantonment Bestiary: The Art of Titian Ramsay Peale. In *Archeological Investigations at Engineer Cantonment: Winter Quarters of the 1819–1820 Long Expedition, Eastern Nebraska*, edited by John R. Bozell, Gayle F. Carlson, and Robert E. Pepperl, pp. 274–302. Publications in Anthropology No. 12. History Nebraska, Lincoln.

Gibbon, Guy, ed. 1982. *Oneota Studies.* Publications in Anthropology No. 1. University of Minnesota, Minneapolis.

Gibbon, Guy. 2003. *The Sioux: The Dakota and Lakota Nations*. Blackwell, Malden, MA.

Gibbon, Guy. 2012. *Archaeology of Minnesota: The Prehistory of the Upper Mississippi River Region.* University of Minnesota Press, Minneapolis.

Gilman, Carolyn. 2008. Mystery of the Indian Map: Decoding a Distant Time and Culture. *Gateway: The Quarterly Magazine of the Missouri Historical Society* 28:9–21.
The Globe [Washington, DC.]. 1837a. Indian Council. October 4:3.
The Globe [Washington, DC.]. 1837b. Indian Delegations Meet the President. September 28:3.
The Globe [Washington, DC.]. 1837c. Ioway and Sac and Fox Presentations. October 7:3.
Goodson, Christina Faye. 2019. *Iro Tųwahi Wisahma Nąha*: The Seventh Generation, Understanding Jiwere Language Status and Reclamation through Community Input. Master's thesis, Department of Anthropology, University of Oklahoma, Norman.
GoodTracks, Jimm G. 2024a. Baxoje, Jiwere-Ñut^achi Ich^e, Ioway, Otoe-Missouria Language. https://iowayotoelang.nativeweb.org/.
GoodTracks, Jimm G. 2024b. BJM Ich^e Wawagaxe IOM Dictionary. https://iowayotoelang.nativeweb.org/dictionary.htm.
GoodTracks, Jimm, Bryan James Gordon, and Saul Schwartz. 2016. Perspectives on Chiwere Revitalization. In *Advances in the Study of Siouan Languages and Linguistics*, edited by Catherine Rudin and Brian J. Gordon, pp. 133–165. Language Science Press, Berlin, Germany.
Gosden, Chris, and Yvonne Marshall. 1999. The Cultural Biography of Objects. *World Archaeology* 31(2):169–178.
Gradwohl, David M. 1995. Mildred Mott Wedel 1912–1995. *Plains Anthropologist* 40(154):399–403.
Gradwohl, David M. 1997. Pioneer Woman in Iowa Archaeology and Prairie-Plains Ethnohistory: Mildred Mott Wedel. *Journal of the Iowa Archeological Society* 44:1–6.
Grantham, Larry. 1993. The Illini Village of the Marquette and Jolliet Voyage of 1673. *Missouri Archaeologist* 53:1–20.
Great Plains Action Society. 2020. Riverland Native Voter Project. https://www.greatplainsaction.org/2020-media.
Great Plains Action Society. 2021. Riverland Native Voter Zine: An Indigenous Perspective and Guide on Native Voting. https://www.greatplainsaction.org/_files/ugd/b1ee4e_0cab4293e570473f854477538017650b.pdf.
Green, Michael D. 1983. "We Dance in Opposite Directions": Mesquakie (Fox) Separatism from the Sac and Fox Tribe. *Ethnohistory* 30(3):129–140.
Green, William, ed. 1995. *Oneota Archaeology: Past, Present, and Future.* Report 20. Office of the State Archaeologist, University of Iowa, Iowa City.
Green, William. 2001. Plate 18, Ioway Indian, 1837. In *An Atlas of Early Maps of the American Midwest*, Part II, compiled by W. Raymond Wood, pp. 14–17. Scientific Papers Vol. 29. Illinois State Museum, Springfield.
Green, William. 2014. Identity, Ideology, and the Effigy Mound–Oneota Transformation. *Wisconsin Archeologist* 95(2):44–72.
Green, William, and Shirley J. Schermer. 2015. Introduction: NAGPRA Consultation and Cultural Affiliation in Iowa. In *Oneota Historical Connections: Working Together in Iowa*, edited by Shirley J. Schermer, William Green, Larry J. Zimmerman, Linda Forman, and Robin M. Lillie, pp. 3–8. Report 24. Office of the State Archaeologist, University of Iowa, Iowa City.

Greene, Candace S. 2009. *One Hundred Summers: A Kiowa Calendar Record.* University of Oklahoma Press, Norman.

Greene, Candace S., and Russell Thornton, eds. 2007. *The Year the Stars Fell: Lakota Winter Counts at the Smithsonian.* University of Nebraska Press, Lincoln.

Griffin, James B. 1937. The Archaeological Remains of the Chiwere Sioux. *American Antiquity* 2(3):180–181.

Grim, Ronald E., and Allison K. Lange. 2019. *America Transformed: Mapping the 19th Century.* Norman B. Leventhal Map and Education Center, Boston Public Library, Boston, MA.

Grimm, Thaddeus. 1985. Time-Depth Analysis of Fifteen Siouan Languages. *Siouan and Caddoan Linguistics* 5:12–27.

Grumet, Robert S. 1998. An Interview with Anthony F. C. Wallace. *Ethnohistory* 45(1):103–127.

Gullett, Michelle C. 1994. "If Even a Few Are Reclaimed, the Labor Is Not Lost": William Hamilton's Life among the Iowa and Omaha Indians. Master's thesis, Department of History, University of Nebraska at Omaha.

Gussow, Zachary. 1954. The Contribution of Associations to Evolutionary Changes in Culture in Four African Societies. PhD dissertation, Faculty of Political Science, Columbia University, New York.

Gussow, Zachary. 1974a. An Anthropological Report on Indian Use and Occupancy of Royce Areas 69 and 120. In *Sac, Fox, and Iowa Indians I,* pp. 29–120. Garland, New York.

Gussow, Zachary. 1974b. An Ethnological Report on the Historic Habitat of the Sauk, Fox, and Iowa Indians. In *Sac, Fox, and Iowa Indians I,* pp. 121–184. Garland, New York.

Gussow, Zachary. 1989. *Leprosy, Racism, and Public Health: Social Policy in Chronic Disease Control.* Westview Press, Boulder, CO.

Hall, Robert L. 1962. *The Archeology of Carcajou Point.* 2 vols. University of Wisconsin Press, Madison.

Hall, Robert L. 1993. Red Banks, Oneota and the Winnebago: Views from a Distant Rock. *Wisconsin Archeologist* 74(1–4):10–79.

Hall, Robert L. 1995. Relating the Big Fish and the Big Stone: The Archaeological Identity and Habitat of the Winnebago in 1634. In *Oneota Archaeology: Past, Present, and Future,* edited by William Green, pp. 19–30. Report 20. Office of the State Archaeologist, University of Iowa, Iowa City.

Hall, Robert L. 1997. *An Archaeology of the Soul: North American Indian Belief and Ritual.* University of Illinois Press, Urbana.

Hallowell, A. Irving. 1937. Temporal Orientation in Western Civilization and in a Pre-Literate Society. *American Anthropologist* 39(4):647–670.

Hamilton, William, and Samuel M. Irvin. 1843. *An Elementary Book of the Ioway Language.* Ioway and Sac Mission Press, Indian Territory.

Harjo, Suzan Shown, ed. 2014. *Nation to Nation: Treaties between the United States and American Indian Nations.* National Museum of the American Indian, Smithsonian Institution, Washington, DC.

Harley, J. B. 2001. *The New Nature of Maps: Essays in the History of Cartography*. Johns Hopkins University Press, Baltimore, MD.

Harn, Alan D., and Sally McClure. 2012. *Six Hundred Generations There: Archaeological and Historical Perspectives on Life at Emiquon, the Nature Conservancy and U.S. Fish and Wildlife Service Properties, Fulton County, Illinois*. Reports of Investigations No. 57. Illinois State Museum, Springfield.

Harris, R. Cole, ed. 1987. *Historical Atlas of Canada*, Vol. 1: *From the Beginning to 1800*. University of Toronto Press, Toronto.

Haury-Artz, Chérie. 2014. Iowaville Faunal Analysis. In "Iowaville, a 1765–1820s Báxoje (Ioway) Village," edited by Cynthia L. Peterson. Special issue, *Journal of the Iowa Archeological Society* 61:57–64.

Haury-Artz, Chérie. 2016. *A River of Unrivaled Advantages: Life along the Lower Des Moines River*, 2nd ed. Office of the State Archaeologist, University of Iowa, Iowa City. https://publications.iowa.gov/22701/1/unrivaled-advantages.pdf.

Henige, David. 1974. *The Chronology of Oral Tradition: Quest for a Chimera*. Clarendon Press, Oxford, England.

Henige, David. 2007. "This Is the Place": Putting the Past on a Map. *Journal of Historical Geography* 33(2):237–253.

Henning, Dale R. 1992. Cultural Adaptations to the Prairie Environment: The Ioway Example. In *Proceedings of the Twelfth North American Prairie Conference: Recapturing a Vanishing Heritage*, edited by Daryl D. Smith and Carol A. Jacobs, pp. 193–194. University of Northern Iowa, Cedar Falls.

Henning, Dale R. 1998a. Managing Oneota: A Reiteration and Testing of Contemporary Archeological Taxonomy. *Wisconsin Archeologist* 79(2):9–28.

Henning, Dale R. 1998b. The Oneota Tradition. In *Archaeology on the Great Plains*, edited by W. Raymond Wood, pp. 345–414. University Press of Kansas, Lawrence.

Henning, Dale R. 2003. The Archeology and History of Ioway/Oto Exchange Patterns, 1650–1700. *Journal of the Iowa Archeological Society* 50:199–221.

Henning, Dale R., and Ronald C. Schirmer. 2020. Cahokia and the Northwest Quarter. In *Cahokia in Context: Hegemony and Diaspora*, edited by Charles H. McNutt and Ryan M. Parish, pp. 128–160. University Press of Florida, Gainesville.

Henning, Dale R., and Gerald F. Schnepf. 2014. *Blood Run: The "Silent City."* Iowan Books, Des Moines, IA.

Henning, Dale R., and Thomas D. Thiessen. 2004a. Regional Prehistory. In *Dhegihan and Chiwere Siouans in the Plains: Historical and Archaeological Perspectives*, edited by Dale R. Henning and Thomas D. Thiessen, pp. 381–398. *Plains Anthropologist* 49, Memoir 36.

Henning, Dale R., and Thomas D. Thiessen. 2004b. Summary and Conclusions. In *Dhegihan and Chiwere Siouans in the Plains: Historical and Archaeological Perspectives*, edited by Dale R. Henning and Thomas D. Thiessen, pp. 591–601. *Plains Anthropologist* 49, Memoir 36.

Henning, Joel. 2008. Chicago Marks the Spot for Two Shows about Maps. *Wall Street Journal*, January 15. https://www.wsj.com/articles/SB120036995826490669.

Henry, Thomas R. 1959. Vistas in Science: Strange Madness in Far North. *Evening Star* [Washington, DC], January 5:8.

Herring, Joseph B. 1987. Presbyterian Ethnologists among the Iowa and Sac Indians, 1837–1853. *American Presbyterians* 65(3):195–203.

Herring, Joseph B. 1990. *The Enduring Indians of Kansas: A Century and a Half of Acculturation.* University Press of Kansas, Lawrence.

Herzberg, Ruth, and John Pearson. 2001. *The Guide to Iowa's State Preserves.* University of Iowa Press, Iowa City.

Hicks, Frederick Charles. 1904. A Biographical Sketch of Thomas Hutchins. In *A Topographical Description of Virginia, Pennsylvania, and North Carolina* by Thomas Hutchins, edited by Frederick Charles Hicks, pp. 7–51. Burrows Brothers, Cleveland.

Hill, Edward E. 1974. *The Office of Indian Affairs, 1824–1880: Historical Sketches.* Clearwater, New York.

Hisatake, Tetsuya. 1986. Indigenous Maps, Cosmology, and Spatial Recognition of the North American Indian: With Special Reference to the Ojibway around Lake Superior. In *Cosmology, Epistemology and the History of Geography,* edited by Hideki Nozawa, pp. 1–25. Institute of Geography, Kyushu University, Fukuoka, Japan.

Hoig, Stan. 2008. *The Chouteaus: First Family of the Fur Trade.* University of New Mexico Press, Albuquerque.

Hollinger, R. Eric. 2015. Archaeology and Ethnohistory in Northeastern Iowa. In *Oneota Historical Connections: Working Together in Iowa,* edited by Shirley J. Schermer, William Green, Larry J. Zimmerman, Linda Forman, and Robin M. Lillie, pp. 55–69. Report 24. Office of the State Archaeologist, University of Iowa, Iowa City.

Hollinger, R. Eric. 2018. Conflict and Culture Change on the Plains: The Oneota Example. In *Archaeological Perspectives of Warfare on the Great Plains,* edited by Andrew J. Clark and Douglas B. Bamforth, pp. 267–274. University Press of Colorado, Louisville, CO.

Hollinger, R. Eric, and David W. Benn, eds. 1998. "Oneota Taxonomy: Papers from the Oneota Symposium of the 54th Plains Anthropological Conference." Special issue, *Wisconsin Archeologist* 79(2).

Holm, Tom, J. Diane Pearson, and Ben Chavis. 2003. Peoplehood: A Model for the Extension of Sovereignty in American Indian Studies. *Wicazo Sa Review* 18(1):7–24.

Hoover, H. D. 2004. *The History of Iowa in the Art of Maps* (exhibit guide). University of Iowa Museum of Art, Iowa City.

Hull, Kathleen L. 2005. Process, Perception and Practice: Time Perspectivism in Yosemite Native Demography. *Journal of Anthropological Archaeology* 24(4):354–377.

Hutchins, Thomas. 1778. A New Map of the Western Parts of Virginia, Pennsylvania, Maryland, and North Carolina. . . . In *A Topographical Description of Virginia, Pennsylvania, and North Carolina. . . .* J. Almon, London.

Hyde, Anne F. 2022. *Born of Lakes and Plains: Mixed-Descent Peoples and the Making of the American West.* Norton, New York.

Indian Land Tenure Foundation. 2024. U.S. Treaty Search. http://portal.treatysigners.org/us/SitePages/Signature%20Search.aspx.

Indigenous Mapping Collective. 2024. https://www.indigenousmaps.com/.

Ingold, Tim. 1993. The Temporality of the Landscape. *World Archaeology* 25(2):152–174.
Iowa Department of Natural Resources. 2000. *Iowa: Portrait of the Land.* Iowa Department of Natural Resources, Des Moines. https://publications.iowa.gov/29543/1/Iowa_Portrait_of_the_Land.pdf.
Iowa Department of Natural Resources. 2024. Water Trail Context. https://www.iowadnr.gov/media/7051/download.
Iowa Tribe of Kansas and Nebraska. 2023. *Náwo Wapánagun Hinmányiwi: Pathways to Climate Resilience.* Iowa Tribe of Kansas and Nebraska, White Cloud, KS. https://publuu.com/flip-book/199107/482028.
Iowa Tribe of Kansas and Nebraska. 2024a. https://iowatribeofkansasandnebraska.com/.
Iowa Tribe of Kansas and Nebraska. 2024b. Treaties. https://iowatribeofkansasandnebraska.com/government/treaties/.
Iowa Tribe of Oklahoma. 2024. https://iowanation.org/.
Ioway Cultural Institute. 2024a. https://ioway.nativeweb.org/.
Ioway Cultural Institute. 2024b. Language: On the Ioway Language. http://ioway.nativeweb.org/language/onlanguage.htm.
Irvin, S. M., and W. Hamilton. 1853. Iowa and Sac Tribes. In *Information Respecting the History, Condition and Prospects of the Indian Tribes of the United States,* Part III, by Henry R. Schoolcraft, pp. 259–276. Lippincott, Grambo, Philadelphia.
Jackson, Rachel, and Phil Bratta. 2020. Decolonial Directions: Rivers, Relationships, and Realities of Community Engagement on Indigenous Lands. *Journal of Multimodal Rhetorics* 4(1):50–86.
Jenkinson, Clay, ed. 2018. "A Major Discovery: The Arikara Too Né's Lewis and Clark Map." Special Issue, *We Proceeded On* 44(2):6–39.
Jensen, Richard E. 1971. National Register of Historic Places Inventory-Nomination Form, Yutan Site (25 SD 1). Manuscript on file, Nebraska State Historical Society, Lincoln.
Jensen, Richard E. 1998. *The Fontenelle and Cabanné* Trading Posts: The History and Archeology of Two Missouri River Sites, 1822–1838. Publications in Anthropology No. 11. Nebraska State Historical Society, Lincoln.
Johnson, Leslie Main. 2010. *Trail of Story, Traveller's Path: Reflections on Ethnoecology and Landscape.* AU Press, Athabasca University, Edmonton.
Johnson, Linda. 2009. *The Kandik Map.* University of Alaska Press, Fairbanks.
Jones, Dorothy V. 1982. *License for Empire: Colonialism by Treaty in Early America.* University of Chicago Press, Chicago.
Joyce, Rosemary A. 2019. Materialities and Practices of Persistence: Indigenous Survivance in the Face of Settler Societies. In *Indigenous Persistence in the Colonized Americas: Material and Documentary Perspectives on Entanglement,* edited by Heather Law Pezzarossi and Russell N. Sheptak, pp. 187–206. University of New Mexico Press, Albuquerque.
Joyce, Rosemary A., and Susan D. Gillespie, eds. 2015. *Things in Motion: Object Itineraries in Anthropological Practice.* School for Advanced Research Press, Santa Fe, NM.
Jung, Patrick J. 2016. Lonely Sentinel: A Military History of Fort Madison, 1808–1813. *Annals of Iowa* 75(3):201–233.

Jung, Patrick J. 2018. *The Misunderstood Mission of Jean Nicolet: Uncovering the Story of the 1634 Journey.* Wisconsin Historical Society Press, Madison.

Kane, Lucile M., June D. Holmquist, and Carolyn Gilman, eds. 1978. *The Northern Expeditions of Stephen H. Long: The Journals of 1817 and 1823 and Related Documents.* Minnesota Historical Society Press, St. Paul.

Kansas Humanities Council. 1998. Iowa Tribe Explores Its Roots through Archeology. *Kansas Humanities Council News*, Spring, p. 3.

Kathryn M. Buder Center for American Indian Studies. 2021. *Indigenous Land, Peoples and History of Missouri Brief.* Washington University, St. Louis, MO. https://bpb-us-w2.wpmucdn.com/sites.wustl.edu/dist/a/1072/files/2021/10/Indigenous-Land-Peoples-and-History-of-MO.pdf.

KCCI (Des Moines). 2022. Project Community: Iowa Tribe Receives Land Nearly 2 Centuries after Treaty Forced Them Out. November 30. https://www.kcci.com/article/johnson-county-project-community-iowa-tribe-receives-land-nearly-2-centuries-after-treaty-forced-them-out/42101298.

Kehoe, Alice Beck. 2007. Introduction to the Bison Books Edition. In *Mythology of the Blackfoot Indians* by Clark Wissler and D. C. Duvall, 2nd ed., pp. xiii–xli. University of Nebraska Press, Lincoln.

Kehoe, Alice Beck. 2014a. Manifest Destiny as the Order of Nature. In *Nature and Antiquities: The Making of Archaeology in the Americas,* edited by Philip L. Kohl, Irina Podgorny, and Stefanie Gänger, pp. 186–201. University of Arizona Press, Tucson.

Kehoe, Alice Beck. 2014b. *A Passion for the True and Just: Felix and Lucy Kramer Cohen and the Indian New Deal.* University of Arizona Press, Tucson.

Kelderman, Frank. 2019a. *Authorized Agents: Publication and Diplomacy in the Era of Indian Removal.* State University of New York Press, Albany.

Kelderman, Frank. 2019b. Na'hjeNing'e's Rivers: Indigenous Maps, Diplomacy, and the Writing of Ioway Space. *Altre Modernità* 22:43–54.

Kelderman, Frank. 2020. Review of *How the West Was Drawn. Imago Mundi* 72(1):81–82.

Keyes, Charles Reuben. 1927. Prehistoric Man in Iowa. *The Palimpsest* 8(6):185–229.

Keyser, James D., and Michael A. Klassen. 2001. *Plains Indian Rock Art.* University of Washington Press, Seattle.

Kilen, Mike. 2016. The North Raccoon: A River of Controversy and Undiscovered Beauty. *Des Moines Register*, June 16. https://www.desmoinesregister.com/story/money/agriculture/2016/06/16/north-raccoon-river-controversy-and-undiscovered-beauty/85039642/.

Kivett, Marvin F. 1940. Oto Indians Village Sites. Manuscript on file, Nebraska State Historical Society, Lincoln.

Kopytoff, Igor. 1986. The Cultural Biography of Things: Commoditization as a Process. In *The Social Life of Things: Commodities in Cultural Perspective,* edited by Arjun Appadurai, pp. 64–92. Cambridge University Press, Cambridge, England.

Kretzler, Ian, and Sara Gonzalez. 2023. On Listening and Telling Anew: Possibilities for Archaeologies of Survivance. *American Anthropologist* 125(2):310–321.

Krus, Anthony M., John D. Richards, and Robert J. Jeske. 2022. Chronology for Mississippian and Oneota Occupations at Aztalan and the Lake Koshkonong Locality. *American Antiquity* 87(1):124–141.

Kurz, Rudolph Friederich. 1937. *Journal of Rudolph Friederich Kurz: An Account of His Experiences among Fur Traders and American Indians on the Mississippi and Upper Missouri Rivers during the Years 1846 to 1852*, translated by Myrtis Jarrell, edited by J. N. B. Hewitt. Bulletin 115. Bureau of American Ethnology, Smithsonian Institution, Washington, DC.

Kuwanwisiwma, Leigh J., and T. J. Ferguson 2009. *Hopitutskwa* and *Ang Kuktota*: The Role of Archaeological Sites in Defining Hopi Cultural Landscapes. In *The Archaeology of Meaningful Places*, edited by Brenda J. Bowser and María Nieves Zedeño, pp. 90–106. University of Utah Press, Salt Lake City.

La Flesche, Francis, 1884. Letter dated January 15, 1883. In *Sixteenth and Seventeenth Annual Reports of the Trustees of the Peabody Museum of American Archaeology and Ethnology* 3:179–181.

LAGenWeb Archives. 2005. Obituaries, Orleans Parish, Louisiana. http://files.usgw archives.net/la/orleans/obits/1/g-17.txt.

Laluk, Nicholas C. 2024. Place as Indigenized Archaeological Knowledge. In *Indigenizing Archaeology: Putting Theory into Practice*, edited by Emily C. Van Alst and Carlton Shield Chief Gover, pp. 82–95. University Press of Florida, Gainesville.

Lankford, George E. 2017. Nuances of Memory: Historical Legend vs. Legendary History. In *Forging Southeastern Identities: Social Archaeology, Ethnohistory, and Folklore of the Mississippian to Early History South*, edited by Gregory A. Waselkov and Marvin T. Smith, pp. 205–219. University of Alabama Press, Tuscaloosa.

Lappas, Thomas J. 2006. "A Perfect Apollo": Keokuk and Sac Leadership during the Removal Era. In *The Boundaries between Us: Natives and Newcomers along the Frontiers of the Old Northwest Territory, 1750–1850*, edited by Daniel P. Barr, pp. 219–235. Kent State University Press, Kent, OH.

Lee, Robert. 2022. "A Better View of the Country": A Missouri Settlement Map by William Clark. *William and Mary Quarterly* 79(1):89–120.

Lelièvre, Michelle A., and Maureen E. Marshall. 2015. "Because Life It Selfe Is But Motion": Toward an Anthropology of Mobility. *Anthropological Theory* 15(4):434–471.

Lepler, Jessica M. 2013. *The Many Panics of 1837: People, Politics, and the Creation of a Transatlantic Financial Crisis.* Cambridge University Press, New York.

Lewis, G. Malcolm. 1979. The Indigenous Maps and Mapping of North American Indians. *Map Collector* 9:25–32.

Lewis, G. Malcolm. 1980. Indian Maps. In *Old Trails and New Directions: Papers of the Third North American Fur Trade Conference*, edited by Carol M. Judd and Arthur J. Ray, pp. 9–23. University of Toronto Press, Toronto.

Lewis, G. Malcolm. 1984. Indian Maps: Their Place in the History of Plains Cartography. *Great Plains Quarterly* 4(2):91–108.

Lewis, G. Malcolm. 1987. Indian Maps: Their Place in the History of Plains Cartography. In *Mapping the North American Plains: Essays in the History of Cartography*, edited by

Frederick C. Luebke, Frances W. Kaye, and Gary E. Moulton, pp. 63–80. University of Oklahoma Press, Norman.

Lewis, G. Malcolm. 1996. An Early Map on Skin of the Area Later to Become Indiana and Illinois. *British Library Journal* 22(1):66–87.

Lewis, G. Malcolm, ed. 1998a. *Cartographic Encounters: Perspectives on Native American Mapmaking and Map Use.* University of Chicago Press, Chicago.

Lewis, G. Malcolm. 1998b. Frontier Encounters in the Field. In *Cartographic Encounters: Perspectives on Native American Mapmaking and Map Use,* edited by G. Malcolm Lewis, pp. 9–32. University of Chicago Press, Chicago.

Lewis, G. Malcolm. 1998c. Maps, Mapmaking, and Map Use by Native North Americans. In *The History of Cartography,* Vol. 2, Book 3: *Cartography in the Traditional African, American, Arctic, Australian, and Pacific Societies,* edited by David Woodward and G. Malcolm Lewis, pp. 51–182. University of Chicago Press, Chicago.

Lewis, G. Malcolm. 2006. Intracultural Mapmaking by First Nations Peoples in the Great Lakes Region: A Historical Review. *Michigan Historical Review* 32(1):1–17.

Lewis, G. Malcolm. 2014. Postscript: Reflections on a "Five-Street" Journey—ca. 1970–1985. In *Mapping Native America: Cartographic Interactions between Indigenous Peoples, Government, and Academia,* Vol. 3: *Cartography and Indigenous Autonomy,* edited by Daniel G. Cole and Imre Sutton, pp. 331–349. Privately published, San Bernardino, CA.

Lewis, G. Malcolm, and David Woodward, eds. 1998. *The History of Cartography,* Vol. 2, Book 3: *Cartography in the Traditional African, American, Arctic, Australian, and Pacific Societies.* University of Chicago Press, Chicago. https://press.uchicago.edu/books/hoc/HOC_V2_B3/Volume2_Book3.html.

Lewis, Hugh M. 2004. *Robidoux Chronicles: French-Indian Ethnoculture of the Trans-Mississippi West.* Trafford, Victoria, BC.

Lilley, Ian. 2006. Archaeology, Diaspora and Decolonization. *Journal of Social Archaeology* 6(1):28–47.

Limerick, Patricia Nelson. 1987. *The Legacy of Conquest: The Unbroken Past of the American West.* Norton, New York.

Lockard, Ray W., Edward Riley, and George Hamilton. 1921. *Iowa Corn Song* (sheet music). Riley, Des Moines, IA.

Louis, Renee Pualani, Jay T. Johnson, and Albertus Hadi Pramono, eds. 2012. "Indigenous Cartographies and Counter-Mapping." Special Issue, *Cartographica* 47(2):77–134.

Ludwickson, John, Donald Blakeslee, and John O'Shea. 1987. *Missouri National Recreational River: Native American Cultural Resources.* Publications in Anthropology No. 3. Wichita State University, Wichita, KS.

Lurie, Nancy Oestreich. 1978a. The Indian Claims Commission. *Annals of the American Academy of Political and Social Science* 436:97–110.

Lurie, Nancy Oestreich. 1978b. Winnebago. In *Handbook of North American Indians,* Vol. 15: *Northeast,* edited by Bruce G. Trigger, pp. 690–707. Smithsonian Institution, Washington, DC.

Lurie, Nancy Oestreich. 1985. Epilog. In *Irredeemable America: The Indians' Estate and Land Claims*, edited by Imre Sutton, pp. 363–382. University of New Mexico Press, Albuquerque.

Lurie, Nancy Oestreich, and Patrick J. Jung. 2009. *The Nicolet Corrigenda: New France Revisited.* Waveland Press, Long Grove, IL.

Lynchburg Virginian. 1837. Indian Council—Signing of Treaties. October 30:4.

Maher, Kimberly. 2014. Ioway No Heart Map of 1837. https://kamaher.wordpress.com/ioway-no-heart-map-of-1837/.

Mandel, Rolfe, and R. Peter Winham. 1992. *A Phase II Evaluation of the North 25th Street to North 16th Street Connector Road in Council Bluffs, Pottawattamie County, Iowa.* Omaha, NE and Sioux Falls, SD. Report on file, Office of the State Archaeologist, University of Iowa, Iowa City.

Mansberger, Floyd. 2013. *Phase I Archaeological Survey of the Proposed 11th Street Commercial Park, Rock Island, Illinois.* Fever River Research, Springfield, IL.

Marchitello, Howard. 1994. Political Maps: The Production of Cartography and Chorography in Early Modern England. In *Cultural Artifacts and the Production of Meaning*, edited by Margaret J. M. Ezell and Katherine O'Brien O'Keeffe, pp. 13–40. University of Michigan Press, Ann Arbor.

Marquette University. 2016. Marquette University to Honor Outstanding Graduates at Alumni National Awards Weekend, April 28–30. https://www.marquette.edu/news-center/2016/marquette-university-to-honor-outstanding-graduates-at-alumni-national-awards-weekend.php.

Marshalltown [Iowa] Evening Times-Republican. 1918. Unveil Monument to Old Indian Chief. June 21:8.

Mason, Kevin. 2023. Iowa History Daily: October 7—an Ioway Map of Iowa. https://www.notesoniowa.com/post/iowa-history-daily-october-7-an-ioway-map-of-iowa.

Mason, Ronald J. 2000. Archaeology and Native American Oral Traditions. *American Antiquity* 65(2):239–266.

Mason, Ronald J. 2006. *Inconstant Companions: Archaeology and North American Indian Oral Traditions.* University of Alabama Press, Tuscaloosa.

Mattison, Ray H. 1958. The Indian Frontier on the Upper Missouri in 1865. *Nebraska History* 39(3):241–266.

Mazrim, Robert F. 2011. *At Home in the Illinois Country: French Colonial Domestic Site Archaeology in the Midwest 1730–1800.* Studies in Archaeology No. 9. Illinois State Archaeological Survey, Urbana.

McDermott, John Francis. 1959. *The Art of Seth Eastman.* Smithsonian Institution, Washington, DC.

McGee, W. J. 1891. The Pleistocene History of Northeastern Iowa. In *Eleventh Annual Report of the United States Geological Survey to the Secretary of the Interior 1889–'90, Part I—Geology*, by J. W. Powell, pp. 188–577. Government Printing Office, Washington, DC.

McGlade, James. 1995. Archaeology and the Ecodynamics of Human-Modified Landscapes. *Antiquity* 69(262):113–132.

McInnis, Henry. 1964. Psychiatry Cuts Stigma of Leprosy. *News and Observer* [Raleigh, North Carolina], April 24:21.

McKenney, Thomas L., and James Hall. 1838a. *History of the Indian Tribes of North America, with Biographical Sketches and Anecdotes of the Principal Chiefs*, Vol. 1. Frederick W. Greenough, Philadelphia.

McKenney, Thomas L., and James Hall. 1838b. *History of the Indian Tribes of North America, with Biographical Sketches and Anecdotes of the Principal Chiefs*, Vol. 2. Frederick W. Greenough, Philadelphia.

McKusick, Marshall B. 2009. Fort Madison, 1808–1813. In *Frontier Forts of Iowa: Indians, Traders, and Soldiers, 1682–1862*, edited by William E. Whittaker, pp. 55–74. University of Iowa Press, Iowa City.

McLeod, Reggie. 1997. Oneota: What's in a Name? *Big River* 5(1):1–3.

Meadows, William C. 2008. *Kiowa Ethnogeography*. University of Texas Press, Austin.

Merrill, Moses. 1835. *First Ioway Reading Book*. Shawnee Baptist Mission, Indian Territory.

Miller, Peter N., and Soon Kai Poh, eds. 2022. *Conserving Active Matter*. Bard Graduate Center, New York.

Minc, Leah D. 1986. Scarcity and Survival: The Role of Oral Tradition in Mediating Subsistence Crises. *Journal of Anthropological Archaeology* 5(1):39–113.

Miner, William Harvey. 1911. *The Iowa*. Torch Press, Cedar Rapids, IA.

Mitchell, Martin D. 2014. Using Mental Map Principles to Interpret American Indian Cartography. *Journal of Geography* 113(1):3–9.

Monmonier, Mark. 1996. *How to Lie with Maps*, 2nd ed. University of Chicago Press, Chicago.

Morrissey, Robert Michael. 2022. *People of the Ecotone: Environment and Indigenous Power at the Center of Early America*. University of Washington Press, Seattle.

Mott, Frank Luther. 1957. Pronunciation of Iowa. *The Palimpsest* 38(3):101–105.

Mott, Mildred. 1938. The Relation of Historic Indian Tribes to Archaeological Manifestations in Iowa. *Iowa Journal of History and Politics* 36(3):227–314.

Moulton, Gary, ed. 2024. *Journals of the Lewis and Clark Expedition Online*. University of Nebraska Press, Lincoln. https://lewisandclarkjournals.unl.edu/.

National Intelligencer [Washington, DC]. 1837. Indian Council. October 9:3.

National Intelligencer [Washington, DC]. 1837. Sioux Indians. October 11:3.

National Park Service. 2022. Effigy Mounds National Monument Becomes a Tribal Sister Park to Ioway Tribal National Park. November 22. https://www.nps.gov/efmo/learn/news/2022-11-28-tribal-sister-park.htm.

Native American Rights Fund. 1976. *Index to Indian Claims Commission Decisions, Includes 1976 Supplement*. Native American Rights Fund, Boulder, CO.

Nebraska Public Media. 2024. The Yutan and Eagle Ridge Sites. https://nebraskastudies.org/en/1500-1799/emergence-of-historic-tribes/yutan-eagle-ridge/.

Nelson, Stanley. 2018. *Chickasaw Historical Atlas*. Chickasaw Press, Ada, OK.

Nicollet, Joseph N. 1842. *Map of the Hydrographical Basin of the Upper Mississippi River*. U.S. Senate, Washington, DC.

Nielsen, Astrid, and Iris Edenheiser, eds. 2013. *Tecumseh, Keokuk, Black Hawk: Portrayals of Native Americans in Times of Treaties and Removals.* Arnoldsche Verlagsanstalt, Stuttgart, Germany.

Nieves Zedeño, María, and Robert Christopher Basaldú. 2004. *Pipestone National Monument, Minnesota: Native American Cultural Affiliation and Traditional Association Study.* Bureau of Applied Research in Anthropology, University of Arizona, Tucson.

Nieves Zedeño, María, and Brenda J. Bowser. 2009. The Archaeology of Meaningful Places. In *The Archaeology of Meaningful Places,* edited by Brenda J. Bowser and María Nieves Zedeño, pp. 1–14. University of Utah Press, Salt Lake City.

Nieves Zedeño, María, Kacy Hollenback, and Calvin Grinnell. 2009. From Path to Myth: Journeys and the Naturalization of Territorial Identity along the Missouri River. In *Landscapes of Movement: Trails, Paths, and Roads in Anthropological Perspective,* edited by James E. Snead, Clark L. Erickson, and J. Andrew Darling, pp. 106–132. University of Pennsylvania Museum of Archaeology and Anthropology, Philadelphia.

Niles' National Register [Washington, DC]. 1837. The Indians at Boston. November 11:166–167.

Nolan, David J. 1992. The Ioway in Illinois? An Historic Archaeological Approach. Manuscript on file, Office of the State Archaeologist, University of Iowa, Iowa City.

Norman B. Leventhal Map and Education Center. 2019. America Transformed: Mapping the 19th Century (exhibition). Boston Public Library, May 4, 2019–May 10, 2020. https://collections.leventhalmap.org/exhibits/25.

O'Briant, Kevin. 2018. Too Né's World: The Arikara Map and Native American Cartography. *We Proceeded On* 44(2):6–15.

Oetelaar, Gerald A., and David Meyer. 2006. Movement and Native American Landscapes: A Comparative Approach. *Plains Anthropologist* 51(199):355–374.

Office of Indian Affairs. 1837. *Annual Report of the Commissioner of Indian Affairs Transmitted with the Message of the President at the Opening of the 2d Session of the 25th Congress 1837–1838.* Office of Indian Affairs, Washington, DC.

Office of the State Archaeologist. 2007a. *Báxoje*: Maps, Material Culture, and Memory: On the Trail of the Ioway. University of Iowa. https://digital.lib.uiowa.edu/islandora/object/ui%3A29586.

Office of the State Archaeologist. 2007b. *Iowa Archaeology Month 2007—Maps, Material Culture, and Memory: On the Trail of the Ioway* (brochure). Office of the State Archaeologist, University of Iowa, Iowa City.

Office of the State Archaeologist. 2019. About HILD. University of Iowa. http://www.iowahild.com/about-hild.html.

Office of the State Archaeologist. 2021. 1837 Ioway Map. University of Iowa. https://iowaarchaeology.org/media/ioway/1837_Ioway_Map.html.

Office of the State Archaeologist. 2022. Iowa Ancient Trails Project. University of Iowa. http://www.uiowacar.com/osaglotrails/ancient-trails-tours-home/about-the-project.

Office of the State Archaeologist. 2024. Community Program Menu: The 1837 Ioway Map. University of Iowa. https://archaeology.uiowa.edu/services/education-and-interpretation/public-programming#the-1837-ioway-map.

Office of the State Archaeologist. 2025. A Tribute to Lance Foster of the Iowa Tribe of Kansas and Nebraska. January 14. https://archaeology.uiowa.edu/news/2025/01/tribute-lance-foster-iowa-tribe-kansas-and-nebraska.

Oklahoma State University Library Digital Collections. 2024. Indian Claims Commission Decisions. https://dc.library.okstate.edu/digital/collection/p17279coll10.

Olshin, Benjamin B. 2022. Indigenous Mapping: Cultural and Psychological Sources. *The Portolan* 114:22–35.

Olson, Greg. 2005. Navigating the White Road: White Cloud's Struggle to Lead the Ioway along the Path of Acculturation. *Missouri Historical Review* 99(2):93–114.

Olson, Greg. 2008. *The Ioway in Missouri*. University of Missouri Press, Columbia.

Olson, Greg. 2014. *Great Walker, Ioway Leader*. Truman State University Press, Kirksville, MO.

Olson, Greg. 2016. *Ioway Life: Reservation and Reform 1837–1860*. University of Oklahoma Press, Norman.

Olson, Greg. 2024. The Ioways. In *Missouri Encyclopedia*, State Historical Society of Missouri. https://missouriencyclopedia.org/groupsorganizations/ioways.

O'Neal, Charles F. 1958. The Ethnohistory of the Ioway. Master's thesis, Department of Sociology and Anthropology, State University of Iowa, Iowa City.

O'Shea, John M., and John Ludwickson. 1992. *Archaeology and Ethnohistory of the Omaha Indians: The Big Village Site*. University of Nebraska Press, Lincoln.

Ostler, Jeffrey. 2019. *Surviving Genocide: Native Nations and the United States from the American Revolution to Bleeding Kansas*. Yale University Press, New Haven, CT.

O'Sullivan, John L. 1845. Annexation. *United States Magazine and Democratic Review* 17(1):5–10.

Our Iowa Heritage. 2022. Honoring the Ioway Tribe of Johnson County. https://ouriowaheritage.com/honoring-the-ioway-tribe-of-johnson-county/.

Overstreet, David F. 1995. The Eastern Wisconsin Oneota Regional Continuity. In *Oneota Archaeology: Past, Present, and Future*, edited by William Green, pp. 33–64. Report 20. Office of the State Archaeologist, University of Iowa, Iowa City.

Oxford English Dictionary. 1971. *The Compact Edition of the Oxford English Dictionary*. Oxford University Press, Oxford, England.

Oxford University Press. 2024. Oxford Languages. https://languages.oup.com/google-dictionary-en/.

Palmer, Mark H. 2016. Kiowa Storytelling around a Map. In *The Digital Arts and Humanities: Neogeography, Social Media and Big Data Integrations and Applications*, edited by Charles Travis and Alexander von Lünen, pp. 63–73. Springer, Switzerland.

Palmer, Mark H., Sarah Frost, Grace Martinez, and Lasya Venigalla. 2021. Art and Argument: Indigitization of a Kiowa Historical Map for Teaching and Research. *ISPRS: International Journal of Geo-Information* 10:746. https://doi.org/10.3390/ijgi10110746.

Parks, Douglas R., and Robert L. Rankin. 2001. Siouan Languages. In *Plains*, Vol. 13: *Handbook of North American Indians*, edited by Raymond J. DeMallie, pp. 94–114. Smithsonian Institution, Washington, DC.

Pearce, Christina E., and William Green. 2014. Plant Remains from Iowaville. In "Iowaville, a 1765–1820s Báxoje (Ioway) Village," edited by Cynthia L. Peterson. Special issue, *Journal of the Iowa Archeological Society* 61:47–56.

Pearce, Margaret Wickens. 2014. The Last Piece Is You. *Cartographic Journal* 51(2):107–122.

Pearce, Margaret Wickens, and Renee Pualani Louis. 2008. Mapping Indigenous Depth of Place. *American Indian Culture and Research Journal* 32(3):107–126.

Pepperl, Robert E., and John R. Bozell. 2018. The Long Expedition and Engineer Cantonment. In *Archeological Investigations at Engineer Cantonment: Winter Quarters of the 1819–1820 Long Expedition, Eastern Nebraska*, edited by John R. Bozell, Gayle F. Carlson, and Robert E. Pepperl, pp. 9–48. Publications in Anthropology No. 12. History Nebraska, Lincoln.

Peterson, Cynthia L. 2009. Historical Tribes and Early Forts. In *Frontier Forts of Iowa: Indians, Traders, and Soldiers, 1682–1862*, edited by William E. Whittaker, pp. 12–29. University of Iowa Press, Iowa City.

Peterson, Cynthia L., ed. 2012. *Archaeological Study of Iowaville, a 1765–1824 Ioway (Báxoje) Village in Van Buren County, Iowa*. Contract Completion Report 1956. Office of the State Archaeologist, University of Iowa, Iowa City.

Peterson, Cynthia L., ed. 2014. "Iowaville, a 1765–1820s Báxoje (Ioway) Village." Special issue, *Journal of the Iowa Archeological Society* 61:1–77.

Pettrich, Ferdinand. 1842. *Portraits of Distinguished Indians from Several Tribes Who Visited Washington in 1837*. Edward Weber, Baltimore, MD.

Pieratos, Nikki A., Sarah S. Manning, and Nick Tilse. 2021. Land Back: A Meta Narrative to Help Indigenous People Show Up as Movement Leaders. *Leadership* 17(1):47–61.

Plank, Pryor. 1908. The Iowa, Sac and Fox Indian Mission and Its Missionaries, Rev. Samuel M. Irvin and Wife. *Transactions of the Kansas State Historical Society* 10:312–325.

Pond, G. H. 1852. Iowa Indians and Mounds. *Annals of the Minnesota Historical Society*, 1852:23–24.

Prior, Jean C. 1991. *Landforms of Iowa*. University of Iowa Press, Iowa City.

Prucha, Francis Paul. 1995. *The Great Father: The United States Government and the American Indians*, Vol. 1. University of Nebraska Press, Lincoln.

Public Ledger [Philadelphia]. 1837. Indians. October 27:1.

Radin, Paul. 1923. The Winnebago Tribe. In *Thirty-Seventh Annual Report of the Bureau of American Ethnology, 1915–1916*, pp. 35–560. Smithsonian Institution, Washington, DC.

Rankin, Robert L. 2015. Oneota, Historical Linguistics, and the Ioway, Otoe-Missouria, and Winnebago Peoples. In *Oneota Historical Connections: Working Together in Iowa*, edited by Shirley J. Schermer, William Green, Larry J. Zimmerman, Linda Forman, and Robin M. Lillie, pp. 103–112. Report 24. Office of the State Archaeologist, University of Iowa, Iowa City.

Rankin, Robert L. 2021. On Siouan Chronology. In *Siouan Languages and Linguistics: Selected Papers by Robert L. Rankin*, edited by David S. Rood and John P. Boyle, pp. 262–291. Brill, Leiden.

Ray, Arthur J. 2016. *Aboriginal Rights Claims and the Making and Remaking of History*. McGill-Queen's University Press, Montreal.

Reddin, Paul. 1999. *Wild West Shows*. University of Illinois Press, Urbana.

Richardson, William P. 1852. Report No. 22 to D. D. Mitchell, September 30, 1852. In *Annual Report of the Commissioner of Indian Affairs for the Year 1852*, pp. 70–72. U.S. Senate, Washington, DC.

Ritterbush, Lauren W. 2002. Drawn by the Bison: Late Prehistoric Native Migration into the Central Plains. *Great Plains Quarterly* 22(4):259–270.

Roberts, Timothy E., and Christy S. Rickers. 1999. Historical Iowa Settlement in the Grand River Basin of Iowa and Missouri. *Missouri Archaeologist* 57:1–36.

Robeson, George F. 1926. Fur Trade in Early Iowa. *The Palimpsest* 6(1):14–29.

Rogers, Richard, and Oscar Hammerstein II. 1945. All I Owe Ioway. In *State Fair* (film). 20th Century Fox, Los Angeles.

Rosenthal, Harvey D. 1985. Indian Claims and the American Conscience: A Brief History of the Indian Claims Commission. In *Irredeemable America: The Indians' Estate and Land Claims*, edited by Imre Sutton, pp. 35–70. University of New Mexico Press, Albuquerque.

Rose-Redwood, Reuben, Natchee Blu Barnd, Annita Hetoevėhotohke'e Lucchesi, Sharon Dias, and Wil Patrick, eds. 2020. "Decolonizing the Map." Special Issue, *Cartographica* 55(3):151–214.

Rouse, Anderson. 2012. Re-Examining American Indian Time Consciousness. https://www.academia.edu/7329888/ReexaminingAmericanIndianTimeConsciousness.

Rowntree, Lester B. 1996. The Cultural Landscape Concept in American Historical Geography. In *Concepts in Human Geography*, edited by Carville Earle, Kent Mathewson, and Martin S. Kenzer, pp. 127–160. Rowman and Littlefield, Lanham, MD.

Royce, Charles C. 1899. Indian Land Cessions in the United States. In *Eighteenth Annual Report of the Bureau of American Ethnology to the Secretary of the Smithsonian Institution, 1897–'97*, Part II, by J. W. Powell, pp. 521–964. Smithsonian Institution, Washington, DC.

Rundle, Kelly, and Tammy Rundle, dirs. 2007–2013. *Lost Nation: The Ioway*. 3-part documentary film series. Fourth Wall Films, Moline, IL.

Ruoff, A. Lavonne Brown. 2005. Eastman's Maternal Ancestry: Letter from Charles Alexander Eastman to H. M. Hitchcock, September 8, 1927. *Studies in American Indian Literature* 17(2):10–17.

Ryden, Kent. 1993. *Mapping the Invisible Landscape: Folklore, Writing, and the Sense of Place.* University of Iowa Press, Iowa City.

Saunt, Claudio. 2020. *Unworthy Republic: The Dispossession of Native Americans and the Road to Indian Territory.* Norton, New York.

Scherer, Joanna C., and Thierry Veyrié. 2024. A Foot in the Field, a Foot in the Archive, and a Keen Editorial Eye: The Making of an Ethnohistorian. In *Great Plains Ethnohistory: New Interdisciplinary Approaches*, edited by Rani-Henrik Andersson, Logan Sutton, and Thierry Veyrié, pp. 24–54. University of Nebraska Press, Lincoln.

Schermer, Shirley J., William Green, Larry J. Zimmerman, Linda Forman, and Robin J. Lillie, eds. 2015. *Oneota Historical Connections: Working Together in Iowa.* Report 24. Office of the State Archaeologist, University of Iowa, Iowa City.

Schoolcraft, Henry R. 1845. *Oneóta, or Characteristics of the Red Race in America.* Wiley and Putnam, New York.

Schoolcraft, Henry R. 1853. *Information Respecting the History, Condition and Prospects of the Indian Tribes of the United States,* Part III. Lippincott, Grambo, Philadelphia.

Schwartz, Saul. 2008. Iowaville in Perspectives: Expansive Ethnohistory at an Ioway Indian Village. Honors thesis, Departments of Anthropology and History, Beloit College, Beloit, WI.

Schwartz, Saul. 2012. Iowaville Historic Context. In *Archaeological Study of Iowaville, a 1765–1824 Ioway (Baxoje) Village in Van Buren County, Iowa,* edited by Cynthia L. Peterson, pp. 4–32. Contract Completion Report 1956. Office of the State Archaeologist, University of Iowa, Iowa City.

Schwartz, Saul. 2018a. The Predicament of Language and Culture: Advocacy, Anthropology, and Dormant Language Communities. *Linguistic Anthropology* 28(3):332–355.

Schwartz, Saul. 2018b. Writing Chiwere: Orthography, Literacy, and Language Revitalization. *Language and Communication* 61(2):75–87.

Schwartz, Saul. 2021. Legacy Materials and Cultural Facework: Obscenity and Bad Words in Siouan Language Documentation. *Language Documentation and Description* 21:166–198.

Schwartz, Saul, and William Green. 2013. Middle Ground or Native Ground? Material Culture at Iowaville. *Ethnohistory* 60(4):537–565.

Segal, Zef, and Bram Vannieuwenhuyze, eds. 2020. *Motion in Maps, Maps in Motion: Mapping Stories and Movement through Time.* Amsterdam University Press, Amsterdam.

Shepard, Robert C., Patrick Bitterman, J. Clark Archer, and Fred M. Shelley. 2024. *Atlas of Iowa.* University of Iowa Press, Iowa City.

Shield Chief Gover, Carlton Quinn. 2024. The Seeds of Ethnogenesis: An Indigenous Archaeology of Central Plains Village Formation. PhD dissertation, Department of Anthropology, University of Colorado, Boulder.

Shillcock, George. 2022. Indigenous Tribe That Gave Iowa Its Name Has Land Again in the State: Here's How It Happened. *Iowa City Press-Citizen,* September 26. https://ouriowaheritage.com/honoring-the-ioway-tribe-of-johnson-county/.

Short, John Rennie. 2009. *Cartographic Encounters: Indigenous Peoples and the Exploration of the New World.* Reaktion, London.

Sine, Mae Murray. 2008a. Native Ioway History Week 2008—Ioway Gifts. *Lost Nation: The Ioway,* October 6. https://docublogger.typepad.com/ioway/2008/10/native-ioway-hi.html.

Sine, Mae Murray. 2008b. Native Ioway History Week—2008, No Heart Statue Dedicated. *Lost Nation: The Ioway,* October 9. https://docublogger.typepad.com/ioway/2008/10/no-heart-statue.html.

Skinner, Alanson B. 1925. Traditions of the Ioway Indians. *Journal of American Folk-Lore* 38(150):425–506.

Skinner, Alanson B. 1926. Ethnology of the Ioway Indians. *Bulletin of the Public Museum of the City of Milwaukee* 5(4):181–354.

Sletto, Bjørn, ed. 2009. "Indigenous Cartographies." Special Issue, *Cultural Geographies* 16(2):147–277.

Smith, Anthony D. 1986. *The Ethnic Origins of Nations.* Blackwell, Oxford, England.

Smithsonian National Museum of the American Indian. 2024. The Removal Act. https://americanindian.si.edu/americans/#stories/the-removal-act.

Snead, James E., Clark L. Erickson, and J. Andrew Darling, eds. 2009. *Landscapes of Movement: Trails, Paths, and Roads in Anthropological Perspective.* University of Pennsylvania Museum of Archaeology and Anthropology, Philadelphia.

Soikkeli, Laura M. 1999. William Clark's 1814 Map of Central Missouri. *Missouri Archaeological Society Quarterly* 16(1):4–12.

Speth, Janet M. 2000. The Site Complex at Red Banks (47-BR-4/BR-31), Brown County, Wisconsin, as Seen through Collections at the Neville Public Museum. Manuscript on file, Neville Public Museum, Green Bay, WI.

Springer, James Warren, and Stanley R. Witkowski. 1982. Siouan Historical Linguistics and Oneota Archaeology. In *Oneota Studies*, edited by Guy E. Gibbon, pp. 69–83. Publications in Anthropology No. 1. University of Minnesota, Minneapolis.

Stahle, R. L. 1966. Ferdinand Pettrich in America. *Pennsylvania History* 33(4):388–411.

State Historical Society of Iowa. 1920. The Sac and Fox Treaty of 1842. *Annals of Iowa* 12(5):375–381.

Steinauer-Scudder, Chelsea, Adam Loften, and Emmanuel Vaughan-Lee. 2018. Counter Mapping. *Emergence Magazine*, December 2. https://emergencemagazine.org/film/counter-mapping/.

Steinke, Christopher. 2014. "Here Is My Country": Too Né's Map of Lewis and Clark in the Great Plains. *William and Mary Quarterly* 71(4):589–611.

Stevenson, Katherine. 1994. Chronological and Settlement Aspects of the Valley View Site (47 Lc 34). *Wisconsin Archeologist* 75(3–4):237–294.

Stevenson, Winona. 1993. Beggars, Chickabobbooags, and Prisons: Paxoche (Ioway) Views of English Society, 1844–45. *American Indian Culture and Research Journal* 17(4):1–23.

Stillwater [Oklahoma] Daily News-Press. 1956. Aged Indian Dies Saturday. January 15:2.

Stillwater [Oklahoma] News-Press. 1959. Emma Kent, 91, Rites on Sunday. October 8:2.

StoryMaps. 2024. ArcGIS StoryMaps. https://storymaps.arcgis.com/.

Stout, David B. 1953. Plans for an Archaeological Program at the State University of Iowa. *Journal of the Iowa Archeological Society* 3(1):8–12.

Stout, David B. 1974. An Anthropological Report on the Indian Occupancy of Royce Area 262. In *Sac, Fox, and Iowa Indians II: Indians of E. Missouri, W. Illinois, and S. Wisconsin, from the Proto-Historic Period to 1804.* Garland, New York.

Straffin, Dean F. 1972. Iowaville: A Possible Historic Ioway Site on the Lower Des Moines River. *Proceedings of the Iowa Academy of Science* 79(1):44–46.

Studio1:1. 2023. *Maps for Native Truths: Our Voices, Our Stories* (exhibition). https://www.studio1to1.net/field.

Sugden, John. 1985. *Tecumseh's Last Stand.* University of Oklahoma Press, Norman.

Sundstrom, Linea, and Glen Fredlund. 1999. The Crazy Mule Maps: A Northern Cheyenne's View of Montana and Western Dakota in 1878. *Montana: The Magazine of Western History* 49(1):46–57.

Tanner, Helen Hornbeck, ed. 1986. *Atlas of Great Lakes Indian History.* University of Oklahoma Press, Norman.

Tanner, Henry S. 1829. *United States of America.* H. S. Tanner, Philadelphia.

Tardieu, P. F. 1820. *United States of N*th*. America.* P. F. Tardieu, Paris.

Taylor, Anne, David Gadsden, Joseph Kerski, and Heather Guglielmo, eds. 2017. *Tribal GIS: Supporting Native American Decision-Making,* 2nd ed. ESRI Press, Redlands, CA.

Taylor, D. R. Fraser, and Romola V. Thumbadoo, eds. 2021. "Mapping Indigenous Knowledge in the Digital Age." Special issue, *ISPRS: International Journal of Geo-Information* 11. https://www.mdpi.com/journal/ijgi/special_issues/Indigenous_Knowledge.

Taylor, William Timothy Treal, plus 88 authors. 2023. Early Dispersal of Domestic Horses into the Great Plains and Northern Rockies. *Science* 379(6639):1316–1323.

Temple, Wayne C. 1966. *Indian Villages of the Illinois Country.* Scientific Papers Vol. 2, Part 2. Illinois State Museum, Springfield.

Temple, Wayne C., comp. 1975. *Indian Villages of the Illinois Country. Atlas. Supplement.* Scientific Papers Vol. 2, Part 1. Illinois State Museum, Springfield.

Theler, James L., and Robert F. Boszhardt. 2003. *Twelve Millennia: Archaeology of the Upper Mississippi River Valley.* University of Iowa Press, Iowa City.

Thiessen, Thomas D. 1988. Who Lived at Blood Run? A Review of the Historical and Traditional Evidence. Manuscript on file, Office of the State Archaeologist, University of Iowa, Iowa City.

Thiessen, Thomas D. 2004. Traditional and Historical Summary. In *Central Siouans in the Northeastern Plains: Oneota Archaeology at the Blood Run Site,* edited by Dale R. Henning and Thomas D. Thiessen, pp. 355–380. *Plains Anthropologist* 49, Memoir 36.

Thorne, Tanis C. 1996. *The Many Hands of My Relations: French and Indians on the Lower Missouri.* University of Missouri Press, Columbia.

Thornton, Thomas F. 2008. *Being and Place among the Tlingit.* University of Washington Press, Seattle.

Thrower, Norman J. W. 1996. *Maps and Civilization: Cartography in Culture and Society.* University of Chicago Press, Chicago.

Thrush, Coll. 2017. *Native Seattle: Histories from the Crossing-Over Place,* 2nd ed. University of Washington Press, Seattle.

Thwaites, Reuben Gold, ed. 1900. *The Jesuit Relations and Allied Documents: Travels and Explorations of the Jesuit Missionaries in New France, 1610–1791,* Vol. 60: *Lower Canada, Illinois, Iroquois, Ottawas: 1675–1677.* Burrows Brothers, Cleveland.

Thwaites, Reuben Gold, ed. 1905. *Early Western Travels 1748–1846,* Vol. 17: *Part IV of James's Account of S. H. Long's Expedition 1819–1820.* Arthur H. Clark, Cleveland.

Trabert, Sarah, Matthew E. Hill Jr., and Margaret E. Beck. 2023. Movement or Diaspora? Understanding a Multigenerational Puebloan and Ndee Community on the Central Great Plains. *Open Archaeology* 9:20220288.

Trager, George L. 1974. David Bond Stout 1913–1968. *American Anthropologist* 76(1):73–75.

Transeau, Edgar Nelson. 1935. The Prairie Peninsula. *Ecology* 16(3):423–437.

Treat, Patricia A. 1983. Plate 16: Oto Indian (or Gero-Schunu-Wy-Ha). In *An Atlas of Early Maps of the American Midwest*, compiled by W. Raymond Wood, n.p. Scientific Papers Vol. 18. Illinois State Museum, Springfield.

Trow, Tom, and Dan Wendt. 2021. "There Is Flint": Rediscovering the Grand Meadow Chert Quarry (video). Minnesota Archaeological Society. https://www.youtube.com/watch?v=JhAv-y2zNZc&t=2200s.

Tuan, Yi-Fu. 1975. Place: An Experiential Perspective. *Geographical Review* 65(2):151–165.

Tucker, Sarah J., comp. 1942. *Indian Villages of the Illinois Country*, Part I: *Atlas*. Scientific Papers Vol. 2, Part 1. Illinois State Museum, Springfield.

Turnbull, David. 1989. *Maps Are Territories, Science Is an Atlas*. Deakin University Press, Geelong, Victoria, Australia. Republished 1993, University of Chicago Press, Chicago.

Urban, Greg. 2016. Anthony F. C. Wallace 1923–2015. *Biographical Memoirs*. National Academy of Sciences, Washington, DC. https://www.nasonline.org/wp-content/uploads/2024/06/wallace-anthony.pdf.

U.S. Congress. 1954. *Termination of Federal Supervision over Certain Tribes of Indians*. Government Printing Office, Washington, DC.

U.S. Congress, Office of Technology Assessment. 1988. *Book Preservation Technologies*. OTA-375. Government Printing Office, Washington, DC.

U.S. Geological Survey. 2024. *National Atlas of the United States of America, Rivers and Lakes Unlabeled*. Originally at nationalatlas.gov. Accessible at https://web.archive.org/web/20160412234705/http://nationalmap.gov/small_scale/printable/images/pdf/outline/rivers_lakes(u).pdf.

U.S. Indian Claims Commission. 1979. *Final Report*. Government Printing Office, Washington, DC.

van de Logt, Mark. 2023. *Between the Floods: A History of the Arikaras*. University of Oklahoma Press, Norman.

Vansina, Jan. 1985. *Oral Tradition as History*. University of Wisconsin Press, Madison.

Vermont Mercury [Woodstock, Vermont]. 1837. The Indian Warriors. November 3:3.

Viola, Herman J. 1976. *The Indian Legacy of Charles Bird King*. Smithsonian Institution Press, Washington, DC.

Viola, Herman J. 1981. *Diplomats in Buckskins: A History of Indian Delegations in Washington City*. Smithsonian Institution Press, Washington, DC.

Vizenor, Gerald. 1998. *Fugitive Poses: Native American Indian Scenes of Absence and Presence*. University of Nebraska Press, Lincoln.

Vizenor, Gerald. 2008. Aesthetics of Survivance: Literary Theory and Practice. In *Survivance: Narratives of Native Presence*, edited by Gerald Vizenor, pp. 1–23. University of Nebraska Press, Lincoln.

Vizenor, Gerald. 2015. The Unmissable: Transmotion in Native Stories and Literature. *Transmotion* 1(1):63–75.

Vogel, Virgil J. 1983. *Iowa Place Names of Indian Origin*. University of Iowa Press, Iowa City.

Vollmar, Rainer. 1981. *Indianische Karten Nordamerikas: Beiträge zur historischen Kartographie vom 16. bis zum 19. Jahrhundert.* Dietrich Reimer Verlag, Berlin, West Germany.

Vollmar, Rainer. 1982. Kartenanfertigung und Raumauffassung nordamerikanische Indianer. *Geographische Rundschau* 34(7):302–307.

Wagner, Mark J. 2011. *The Rhodes Site: A Historic Kickapoo Village on the Illinois Prairie.* Studies in Archaeology No. 5. Illinois State Archaeological Survey, Urbana.

Wagner, Mark J., Elaine Bluhm Herold, and Richard L. Fishel, eds. 2023. *The Crawford Farm Site (11RI81): The 1958–1961 University of Illinois Excavations at the Great Sac Town of Saukenauk.* Technical Report No. 199. Illinois State Archaeological Survey, Urbana.

Wallace, Anthony F. C. 1970. *Prelude to Disaster: The Course of Indian-White Relations Which Led to the Black Hawk War of 1832.* Illinois State Historical Library, Springfield.

Wallace, Anthony F. C. 2005. The Consciousness of Time. *Anthropology of Consciousness* 16(2):1–15.

Warhus, Mark, ed. 1993. "Cartographic Encounters: An Exhibition of Native American Maps from Central Mexico to the Arctic." Special Issue, *Mapline* (Herman Dunlap Center for the History of Cartography, Newberry Library, Chicago) 7:1–24.

Warhus, Mark. 1994. *Another America: An Exhibition of Native American Maps* (exhibition brochure). Milwaukee, WI.

Warhus, Mark. 1997. *Another America: Native American Maps and the History of Our Land.* St. Martin's Press, New York.

Warren, Stephen. 2014. *The Worlds the Shawnees Made: Migration and Violence in Early America.* University of North Carolina Press, Chapel Hill.

Waselkov, Gregory A. 1989. Indian Maps of the Colonial Southeast. In *Powhatan's Mantle: Indians in the Colonial Southeast,* edited by Peter H. Wood, Gregory A. Waselkov, and M. Thomas Hatley, pp. 292–343. University of Nebraska Press, Lincoln.

Watkins, Albert. 1913. First Steamboat Trial Trip up the Missouri. *Collections of the Nebraska State Historical Society* 17:200–201.

Watkins, Eugene. 2012. Fort Madison: America's Frontier Outpost 1808–1813. Manuscript on file, Office of the State Archaeologist, University of Iowa, Iowa City.

Wedel, Mildred Mott. 1959. Oneota Sites on the Upper Iowa River. *Missouri Archaeologist* 21(2–4):1–181.

Wedel, Mildred Mott. 1961. Indian Villages on the Upper Iowa River. *The Palimpsest* 42(12):561–592.

Wedel, Mildred Mott. 1976. Ethnohistory: Its Payoffs and Pitfalls for Iowa Archeologists. *Journal of the Iowa Archeological Society* 23:1–44.

Wedel, Mildred Mott. 1978. A Synonymy of Names for the Ioway Indians. *Journal of the Iowa Archeological Society* 25:49–77.

Wedel, Mildred Mott. 1981. The Ioway, Oto, and Omaha Indians in 1700. *Journal of the Iowa Archeological Society* 28:1–13.

Wedel, Mildred Mott. 1982. The Wichita Indians in the Arkansas River Basin. In *Plains Indian Studies: A Collection of Essays in Honor of John C. Ewers and Waldo R. Wedel,* edited by Douglas H. Ubelaker and Herman J. Viola, pp. 118–135. Smithsonian Contributions to Anthropology 30. Smithsonian Institution, Washington, DC.

Wedel, Mildred Mott. 1986. Peering at the Ioway Indians through the Mists of Time: 1650–circa 1700. *Journal of the Iowa Archeological Society* 33:1–74.

Wedel, Mildred Mott. 1988. The 1804 "Old Ioway Village" of Lewis and Clark. *Journal of the Iowa Archeological Society* 35:70–71.

Wedel, Mildred Mott. 2001. Iowa. In *Plains*, Vol. 13: *Handbook of North American Indians*, edited by Raymond J. DeMallie, pp. 423–446. Smithsonian Institution, Washington, DC.

Wedel, Mildred Mott, and Raymond J. DeMallie. 1980. The Ethnohistorical Approach in Plains Area Studies. In *Anthropology on the Great Plains*, edited by W. Raymond Wood and Margot Liberty, pp. 110–128. University of Nebraska Press, Lincoln.

Weik, Terrance, ed. 2019. *The Archaeology of Removal in North America.* University Press of Florida, Gainesville.

Whelan, Mary K. 2003. The 1837 Ioway Indian Map Project: Using Geographic Information Systems to Integrate History, Archaeology, and Landscape. Master's thesis, Geographic Information Science, University of Redlands, Redlands, CA. https://doi.org/10.26716/redlands/master/2003.18.

Whelan, Mary K. 2024. The 1837 Ioway Indian Map Project. The Digital Archaeological Record, id: 6309. https://core.tdar.org/project/6309/the-1837-ioway-indian-map-project.

Whiteley, Peter M. 2002. Archaeology and Oral Tradition: The Scientific Importance of Dialogue. *American Antiquity* 67(3):405–415.

Whitman, William. 1937. *The Oto*. Columbia University Contributions to Anthropology 28. Columbia University Press, New York.

Whitman, William. 1938. Origin Legends of the Oto. *Journal of American Folk-Lore* 51(200):173–205.

Whitney, Ellen M., ed. 1973. *The Black Hawk War 1831–1832*, Vol. 2: *Letters and Papers, Part I, April 30, 1831–June 23, 1832.* Collections of the Illinois State Historical Library Vol. 36. Springfield.

Whittaker, William E. 2008. Searching for Quashquame's Village. *Newsletter of the Iowa Archeological Society* 58(4):1–4.

Whittaker, William E. 2015. Determining the Age of GLO-Mapped Trail Networks: A GIS Analysis of Northern Iowa. *Midcontinental Journal of Archaeology* 40(2):134–148.

Whittaker, William E. 2016. An Analysis of Historic-Era Indian Locations in Iowa. *Midcontinental Journal of Archaeology* 41(2):159–185.

Whittaker, William E., Lynn M. Alex, and Mary C. De La Garza. 2015. *The Archaeological Guide to Iowa.* University of Iowa Press, Iowa City.

Whittaker, William E., and Mark L. Anderson. 2008. Wanampito: An Early Ioway Site? *Newsletter of the Iowa Archeological Society* 58(1):4–5.

Whittaker, William E., and John Doershuk. 2010. Where Were the Chemin des Voyageurs? *Newsletter of the Iowa Archeological Society* 60(4):4–5.

Wigan, Kären, and Caroline Winterer, eds. 2020. *Time in Maps: From the Age of Discovery to Our Digital Era.* University of Chicago Press, Chicago.

Wigginton, Caroline. 2022. *Indigenuity: Native Craftwork and the Art of American Literatures.* University of North Carolina Press, Chapel Hill.

Willis, N. P. 1837. Washington in the Session. *New York Mirror*, March 4:284.

Willow, Anna J. 2013. Doing Sovereignty in Native North America: Anishinaabe Counter-Mapping and the Struggle for Land-Based Self-Determination. *Human Ecology* 41(6):871–884.

Winther, Rasmus Grønfeldt. 2020. *When Maps Become the World*. University of Chicago Press, Chicago.

Witgen, Michael John. 2022. *Seeing Red: Indigenous Land, American Expansion, and the Political Economy of Plunder in North America*. University of North Carolina Press, Chapel Hill.

Withrow, Randall M. 2012. *The Wever Bypass Excavations: Highway Archaeology along the Great River Road in Southeast Iowa*. Iowa Department of Transportation, Ames. https://iowadot.gov/ole/documents/Booklet%20-%20Wever%20Bypass%20Excavations.pdf.

Wood, Denis. 1992. *The Power of Maps*. Guilford, New York.

Wood, W. Raymond. 1990. Ethnohistory and Historical Method. In *Archaeological Method and Theory*, Vol. 2, edited by Michael B. Schiffer, pp. 81–109. University of Arizona Press, Tucson.

Wood, W. Raymond. 2002. Early Maps of the American Midwest. *Living Museum* 64(1):3–7.

Worley, Sally. 2021. Reflecting on History to Create Resilient Paths Forward. Practical Farmers of Iowa, April 22. https://practicalfarmers.org/2021/04/reflecting-on-history-to-create-resilient-paths-forward/.

Young, J. H. 1831. *Map of the United States*. S. Augustus Mitchell, Philadelphia.

Zerubavel, Eviatar. 2003. *Time Maps: Collective Memory and the Social Shape of the Past*. University of Chicago Press, Chicago.

Zimmer, Eric Steven. 2024. *Red Earth Nation: A History of the Meskwaki Settlement*. University of Oklahoma Press, Norman.

Zimmerman, Larry, and Dawn Makes Strong Move. 2008. Archaeological Taxonomy, Native Americans, and Scientific Landscapes of Clearance: A Case Study from Northeastern Iowa. In *Landscapes of Clearance: Archaeological and Anthropological Perspectives*, edited by Angèle Smith and Amy Gazin-Schwartz, pp. 190–211. Left Coast Press, Walnut Creek, CA.

Index

Note: Page numbers in italics refer to figures